VISUAL
LEADERS
NEW TOOLS FOR
VISIONING, MANAGEMENT,
& ORGANIZATION CHANGE
VIRTUAL WORK
VISUAL MEETINGS
COLLABORATION
DESIGN THINKING
STORYMAPS
MODELS
strategy
implementation
VISUAL LANGUAGE
STARTUPS
GROWTH ORGS
INSTITUTIONS
DAVID SIBBET

This book is printed on acid-free paper.

Published by John Wiley & Sons, Inc., Hoboken, New Jersey.
Published simultaneously in Canada.

For general information on our other products and services or for technical support, please contact our Customer Care Department within the United States at (800) 762–2974, outside the United States at (317) 572–3993 or fax (317) 572–4002.

Wiley publishes in a variety of print and electronic formats and by print-on-demand. Some material included with standard print versions of this book may not be included in e-books or in print-on-demand. If this book refers to media such as a CD or DVD that is not included in the version you purchased, you may download this material at http://booksupport.wiley.com. For more information about Wiley products, visit www.wiley.com.

ISBN 978-1-118-47165-4 (pbk); ISBN 978-1-118-49422-6 (ebk); ISBN 978-1-118-49423-3 (ebk); ISBN 978-1-118-49424-0 (ebk)

Printed in the United States of America.
10 9 8 7 6 5 4 3 2 1

This book is dedicated to all the young leaders who are taking on the challenges of this century through their many organizations, and to my leadership team at The Grove, who will be taking this work forward in the future.

Contents

Part Three:

Power Tools for Visual Leaders

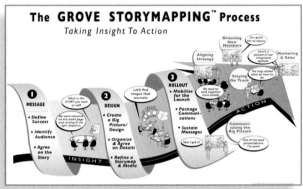

Part Four:

Managing the New Media

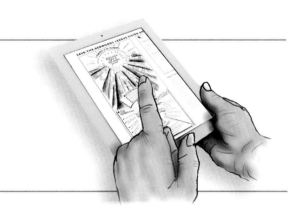

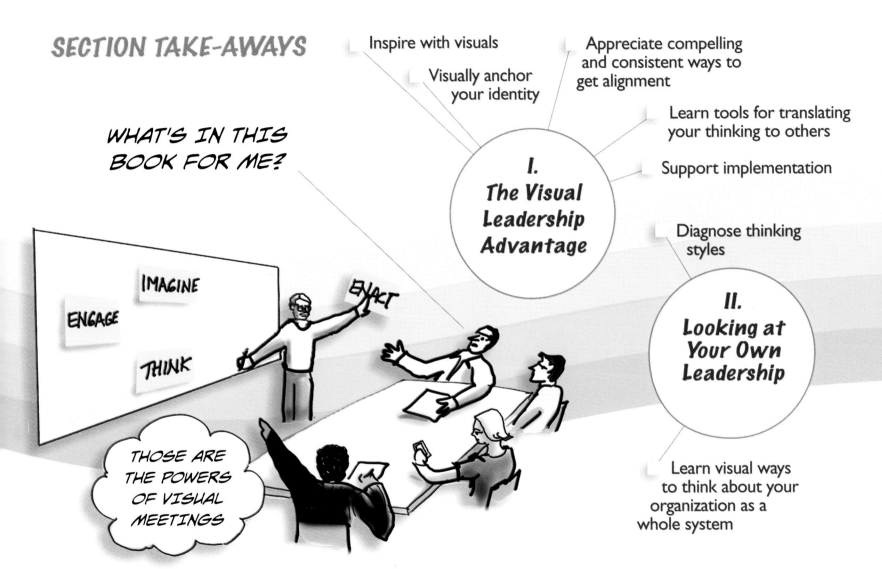

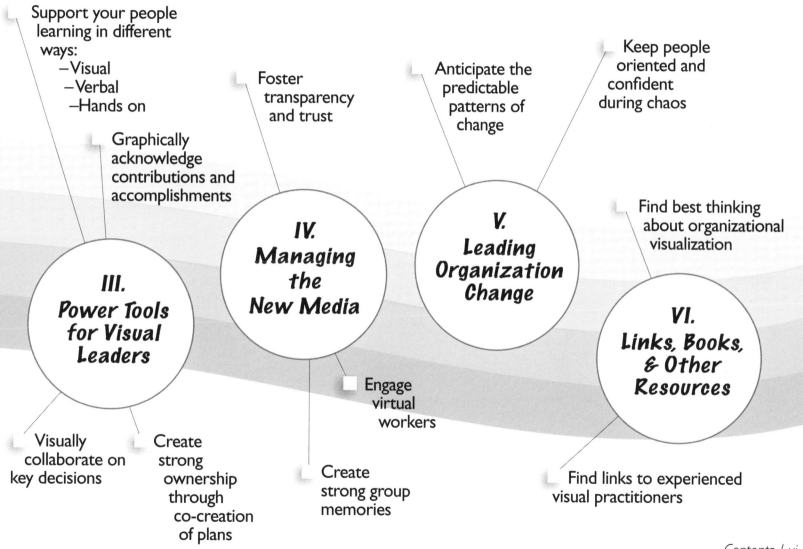

Support your people learning in different ways:
—Visual
—Verbal
—Hands on

Graphically acknowledge contributions and accomplishments

Foster transparency and trust

Anticipate the predictable patterns of change

Keep people oriented and confident during chaos

III. Power Tools for Visual Leaders

IV. Managing the New Media

V. Leading Organization Change

Find best thinking about organizational visualization

VI. Links, Books, & Other Resources

Engage virtual workers

Visually collaborate on key decisions

Create strong ownership through co-creation of plans

Create strong group memories

Find links to experienced visual practitioners

Introduction
Tracking a Visual Revolution

If you picked up this book, you are probably interested in visualization and leadership. Perhaps you've experienced visual meetings in which a facilitator used large graphic displays to record conversations. Maybe you are being asked to pitch a new business plan or convince a partner to affiliate with your organization and suspect that visuals might help. Maybe you've just been promoted to a manager position and need to align your people so that you can meet your targets. Or you might love sticky notes to organize your thoughts.

You might have noticed that the younger generation is unabashedly visual. Videos, digital photos, graphics, interactive maps, games, movies, and websites are taken for granted. It's all happening in the context of a larger revolution in visualization that is happening in data visualization, graphic design, and visual facilitation. So let's assume you get the visual part.

Do You Need to Draw?

If you are thinking, "I can't draw. I can't use these tools. This book is for facilitators," then you are precisely who this book is intended for. Leaders, more than ever, need to know how to use visual tools, manage visual practitioners and their work, and understand how to help their entire organization be visually literate—especially if you don't think of yourself as being skillful visually.

But we'll look at evidence to show that you are already a highly visual person, even if it isn't your preferred way to think consciously. We'll explore how you can take advantage of the visual revolution in very creative ways without being the one who does the drawing and designing. We'll look at how you can work with visual practitioners to focus their support to get the best results. And you'll learn how you can upgrade your own thinking about how metaphor and mental models work to filter and focus communications. Visualization is a critical part of leadership excellence in our times. The purpose of this book is to provide you with both understanding and practices that assure you can take full advantage of this revolution.

I CAN'T DRAW, SO WHY SHOULD I READ THIS BOOK?

1. TO CREATE ALIGNMENT AND OWNERSHIP

2. TO THINK BIG PICTURE

3. TO REMEMBER OUR PLANS

4. AND TO SHOW PEOPLE HOW THEY CAN HELP US GET RESULTS

New Managers
Team Leaders
Department Heads
Unit Leaders
Supervisors
Directors
Group Leaders
Executives
Community Leaders
Nonprofit Directors
Entrepreneurs
Executive Coaches
Board Chairs
Executive Assistants
Business HR Staff
Management Consultants
&
Visual Practitioners
who work with leaders

This Book Is for Leaders and Managers

You may also be wondering if you are a leader and if this book addresses your types of challenges. My mentors insist that leadership and management go together, in that most leaders need to manage execution in addition to helping shape direction and goals. In this regard, this book will share tools for visioning and strategy—key jobs of designated leaders—but also include tools that are terrific for implementation. This, however, is not a book about leadership in general—there are many fine ones already in print (noted in the last section on links and resources). But there are few books, if any, focusing on visual leadership directly.

You'll Meet Unsung Heroes

Visual leaders are collaborators who are often unsung heroes. You'll meet Betsy Stites and Pam Hull at Health East Care System in St. Paul, Minnesota; Evert Lindquist, professor of public administration at University of Victoria; David Warren, a TEDx consultant in Santa Cruz; Luke Hohmann of Innovation Games Company; Don Neubacher, superintendent of Yosemite National Park; and John Schiavo, former chief executive officer of Otis Spunkmeyer. None of them use markers much. However, they "get" the importance of their organizations using visuals to get results and make it possible for the people who work with them to embrace visual communications in an ongoing and productive way. These are all people who are taking advantage of visual facilitation—a broad category of visualizing aimed at support group communications, decision making, and organization development.

Are You a Visual Thinker?

Dan Roam wrote the popular (and recommended) book *Back of Napkin: Solving Problems and Selling Ideas with Pictures*. He likes to conduct informal polls in his workshops, asking, "Who are black-pen people, who are yellow-pen people, and who are red-pen people?" Well, you can't answer this without knowing what he means. Black-pen people are those who can't resist using a whiteboard or flip chart if it is available to express their ideas. Dan says about 25 percent of people are in this category. The yellow-pen people are people who can't resist highlighting and riffing off the diagrams and drawings others make. Dan claims about 50 percent fall in this category. Lots of leaders fall here, and rely on skilled facilitators and staff for the black pens. Red-pen people are those who think graphics oversimplify things. Often they are experts who resist working in a collaborative way. Some get really irritated with visualization. Dan says a good 20 to 25 percent are in this category. Which are you?

This book is written squarely for the black-pen and yellow-pen people. But even if you are a red-pen person, you might appreciate the value of visualization by the time you are through. Think of becoming aware of your own mental filters and lenses as a visualization challenge. Consider that the activity of drawing is actually as much a process of thinking as it is of producing an artifact of that process. There is tremendous subtlety in the challenge of visualizing something—especially systemic things like end-to-end processes, scenarios, and infrastructures. No matter what kind of leader you are, visualization is a development that you would want at least to be aware of.

Big Picture of Visualization

Appreciate as you begin to read this book that it is dealing with the leading edge of a very large phenomenon. For some the word visualization only suggests computer analysis of large data streams. For others it means scientific visualization. For others it means sharing pictures on smartphones. For many it means using visuals to facilitate meetings. As with any field you are trying to understand, it is helpful to have a map, so we begin with one. Evert Lindquist, director of the School of Public Administration at the University of Victoria in British Columbia, created one as a way to help analysts who were advising policy makers understand how they might use

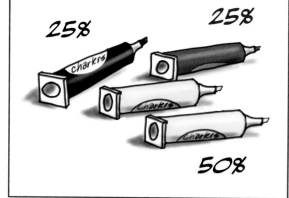

ARE YOU A BLACK-PEN, YELLOW-PEN, OR RED-PEN PERSON?

❏ **BLACK:** Can't resist drawing and sketching when charts and whiteboards are available.

❏ **YELLOW:** Can't resist highlighting and commenting on others' drawings.

❏ **RED:** Gets annoyed at simple drawings of complex subjects.

25% 25% 50%

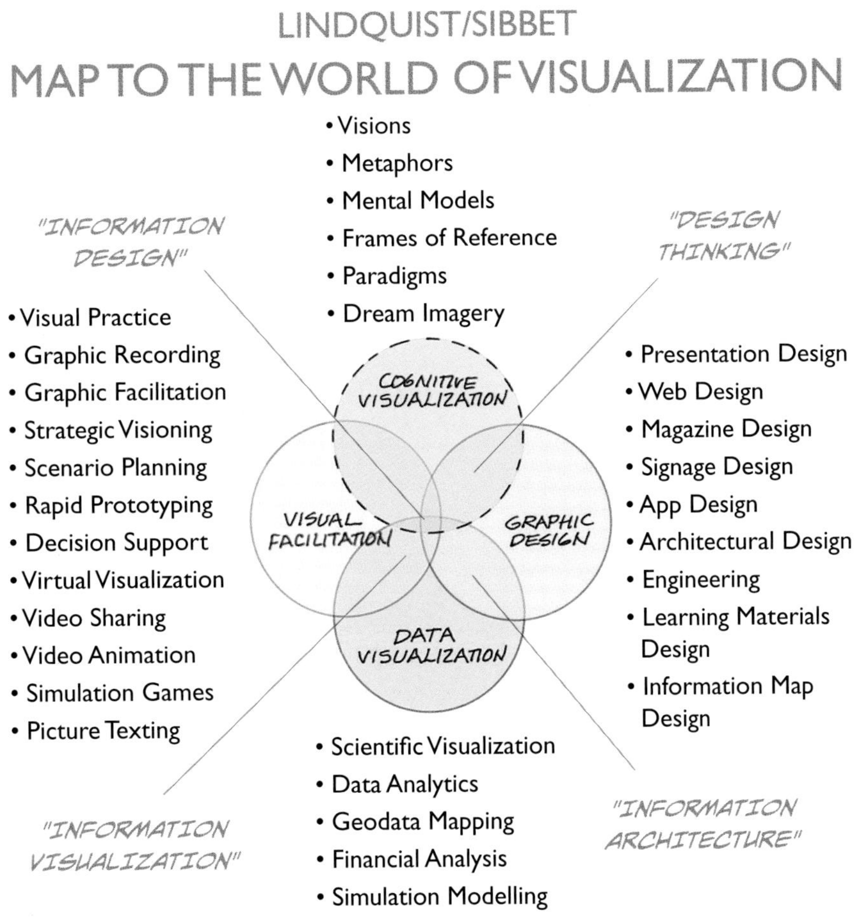

LINDQUIST/SIBBET
MAP TO THE WORLD OF VISUALIZATION

- Visions
- Metaphors
- Mental Models
- Frames of Reference
- Paradigms
- Dream Imagery

"INFORMATION DESIGN"

- Visual Practice
- Graphic Recording
- Graphic Facilitation
- Strategic Visioning
- Scenario Planning
- Rapid Prototyping
- Decision Support
- Virtual Visualization
- Video Sharing
- Video Animation
- Simulation Games
- Picture Texting

"DESIGN THINKING"

- Presentation Design
- Web Design
- Magazine Design
- Signage Design
- App Design
- Architectural Design
- Engineering
- Learning Materials Design
- Information Map Design

COGNITIVE VISUALIZATION

VISUAL FACILITATION

GRAPHIC DESIGN

DATA VISUALIZATION

"INFORMATION VISUALIZATION"

- Scientific Visualization
- Data Analytics
- Geodata Mapping
- Financial Analysis
- Simulation Modelling

"INFORMATION ARCHITECTURE"

This diagram is a collaboration between Evert Lindquist, director and professor of the School of Public Administration, University of Victoria, Canada, and myself. Bear in mind that terms and boundaries are fluid and under continual evolution and debate.

---

visuals to do a better job. His survey of the field led him to identify three domains. They are mapped on this page.

1. **Data Visualization:** This domain includes scientific visualization of all kinds, financial and data analytics, modeling, geodata mapping, and all the other kinds of visualization that rely on powerful visualization software. This book is not about this subject, although the problem of communicating analytical results with decision makers is.

2. **Graphic Design:** Everything that is made in the physical world and the world of media is designed by someone. Architects, engineers, software designers, Web designers, graphic designers, and many other professionals use visualization as a core skill in the work they do, and their products are visual. This has been true for a long time, but until recently, most of the lore about the methods and techniques of these professions has been confined to professional schools. However, since the 1970s these ways of working have been spreading beyond the bounds of design, giving rise to "design thinking" as an accepted skill for leaders.

3. **Visual Facilitation:** This is a term for the growing practice of visually facilitating strategic planning, strategy implementation, team building, group problem solving, and the many types of group work. The International Forum of Visual Practitioners, an association

of full-time professional graphic recorders and facilitators, is in its seventeenth year, with thousands of independent practitioners. Almost all large and small consulting firms now use visualization actively for strategic decision support, innovation, strategy development, and planning of all types. Most large companies have innovation and research centers that live with these kinds of tools. This is the field that this book is primarily about, because its tools are some of the most powerful for visual leaders to understand.

When Evert shared his diagram with me initially, I recognized a deeply embedded archetype at work, with one element missing. (An archetype is a pattern that is very widespread and commonly understood). The missing one was the other end of the data-visualization continuum, which is the domain that exists between the ears, in the imagination of people using these tools. It includes how visualization works in our cognitive processes, with the more structured aspect being the world of mental models and metaphors. Here it is included as a fourth domain, a branch of cognitive science, and labeled cognitive visualization. What does it include?

4. **Cognitive Visualization:** This includes personal visions, metaphors, mental models, and other frames of reference that guide and shape our behavior. It is the connection of these to their outer manifestations on charts and in media that makes visual material meaningful. It is an essential domain to include! Peter Senge, in his popular book *The Fifth Discipline: The Art and Practice of the Learning Organization,* identifies visioning, mental models, and systems thinking as three of the five disciplines (along with teamwork and personal accountability). These are all visually based and refer to the structured ways in which we filter and interpret information. With visioning we imagine opportunities and future states. We elevate metaphors to become mental models that filter our information. We understand our organization systems and the way they work through these internal lenses.

As you can see, this is a huge universe to consider. This book focuses the two domains most relevant to active leadership—the cognitive visualization and visual-facilitation domains—and seven essential tools that, in 40 years of visualizing experience, have emerged as the basic ones that a leader should understand. Within this framework we'll look at insights, practices, and tools that any leader can use.

You'll be Able to Use This Book in Three Ways

This book focuses on the two domains most relevant to active leadership—the cognitive visualization and visual-facilitation domains—and seven essential tools that, in 40 years of visualizing experience, have emerged as the basic ones that a leader should understand.

1. **Upgrading your personal perspective and thinking:** Starting with yourself is always a good practice in leadership. Visualization is a doorway to insight about your own visions, strategies, and implementation plans. It is a path to appreciating the interconnection and wholeness of things. This book should help you understand what kind of organization you are leading and what types of awareness and frames of mind are helpful. Several very powerful explanatory frameworks are visualized in this book, with invitations to use them to explore your own perceptions about the organization you lead—be it a team, a unit within a larger organization, or the whole organization.

2. **Communicating directions and plans:** Visualization becomes a power tool when it comes to communicating with others about what they should be doing and how all the pieces and parts of your organizations work together and how events flow over time to get results. You'll get lots of ideas that you can use personally to implement plans and support change without needing to be an expert at drawing or creating visuals. The concepts apply to both face-to-face and virtual communications. You'll also be able to think through the various tools and platforms that are available for visual facilitation.

3. **Empowering organizational learning and creativity:** Encouragement of visual meetings and visual team methods throughout your organization directly addresses the need for increased creativity, innovation, and operational excellence. People learn and change best when engaged in processes that are interactive, discovery-oriented, and adaptive. You'll learn how to get your direct reports and other key leaders to embrace visual language and experience acceleration in understanding and collaboration.

Organization of Visual Leaders

Part One: The Visual Leader Advantage will orient you to why it's such an advantage to use visualization and to the seven tools that are essential to effective visual leadership. This part will also deal with what every manager should know about running visual meetings if you want to work with visual recorders, facilitators, and visual consultants.

Part Two: Looking at Your Own Leadership will invite you to start with your own development—no matter whether you are starting your own company, leading a department or division in one that is already organized, or holding the top positions in business, government, and nonprofits. A leader who is unconscious about his or her own "operating system" for making sense of organization will have far less success than one who is conscious. This part defines some of the key ideas, distinguishing metaphors, models, and operating systems. It introduces the Sustainable Organizations Model™ as a way to determine what kind of organization you lead and how visuals can help. This part ends with seven practical exercises that you can do personally to boost your visual IQ.

The heart of this book is *Part Three: Power Tools for Visual Leaders*. A chapter for each tool reviews case examples, tools, exercises, and virtual adaptations. These tools are about both setting strategy and implementing it. It's written assuming that you can get familiar enough to guide your staff and other leaders in using these tools—not necessarily use them all directly.

Part Four: Managing the New Media looks directly at the role of the leader in regard to new technology. It is no longer advisable for leaders to sit on the sidelines and let technology experts dictate the means by which an organization communicates. Media shapes everyone's perception. It provides advantage to certain ways of thinking and operating and prevents others. We'll look at how you can be a buoy and a beacon in this new world by using your online presence as an "organization cursor" for focusing attention, and also help determine the platforms others will use.

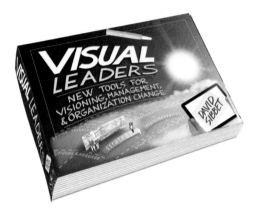

VISUAL LEADERS WILL HELP YOU AND YOUR ORGANIZATION TAKE ADVANTAGE OF THE VISUALIZATION REVOLUTION

Visualization is transforming the world of work and the role of leaders in an age of global communications and increasingly complexity. This book is a guide to increasing your own visual literacy and your ability to help others with theirs. It's full of proven tools that get results.

VISUAL MEETINGS SUPPORTS A GROUP'S CYCLE OF LEARNING

Visual Meetings explains how you can use graphic recording, sticky notes, and idea mapping when imagining, engaging, thinking, or enacting in meetings. It is loaded with very practical and detailed descriptions of how to conduct different visualization activities. It also reviews the Group Graphics Keyboard and the seven archetypal choices for organizing displays.

Part Five: Leading Organization Change illustrates how all the tools considered in previous chapters come to play when you are leading your organization through change. A well-developed, practical map of the stages and tools of change is included in the first chapter. A final chapter considers how you can use visual frameworks and plans to provide safe environments for change, much like a chrysalis for a butterfly during its transformation.

As in *Visual Meetings* and *Visual Teams*, *Visual Leaders* includes a final *Part Six: Links, Books, & Resources*, and it shares the literature on leadership and visualization that inspired this book.

For More Background on Visual Tools

Even though this book is a direct extension of *Visual Meetings* and *Visual Teams*, it is written to be read independently. If, however, you are interested in more detail about the types of visual meeting and visual team tools, techniques, and methods you might want to sponsor in your organization, reviewing these earlier books will add an invaluable layer of richness to your understanding.

Visual Meetings: How Graphics, Sticky Notes, and Idea Mapping Can Transform Group Productivity looks at how people can use visualization to support a cycle of learning and implementation in meetings. It is organized around a simple learning cycle that begins with imagination, moves to engagement, then thinking, then enactment. It was written for anyone who runs meetings, not just professional graphic facilitators, and it concentrates on techniques anyone can use to be visual, even people who aren't skilled at drawing. It describes the Group Graphics Keyboard, an articulation of the seven basic archetypes for displaying information on a chart or screen.

Visual Teams: Graphic Tools for Commitment, Innovation, & High Performance, explores how a team can use visual meeting methods across the whole arc of its work, not only in meetings but also in between. It digs in on new media, virtual work, and the challenge of mobility and suggests that much can be gained by learning to work like designers—using prototypes, interaction, and visualization throughout. It also uses visual language to describe the Drexler/Sibbet Team Performance Model (TPM). The TPM is a widely accepted tool that provides a graphical user interface for thinking about the predictable challenges of both creating and sustaining team performance. *Visual Teams* is a highly illustrated primer for getting results on any kind of team. It also includes chapters on the underlying Theory of Process that informs all three of these books.

Visual Leaders complements the first two books in the series by addressing itself directly to those of you who are responsible for your organization's results overall, not just for team performance and meeting effectiveness. If you end up reading all three books, you will see that the kind of visual thinking suggested here provides an integrated way to think about organizational dynamics from a micro as well as a macro perspective. Finding and helping integrate the confusion of mental models and tools that abound in the space of leadership development has been one of my and The Grove's passion over the years. Visualization has been an essential part of that inquiry.

My Basis for Writing about Visual Leadership

This book is the result of 40 years of direct field experience by myself and a wide network of colleagues worldwide. It is not the product of academic research. Examples are drawn from an exceptionally broad base of direct experience with organizations, both in the Americas and around the world. I've had the good fortune to study both leadership and visualization in tandem, building on eight years of experience-based leadership development with the Coro Center for Civic Leadership in the San Francisco Bay Area. Key elements were cross-sector internships in government, politics, business, labor, media, and community organizations. Leaders in these sectors were our field faculty, in all walks of public life. Coro's cross-sector orientation has continued in my company, The Grove Consultants International's consulting practice, which began in 1977.

VISUAL TEAMS EXPLAINS HOW TO CREATE AND SUSTAIN TEAM PERFORMANCE WITH VISUALS

Visual Teams builds on *Visual Meetings* and shows how to use these methods across the whole arc of a team process, including the parts in between meetings. It also provides a graphical user interface to thinking about team dynamics with the Drexler/Sibbet Team Performance™ Model. The seven challenges of high-performing teams are explained in detail and linked to tools that help meet them. Chapters include detailed stories about different kinds of high-performing visual teams.

ALL IMPROVEMENT IS MADE IN THE OUTLAW AREA ...

Over the years, Buckminster Fuller, one of the most general and inventive of thinkers in our time, has been a great inspiration. I've had a quote from him in my studio since beginning work as a business owner and organization consultant. I've lost its reference, but here is the quote:

"All improvement is made in the outlaw area. You can't reform man, and you can't improve his situation where he is…but when you've made things so good out there in the outlaw area that they can't help getting recognized, then gradually they get drawn in and assimilated."

That's finally happening in regard to visualization in meetings and teams. The new outlaw area is for leaders to be visual *and* visible. So if you are a young leader or a new older leader, or an older leader who is ready for a change, come on in.

We've worked in all types of businesses at all levels, as well as nonprofits, government agencies, and community groups in North and South America, Europe, Africa, and Asia.

Those of us involved in visual facilitation have the unique experience of having our understanding and learning publicly scrutinized every step of the way. As graphic facilitators, we lead management teams visually to understand their visions, strategies, and plans as well as assumptions about the environment, competitors, and work forces. This listening is on record. The feedback is immediate. Sloppy thinking and shallow understanding doesn't last long. As a leader and innovator in the field of organizational development, I care deeply about sharing my learning with the next generation. Telling real stories hedges against the trap many business books find themselves in, which is projecting a kind of "truth" and authority that blankets the fact that the world of organizations and leadership is inherently ambiguous and context dependent. It's important to share knowledge gained from intuitive insight and real experience on the part of those of us who have "been-there-and-done-that" in regard to organizational strategy and change.

Another bias guides this book. It is the assumption that knowledge is created by each of us through our direct experiences not just by learning and repeating concepts. The original idea of *knowledge* is that it is "know-how." It is understanding how to apply ideas in action. This orientation drives wanting to be as accessible as possible with practical suggestions about things you can do yourself. Until you personally play with these ideas and put them into practice yourself you won't really "know" them.

Technology is renewing visualization as a true frontier. You don't have to change your organization to get started. You just need to begin with yourself, and encourage a few others. If enough of us begin leading in this way then maybe our grandchildren will experience a world where organizations are led by people who can sustain a sense of the whole while working on the parts—caring about their interconnections as well as their competitive advantage.

Acknowledgments

Many more people contributed to the ideas in this book than it is possible to acknowledge here. In *Visual Meetings* and *Visual Teams* I acknowledge the many people who have guided me into this work of visualizing as a profession and taught me about meetings and teams. My many colleagues, associates, partners, and team at The Grove Consultants International have been invaluable. I won't repeat those thanks.

In regard to this new work on leadership and organization, there are some people who do deserve special mention. My father, a minister, led five different churches over his active years (which ended when he left Trinity Congregational Church in Weaverville at age 92!). Robert Denton, MD, PhD, my godfather and a country doctor, believed in general medicine and general thinking. His wife Betty Denton, a nurse and research technician, ended up being mayor of our hometown, Bishop, California. Aim Morhardt, my art teacher in high school—a prospector, balladeer, and artist—exemplified creative leadership and saw and believed in the spark in my eye. These people shaped my orientation to public service and leadership.

My specific work in leadership began at the Coro Foundation, now called the Coro Center for Civic Leadership. Coro started in 1942 and pioneered experience-based leadership education. Much of my work has grown from the eight years I spent at Coro in the 1970s. Donald Fletcher, its founder, modeled Socratic learning. William A. Whiteside, the director of the Los Angeles Center where I was a fellow in 1965, went on to create Neighborhood Reinvestment Corporation, a leadership-training organization disguised as a housing rehab program. It replicated in hundreds of cities, through six administrations, and still serves today as NeighborWorks. I am indebted to these men and Coro's large network of leaders for learning to think at a systemic level about metropolitan affairs and leadership.

Michael Doyle and David Straus, co-creators of Interaction Associates, introduced me to facilitation. They both exemplified being thought leaders in an emerging professional field. Early in my work I learned Process Theory with Arthur M. Young's study group at the Institute for the Study of Consciousness in Berkeley, California. Young's theories are a masterful integration of contemporary science and traditional metaphysics and have become the operating system underlying all of my work, including all three of the books in the John Wiley & Sons series on visualization.

Martin Paley, one of the most innovative philanthropists working in community foundations in the 1980s, provided an outstanding example of visual leadership, in supporting graphic facilitation widely but not being a personal practitioner. We worked together in many organization change settings, including the National Council on Foundations. I learned strategy and change work from a group of senior management consultants, all of whom were convinced that visualization was essential to their leadership. Thanks to David Cawood in Vancouver, Rob Eskridge from Growth Management in Southern California, Allan Drexler in Annapolis, Juanita Brown in the San Francisco Bay Area, and Ranny Riley from San Francisco. Rob continues to be a close associate and collaborator. Allan became a partner in developing the Team Performance System. Ranny Riley brought me onto the team that was supporting the creation of Apple University and the Apple Leadership Experience in the early days of John Sculley's tenure. Jim Ewing, our executive development consultant, Lenny Lind, founder of CoVision, and Jim Kouzes, who has gone on to define the core habits of leaders, were all on the Apple team and have remained close colleagues.

Brian O'Neil, the charismatic superintendent of the Golden Gate National Recreation Area, one of the largest national parks in the country, supported visual practices early, and brought The Grove into the transformation of the Presidio as a national park. The Grove continues to work extensively with the national parks. A change team at National Semiconductor in the early 1990s made visualization an anchor in its successful efforts to bring that company back from near-bankruptcy. Supported by CEO Gil Amelio and his consultant, Bob Miles, the change team became skilled visual practitioners and led reengineering and strategy processes organization wide. Special acknowledgment to Kevin Wheeler, head of National University, who attended a Grove workshop and thought the visual way of working would be helpful. Barbara Waugh and Srinivas Sukumar led the human resources and strategy functions, respectively in

Hewlett-Packard (HP) Labs in the 1990s. We worked closely on a multiyear visioning and organization transformation process that was a seedbed for many of the tools that have become standard in this work. Barbara understood the power of "visual listening." Sukumar eventually applied these lessons to cross-cultural work in India and support for California Indians in the San Diego area. In another part of HP, Vivian Wright, a long-time student and very successful manager, has been a pioneer in working virtually, and pushed the envelope on what is possible with visual practice. She continues to inspire by the way she does her virtual global work.

All during the 1990s The Grove was a strategic partner with The Institute for the Future (IFTF), collaborating on a Groupware Users Project that defined the field of collaboration-oriented software and gathered four-dozen large organizations and government agencies in a multiclient project that generated six or seven studies each year. (See Chapter 17 in *Visual Teams* for an overview of the rich learning we experienced). I owe a great deal to Bob Johansen, our leader, and a champion and exemplar of visual leadership. Largely due to his influence and Grove tutelage visualization has become a signature of IFTF.

Tamio Nakano, a director of communications at Hakuhodo advertising in Tokyo, initiated workshopping as a new way to work with clients in Japan and brought visualization forward in the late 1990s. He and his internal team taught me a great deal about cross-cultural visualization. Scott Kriens, when he was CEO of Juniper Networks during a critical period in the early 2000s, used his visual leadership to align the company for growth and transition to a new CEO. John Shiavo, recently retired as CEO of Otis Spunk-meyer, demonstrated how visual leadership could take root at a growing, mid-market company that didn't even have a human resources staff when we started working together. Recently extensive work at Nike, Inc. has confirmed how powerful visual practice can be in a large enterprise. Special thanks goes to Susan Kerosky, Director of Global Procurement, an exemplary and facilitative visual leader. I owe special thanks to Betsy Stites and Pam Hull of HealthEast Care System in St. Paul, Minnesota. They were key leaders in a large visioning and alignment process in the early 2000s and helped me appreciate how Storymapping work could end up cascading and evolving into regular visual practice under their inspired leadership. Their collaboration in telling the full story of the Quality Journey project has grounded this book in an inspiring example of visual leadership in practice. Craig Svendsen, the chief medical quality officer at HealthEast, provided some wonderful validation of the usefulness of visual practice for his self-acknowledged leaning toward "left-brain analysis."

Finally I would like to extend some special thanks to Meryem LeSaget, my long-time colleague from Paris, who helped me early on in the development of the Sustainable Organizations Model. She is a well-known syndicated writer about management and leadership in France, and is passionate about finding and sharing the best ideas in the field. Her support and intellectual partnership have been invaluable.

As my third book with John Wiley & Sons, I've come to deeply appreciate my editor Richard Narramore and his assistant, Lydia Dimitriadis. Richard's patient guidance and detailed work on overall structure and intent provide the critical balance to my protean appetite for big-picture thinking. He is avid about bringing forward tools that emerging managers can really use. I shared his passion. The amount of detail it takes to actually bring a book like this to publication would not be possible without someone like Lydia.

This book and the three-book visualization series would not have been possible, of course, without the full support of my team at The Grove Consultants International—Megan Hinchliffe, Bobby Pardini, Laurie Durnell, Tiffany Forner, Rachel Smith , Tomi Nagai-Rothe, Donna Lafayette, Noel Snow, Andrew Underwood, Ed Palmer, and Thom Sibbet, my oldest son and business colleague since 1985. Jerda Sibbet, my daughter, helped with production. They are the true embodiment of visual practice.

No words can say how important my dear wife, intellectual partner, and poet/teacher Susan has been. We share a rich life of the mind, as well as a large family, gardens, and the arts.

Part One:
The Visual Leader Advantage

Part One:
The Visual Leader Advantage

1: Seven Essential Tools This book begins by reviewing the most essential tools for visualization that a leader should have in his or her toolkit. Part Three will elaborate on these. This overview covers the use of metaphor and models, graphic facilitation, graphic templates, decision theaters, roadmaps, storymaps, video, and what you can do with virtual visualization.

2: Seeing Results in Action This chapter tells the story of visual leaders in a health-care organization who learned to use many of the essential tools indicated in this part. They were not skilled at drawing or experienced at visualization but got terrific results and moved to make visualization a standard way of working in their organization. The case is interleaved with practices you can use right away.

3: How to Run Visual Meetings This chapter covers what every manager should know about how to work with visual meetings and visual practitioners. Leaders set the norms for how everyone relates in meetings. There is creative room for shaping expectations and opportunities if you have a clear idea of what results you would like to achieve.

1. Seven Essential Tools
Metaphors & Models, Visual Meetings, Graphic Templates, Decision Rooms, Roadmaps, Storymaps, & Video

Have you ever set out to learn something new as an adult, say playing a sport or a musical instrument? You probably already know something about whatever you set out to learn, or you wouldn't be attracted to it, but chances are, you didn't learn the underlying discipline or practice enough to be masterful. If you are lucky, you will find a teacher who has experience and knows how to pick just the right foundation elements upon which you can build more proficiency. It's a step-at-a-time process.

If you are young and immersed in visual media already, you'll benefit from seeing what an experienced person like myself has found that works across a broad range of organizations and leaders. You can check to make sure your foundation skills are strong.

If you are more experienced, perhaps having learned to read your own form of "sheet music" for leadership, you can look forward to broadening your repertoire by learning some of the underlying theory and practices that will allow you to improvise in different situations and different organizations.

Beginning with the Tried-and-True

In music, beginning simply and building step by step with the basic elements that every musician knows makes all the difference. The goal, if you are studying jazz, is to have freedom of improvisation. But interestingly, a good teacher will start with the constraint of learning basic melodies, keys, and chords rather than sheet music with all the notes. Sheet music doesn't really teach you what the music is about, or encourage a wide range of possible variations. If you put basics first, in a short time your playing will jump to a whole new level. Visualization tools function just like the basic components of music. As with music you'll learn specific melodies (strategies and practices) that sound great even in their more basic states. This is the approach we'll take in regard

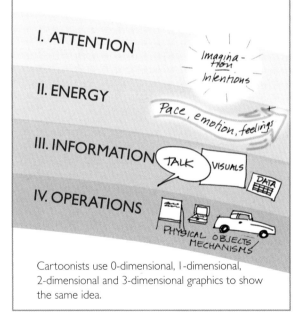

FOUR FLOWS THINKING

The Four Flows framework is a key tool for facilitators, but it also relates to leadership. You may have noticed the band of four shades of blue that run across the opening Parts pages of this and previous books. It is a graphic way of indicating the four ways humans make sense of things. In common terms we talk about spirit, soul, mind, and body. Carl Jung identified these as intuiting, feeling, thinking, and sensing modes of knowing. Here we call them attention, energy, information, and operations. All tools in leadership and management are aimed at handling these singly or in combination.

I. ATTENTION

Imagination - Intentions

II. ENERGY

Pace, emotion, feelings

III. INFORMATION TALK VISUALS DATA

IV. OPERATIONS

PHYSICAL OBJECTS/ MECHANISMS

Cartoonists use 0-dimensional, 1-dimensional, 2-dimensional and 3-dimensional graphics to show the same idea.

to visual leadership. All the way along are stories that explain the "music" and exercises that will teach you the basics. If you practice them as suggested in this book, you'll literally see the results. Because this book is written for leaders and managers, I've included the basics on improving your visual IQ, as well as coaching and guiding your teams to work visually so they don't necessarily rely on you to do it all. This chapter is for orientation, and then each tool will get its own chapter in Part Three. As you begin to get the basic ideas, we will improvise around the edges and you'll hopefully get a sense of the larger world of visualization that awaits. It's every bit as vast as music!

What Is a Visual Tool?

"Tool" is clearly a metaphor. It's used to indicate tangible things you can do to get desired results. Every tool is a product of some intention to do something. With repeated use, a tool will evolve and become refined. A good tool will have a central use but will also be usable for things other than it was intended. For instance, a good hammer could be used to prop open a door. In this book the metaphor of *tool* indicates any distinct, learnable process or practice that can be described and repeated to get an effect, such as the Four Flows framework on this page.

When thinking through all the tools a visual leader can use, it helps to understand the repeating challenges that a leader needs to meet, in any situation, at the broadest level. From the widest possible point of view, your challenge is to focus organizational awareness, support engagement of your people, clarify insights into the right things to be doing, and build ownership in projects and initiatives. A simple Goals of Leadership model is illustrated on the next page (an improvisation on Four Flows). The seven essential tools are ones you can use to meet these goals.

Appreciate that any generalization like this is for the sake of revealing the foundational elements, not all the variations, just as in the music. As you read this chapter let your own experience resonate with the examples and work out your own adaptation of this framework.

Goals of Leadership

Ed Friedrichs, former chief executive officer of Gensler, a very successful, large architecture firm, says, "Leaders focus on doing the right things and managers focus on doing things right. You need both in an organization, even though people often have leanings one way or the other." This book is written for both, so keep both in mind as you look at the five goals illustrated on this page. At the most general level, leaders and managers focus on what needs to be done, with whom, in what time frames, and with what kind of quality.

FOCUSING **A**WARENESS

SUPPORTING **E**NGAGEMENT

CLARIFYING **I**NSIGHTS

BUILDING **O**WNERSHIP

It all adds up to fostering as much understanding of all the right things to be doing distributed as widely as possible throughout your organization. In living systems the DNA instructions are in every cell!

IT ALL ADDS UP TO CREATING **U**NDERSTANDING OF THE RIGHT THINGS TO BE DOING

UNDERSTANDING

ESSENTIAL TOOLS HELP HANDLE THE FLOWS

The seven essential tools are organized in the order in which you would probably learn to deploy them. They nest into each other like chords in music. Here they are visually placed at their center of focus, but like musical chords, they can be played in many different ways.

Each tool is actually a set of tools. Part Three provides specific examples that you can put to use right away along with stories of leaders who have used them successfully. This will give you a sense of where the tools can take you if you learn to use them regularly. Because the intention of this book is to give you enough as a leader to guide your staff and consultants in helping you, these later chapters do not dwell on the technical details, but rather focus on the purpose and expected outcomes that usually attend these approaches.

Top Line

1. METAPHORS & MODELS

2. VISUAL MEETINGS

7. VIDEO & VIRTUAL VISUALS

6. GRAPHIC STORYMAPS

3. GRAPHIC TEMPLATES

5. ROADMAPS & VISUAL PLANS

4. DECISION ROOMS

Bottom Line

What Does It Mean to "Understand"?

You might recognize in the DNA analogy on the previous page a bias toward thinking of organizations as living systems (as distinguished from mechanical systems). In living systems the DNA contains the story of how different parts of the organism should grow and behave. If a cell in a plant finds itself underground, it knows to be a root. If it finds itself at the end of a branch, it becomes a leaf. There is no "central command" in a plant.

The lesson from this analogy is that when people truly know how their work relates to bigger goals and have a fully developed understanding of the way in which they should be doing their job, the organization works more effectively. Developing this general understanding about the right things to do is the primary job of leadership and key power of visual leadership.

The tools shared in this book are some of the most effective ways of creating real understanding from your direct reports and other people concerning the way the organization needs to work. Some of these tools are also about supporting doing things the right way—the manager's job.

You will come to see that the choices of which visual tools are essential focuses on ones that invite *more* rather than less engagement and that empower *more* rather than less understanding. People need to respond to and play with new ideas to create real knowledge. Watching a slide presentation does not support that kind of learning. Working interactively with visualization does—assuming you want to foster awareness, engagement, insight, and ownership— a level of understanding that translates into real results.

Seven Essential Tools for Visual Leaders

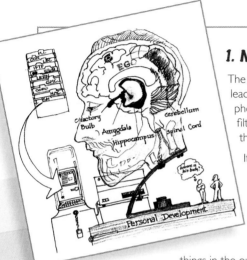

1. METAPHORS & MODELS

The first essential tool set for visual leaders consists of the visual metaphors and models that you use to filter your understanding of how things work in your organization.

If you think about it, your brain has never been outside your skull! All the images, pictures, sounds, smells, and memories have been pulled together out of raw sense data by you! They are all representations of things in the outside world and not the world itself. We understand what we don't know by comparing it with what we do or comparing it with some model we've learned. This is metaphoric thinking. Visual metaphors are the patterns of understanding that we can visualize explicitly. Chapter 7 explores these in some depth.

Key Questions to Ask Yourself

❏ Can I become aware of when I am using metaphoric thinking?

❏ Are the metaphors and mental models that are meaningful to me meaningful to my team and organization?

❏ Do I know how to link my internal ways of thinking with memorable images and stories in visible communications?

❏ Do any of my metaphors and mental models function like the operating system in a computer and can be widely shared?

❏ Will learning to visualize my central metaphors and models help me boost my visual IQ?

2. VISUAL MEETINGS

Visual meetings are ones in which you use visualization actively to inspire, engage, support thinking, and support enactment. It includes both things you as a leader do with visuals and also the visual support you can get from others. The most powerful thing about being interactive with visuals is you get four things right away—even if the charting isn't practiced.

Power of Visual Meetings

IMAGINATION: Visuals spark new thinking.

PARTICIPATION: Engagement increases immediately.

BIG-PICTURE THINKING: Display making is the key to systems thinking, seeing relationships, and developing aligned group understanding.

GROUP MEMORY: Visualizing produces a memorable product that everyone sees being created. Retention increases. Follow-through is stronger.

Chapter 8 will explain this in more detail.

Essential Tools, continued

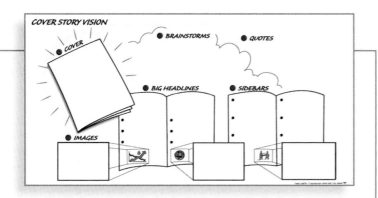

3. GRAPHIC TEMPLATES

An effective way to get visual without facilitators or consultants is to use simple graphic templates for both collecting information and having staff and others report information. The one above is a popular visioning template from The Grove called the "Cover Story Vision Graphic Guide." Many more are covered in Chapter 9.

Graphic templates have prestructured areas for information and are designed to optimize everyone being able to see important relationships.

Benefits of Using Graphic Templates

INSIGHT: Making the graphic template requires that you and your team determine the most relevant information to share.

PANORAMA: Templates placed around a room create a full surround of information so that everyone can see critical relationships.

RETENTION: Templates can be rolled up and unrolled in another room with almost no loss of memory and can stand out from other communications by being big, yet easily shared with digital photography.

4. DECISION ROOMS

Seeing the forest *and* the trees is essential during decision making. As a leader you need to know how to ask staff and others who are supporting you to display critical information in ways that enhance decision making. Much of this involves thinking through what needs to be compared with what. Many of the best tools are large matrixes with sticky notes.

Chapter 10 will show you how to create simple decision rooms you can operate yourself and how to stage more complex ones for larger groups. Decision room design helps enhance your use of visual meeting and graphic template tools.

Here is a mock-up of a management team decision room done in Second Life. It's modeled after The Grove's design space in the Presidio. Some organizations like Procter & Gamble have entire venues like their Gym dedicated to supporting special meetings that are highly visual.

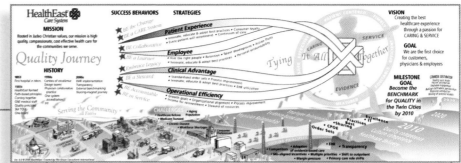

5. ROADMAPS & VISUAL PLANS

Can you imagine project management without timelines and milestones? But many project management tools are too detailed for regular use in your leadership role of keeping attention on the right things and encouraging timely execution. The roadmaps and visual action plans described as an essential tool for visual leaders are high-level visualizations—essentially "freeway maps" (to continue the driving metaphor)—that allow you and the rest of your leadership to tell an aligned overview story about big projects and plans.

The graphic below is a roadmap the National Park Service used to orient the public to its conversion of the Presidio Army Base to a national park, now called the Presidio Trust. Chapter 11 explains how this was created and how you can get staff to create high-level roadmaps and other visual plans that will support implementation.

Key Uses of Roadmaps

COMMITMENT TO IMPLEMENTATION: Get leadership to buy into implementation by having them co-create roadmaps and plans.

PROJECT PACING: Focus your organization on key milestones.

STAKEHOLDER ENGAGEMENT: Be able to explain your process easily to those not directly involved.

6. GRAPHIC STORYMAPS

Large murals and posters that integrate history, visions, challenges, values, critical behaviors, and other key ideas into one graphic are called "storymaps" by The Grove or murals by others. During culture change or any high-impact organizational change, these tools help people link visions and goals to the culture that people experience every day.

You generally create large murals with the help of internal or external information designers. Your role is to guide what story you need to tell and how to use the creation process to align your leadership team. The Quality Journey map is an example. The process, described in Chapter 1, was led by two internal managers who themselves were not information designers but knew who and what needed to be involved.

Key Uses of Storymaps

ALIGNMENT: Use the product to align key language and goals.

CULTURE CHANGE: Engage everyone in understanding what behaviors need to change to reach your visions and goals.

AUTHENTICITY: Provide a way for you and other leaders to show up authentically and personally— and tell your story in a flexible way.

ORGANIZATIONAL DIALOGUE: Iterate storymaps over time to show that you are listening.

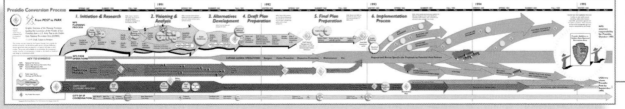

7. VIDEO & VIRTUAL VISUALS

Video, smartphones, and tablets are changing everyone's way of working. As a leader you need to know how to use these tools efficiently, what their advantages are, and how you can make sure your teams have the correct infrastructures for visual work at a distance.

This book isn't about social media, but it will describe how the other six essential tool sets can work virtually on webinars and conferences. It will also explore how you can be a more conscious "cursor" for organizational attention. Video is increasingly a powerful way to accomplish this. There are nice, emerging options beyond very expensive, professional video productions. Chapter 13 explores this area.

Power of Virtual Visuals

FOCUSING ATTENTION: One consequence of having so much digital communication is that it makes it tougher to get through the "noise" and keep everyone's focus on the important things. New media can help if you know how.

PERSONAL TOUCH: Videos capture motion and emotion better than any other medium. There are ways of combining videos with the other tools.

MOBILE MEMORY: If your people can reference key documents in easy, visual ways, it will help them remember.

Questions for a New Visual Leader

The beginning of this chapter compared learning to visualize with learning to play the piano. The essential tools are like the different chords that you can play. All of them use visual notes so to speak—the words, icons, and shapes of graphic language that make it work. As you continue reading keep these questions in mind:

1. How can I use visualization myself as a leader?
2. Which tools should I start with?
3. What is visual language and how does it work?
4. What are the basic rules of improvisation?
5. How can I get others to help me with visualization?

Bring Visual Leadership to Life

As helpful as a four-color book is in showing you different examples of visual work, it does not provide an experience of what it is like having these visuals evolve and develop in real time in a co-creative process. You will have to image that all the way along. To help you, the next chapter reviews a real-life story where many of these tools were used very effectively. This should help you imagine what is possible. Another way is to do the exercises included in this book. The true power of visualizing is in the *ing*—the doing of it. Draw*ing* and diagramm*ing* are actually ways of thinking, just as talking is a way of thinking for some. Chapter Five includes specific exercises you can do to experience this important aspect of visualization yourself.

2. Seeing Results in Action
Why Leaders Get Visual

Betsy Stites and Pam Hull had a problem. They had completed a focused strategy process in their organization, the HealthEast Care System in St. Paul, Minnesota, and decided on a big goal of being the "benchmark of quality in the Twin Cities." The five hospitals and numerous clinics in the system had a good reputation, but rising costs, Medicare, health-care reform, and escalating demands for quality from regulatory bodies and their own consumers were driving them to do more. The problem was how! "There had been a lot of uncertainty," Betsy reflects. "Quality is so etherial. We had to figure out a way to integrate things from an organizational and culture standpoint." Does this sound familiar?

The HealthEast story embodies many examples of how you can respond to such a situation with visual leadership. As a leader you set or inherit goals and then have to galvanize your organization to figure out how to accomplish them. If you are a new leader, this story will give you an idea of

IT'S A REAL MAP!

NOT EXACTLY, BUT
IN THAT SPIRIT!

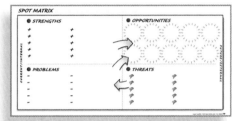
what you will be able to do with a little practice. If you are more experienced, you can affirm what works in practice and pick up some new ideas.

Betsy and Pam were middle managers at HealthEast and were experienced at getting results in their organizations. In 2007 Betsy was an internal organization consultant in charge of leadership development, working across the system to help strengthen the organization and its culture. "It's really an extraordinary organization. We are the most ecumenical health-care system in the United States, a result of merging five different faith-based systems in the 1980s," Betsy noted. But it almost bankrupted them. Coming back had been hard work, but they made it. The steady leadership of their chief executive officer (CEO) and experienced vice presidents (VPs), and a committed organization made the difference. They invested in developing the organization, which was why Betsy, a nurse by training and veteran leader at HealthEast, was focused on culture.

Betsy is gifted with boundless energy and a sparkle that is contagious. She's patient and smart as well. But jollying everyone into working together isn't enough. A strategic ally was Pam Hull, the "system director for strategic development." Pam was strategy-oriented. They had worked the dual focus of strategy and culture all during the 1990s. But Pam had her hands full getting people to align on plans. Health-care systems are notoriously difficult to manage, with built-in tensions between administrators and medical staff, interlaced with hard-pressed nursing professionals—all badgered by legions of stakeholders in business, government and the community.

Betsy Has an Idea

Betsy was introduced to visual practice at a small workshop with Joan McIntosh in Minnesota, where she saw Joan work magic in meetings with graphic facilitation—basically listening to everyone and mapping out the ideas interactively in real time. Joan was trained at The Grove Consultants International, leaders in the field. Pam learned about visualization at a participatory planning workshop in St. Paul, Minnesota. Pam and Betsy began using simple graphic templates to focus planning—things like SPOT charts (shown on the previous page). "A lot of the key people were exposed to this way of working because we really loved the graphic templates," Betsy said. "I'm not good at drawing but always loved Mind Mapping and being visual. We were getting results."

In 2007 Betsy came to a gathering of thought leaders in the field of organization development in California. She was very curious about what else The Grove was working on. She learned about how effective doing large history maps and visions were. Something clicked. "We need to create a visual history of HealthEast and a vision for our quality programs going forward," she wrote in an e-mail in late 2007. "Can you come meet with a group of us and see if this is possible?" In retrospect she said she believed this process of visualizing their way forward would bring everyone to agree on language, concrete actions, *and* how the behavior work she'd been doing on core value linked in one, coherent story capable of being shared. But none of them had actually seen it done.

From this start began a process that led HealthEast to become a visually literate organizational culture, literally seeing its way into getting results. This story contains many of the lessons we need to begin thinking about, and examples of many of the tools described in more detail in later chapters. Many of them can be used independent of a big process like this one.

What Are We Talking About?

Betsy and Pam knew they needed a project team to agree on visualizing the Quality Journey and its links to the overall strategy. They wrote a set of goals and explanation of the approach and convinced the chief medical officer; leaders in nursing, strategy, communications; and the Quality Institute to form a project team to see what could be done. The list of objectives they worked out is shown on the next page. Although the group was positive about visualizing, it had

There are many tools involved with visual leadership. You may have personal favorites. Hopefully this chapter provides a sense of what a whole tool chest looks like. As either a beginning or more experienced leader, having a number of choices allows you to get out of the trap of always looking for nails because all you have is a hammer.

Throughout this book, sidebars like this explain useful tools and visual ideas (like this) that you can put in your kit and used right away, even without using professional facilitators.

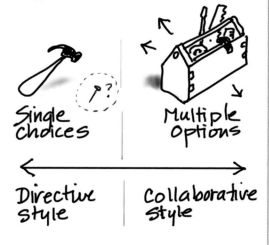

Single Choices
Directive Style

Multiple Options
Collaborative Style

not seen it done large scale on murals. Pam and Betsy met individually with everyone to explain and share samples from other organizations. "The medical staff and quality folks were the most concerned," Betsy says. "They were having trouble communicating how the quality milestone journey was going to be the leading edge of HealthEast's strategy moving forward. They needed a way to explain it and tell the story." When asked how she got people to sign onto the project, Betsy said, "We are pretty well respected in our organization. I think people were going on trust at this point." When they met with Tim Hanson, the CEO, he was cautious, as a good leader of a collegial organization like a health-care system is trained to be. He said he could support it if all the VPs did. This set the bar for Betsy and Pam.

Think about times when you have had a group of key stakeholders who sort of got what you were talking about when you suggested a new idea. It's a common challenge. Do you think a clear, simple communication and a real opportunity results in everyone agreeing? Not usually. Leaders have to repeat things endlessly, especially in regard to overarching visions, goals, and expectations. People are simply full of their own agendas and concerns. It actually takes not only repetition of communications but a successful, immersive experience with something different to get folks moving. This is what Betsy and Pam concluded. The project team needed to see visualization in action and be convinced it would work. (As a reader, you need to be able to imagine this as well, which is why we are starting with a real story that achieved real results.)

First Project Team Meeting

The opportunity for creating a real experience came in late 2007 at a meeting of the new Quality Journey Team in Minnesota. Betsy was on vacation and Pam's boss, the head of strategic planning, came instead. Craig Svendsen, chief medical quality officer and head of the Quality Institute, which was clearly a large stakeholder, had his direct report Karen MacDonald at the

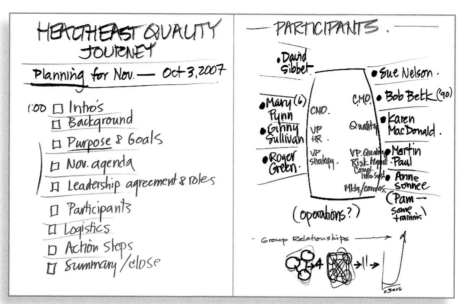

meeting. Because Betsy and Pam were not there, Susan Nelson, a very operationally effective leader in the quality organization, carried the ball. The two flip charts on this page illustrate the agenda of this first meeting and the participants. Watching these being created was, for some, their first experience with what might be possible with visuals.

Metaphors and Maps

These charts are examples of some of the seven essential tools for visual leadership in action. One is **visual facilitation**. Two others are reflected here: **metaphors** and **maps**.

Consider the name used for this project—"The Quality *Journey*." Can you "see" the metaphor? It wasn't an accident that the word *journey* was embedded in the project name. In all the prior strategic planning sessions and process of forming the Quality Institute, people knew full well that the only way they could get alignment and focus from the larger organizations was with a *very* engaging process, over time. It had to be an immersive experience. People simply do not change behavior quickly and don't change if they don't *feel* it's necessary.

At Apple during the early days of the MacIntosh, Steve Jobs had T-shirts printed up with the slogan "The Journey is the Reward." They were prized possessions later. The statement plays with metaphor in a way that kept people focused on the immediate work they needed to do and reframed the idea that visions are only about end states. A key assertion I make in this book is that a visual leader is one who is aware of his or her own metaphoric filters and mental models and is conscious about their use in key organizational communications.

AGENDAS AND SEATING MAPS

Of all the things you can do visually to focus a meeting, putting the agenda and a seating map on flip charts is about as useful as it gets. In startup teams, such as the one at HealthEast, people may know one another, but there are always one or two who aren't so sure (in this case the consultant). You might notice the little drawing below the seating chart. It was drawn to illustrate the complexity of a small group by drawing lines that indicate the number of possible relationships. These two simple charts illustrate three visual meeting methods: visual agendas, seating charts, and flip chart talks.

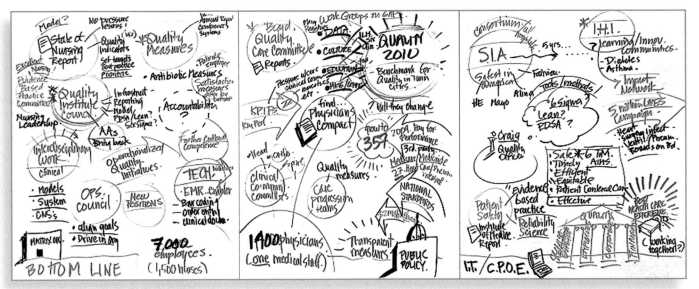

CLUSTER MAP OF QUALITY PROGRAMS AT HEALTHEAST

This cluster map was created on three flip charts while members listened to the HealthEast Quality Journey Team review the different quality programs that existed at the time. No effort was made to evaluate or connect them, but simply juxtapose all the information. This was very simple recording that anyone with decent handwriting could do. But the cumulative effect was to portray a complexity that convinced leadership it needed to spend time on alignment. Team members kept looking at this set of charts, shaking their heads.

Maps are another essential tool. Ones like the small seating chart seem simple, but putting everyone's names on one seating chart made a very clear statement— "We are in this together; we are on one sheet of paper; we are on one team." Maps allow people to see different relationships. We value maps of places we visit when travelling because they help orient us but aren't telling us where to go. (Perhaps the Quality Journey Team saw something in the seating arrangement, but it reflected only where people were actually sitting.) The next part of the meeting convinced the team that large-scale visualization was a promising way to achieve their goals.

Mapping the Quality Programs

The team began to explain some of the different quality programs currently in motion. Three flip charts began to fill up in a cluster format, one of the simplest kinds of maps, with items simply spaced out somewhat evenly without any connections. (The result is shown above.) Its impact was dramatic, even though it was only drawn on three flip charts in a small conference room. You'd have to be in the room to feel the team respond as more and more and more items were added. There really wasn't anyone who could disagree with the need to figure out a way to be more aligned and coordinated. Seeing was believing, in this case. In addition to appreciating the need for the project, the team also had a chance to experience graphic facilitation. Many of the team members had not been exposed to this way of working. They were quite excited. One of the powerful aspects of graphic "listening" of this sort is the way it concretely indicates whether the person doing the writing is hearing what is being said. It models, as no other medium can, that real understanding is the purpose of the engagement. It is a way of leading by listening.

How Can We Involve the Whole System?

The next concern in the Quality Journey Team meeting was having some confidence that the big visualization strategy would work with a larger group. The team needed all the stakeholders to come to the same conclusion it had—that something really needed to change in regard to cooperation between all these well-meaning programs. Historic experience with large meetings didn't necessarily give them confidence. They needed some guidance at this point.

If you get people excited about working visually, they will want to know concretely how the meeting will be run, and will want to believe that it will be successful. You will need to understand visual meeting methods well enough to explain how they work or work with someone who does. In this case Betsy and Pam were depending on consultation to guide the team, and Susan to keep everyone oriented to the practical realities. They knew enough to trust the recommendations they were receiving. If you are thinking, "I don't know enough and don't have the resources to bring in professionals," you can still reach out to other experienced people in your organization for help. This book will accelerate your ability to make good choices about your partners and know how to manage them to get the results you desire.

Choices in a Visual Toolkit

The sketches here and on the following page helped HealthEast team members imagine what was possible at a bigger meeting they were prepared to organize for 65 to 70 key stakeholders.

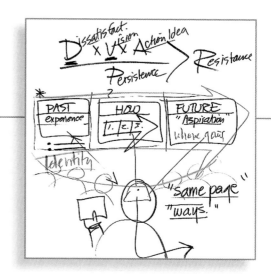

FLIP CHART TALK
$D \times V \times A > R$

One tool in organizational work is the DVA > R model for change. It's an important mental model for leaders to think through the necessary components needed for change to begin. This quick sketch was used to explain it to HealthEast.

DISSATISFACTION: A feeling that current realities need to change.

VISION: A compelling picture of a future opportunity.

ACTION IDEA: Some clear ideas about immediate steps that could credibly move toward the vision.

RESISTANCE: DV&A have to be stronger than R. Resistance and inertia are always present in change.

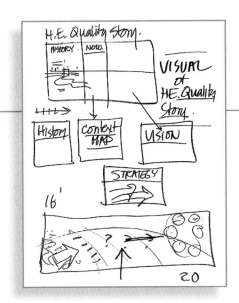

STORYMAPS FOR CHANGE

In the HealthEast case, Betsy and the team were explicit in asking for guidance on how to accomplish their goals.

This chart illustrated two choices for visualizing the DVA aspects of a change story.

1. Work up separate maps.

2. Combine them into one, integrated picture.

Creating simple sketches like this is an important skill for leaders to develop. The drawings do not have to be complicated or in any way refined. They are memory aids to help everyone remember the verbal communication that went with them.

The concepts arise from the repeated interests people have when it comes to listening to leaders talk about plans. Think about your own organization and times when your leaders wanted you to do something new. To successfully convince you, they probably needed to have their story touch on each of the four elements listed here.

1. **History:** People want to know what led up to the current situation. This is especially important for people who fear they will be passed over during changes. It's in the history telling that everyone begins to tune in to the need for change.

2. **Context/Why Change?** People need a story about why they need to change. In Part III we'll dig in to how to work as a leader in these sessions to get people to identify the drivers of change and the key issues, or what some call burning platforms.

3. **Vision:** Imagining the desired future and the benefits of change are also important. Just saying things are a problem doesn't move a situation. There needs to be a pull forward toward something new.

4. **Action Plan:** Even with a clear idea that current reality needs to be changed and that there is a brighter possibility somewhere in the future, people don't move unless they can see clear action steps possible in the near term. These stories are the strategies, the immediate priority goals, and the pictures that suggest a credible path forward.

If you examine the drawing on this page, you can see these choices illustrated very simply. The chart shows how they could either be treated separately or all integrated in one big mural. The project leaders would be able to determine which after the big meeting. We reviewed how the meeting could be structured to draw out everyone's ideas along these four lines. Prior to the meeting, the team had been able to look at samples of what other organizations have done with their visions, so they were confident that these sketches could develop into complete maps. Let's look at the next stages of the story before looking at the final result.

The Big Mapping Meeting

Betsy, Pam, and Susan received approval to stage a meeting with all the VPs and their direct reports—about 65 people from across the five hospitals and related clinics. Seeing the support of the VPs, Tim was now in full support. It was overtly titled the HealthEast Quality Journey Mapping Meeting. It was held in January of 2008. The outcomes and agenda are shown here on the chart.

Leveraging Preparation Activities

A big visualization event is an excuse to do some very important preparation work. Actually, much of the work of enrolling support gets done in these more informal sessions. (Some of the key opportunities afforded by advanced preparation are listed in the sidebar on the next page.) Betsy and Pam were thorough about taking advantage of every one of these opportunities.

All of this happened with no involvement from consultants, except on the day of the event. In specific terms here is what Betsy and Pam had to do to get the buy-in:

1. Talk about the work they'd been doing with templates
2. Share samples of visual storymaps from other organizations
3. Meet individually with everyone
4. Meet individually with the CEO
5. Meet individually with the operation VPs
6. Hold a joint meeting with VPs and leadership presenting the idea

PREP TEAM OPPORTUNITIES

In the picture above are Susan Nelson, Betsy Stites, Pam Hull and a participant (left to right). Part of their leadership work was making sure all the staging and logistics were taken care of and the higher up leaders were briefed. They also made sure that as many people as possible were involved in helping the consultant so that they could learn from the experience.

The picture to the left shows one of the staff filling out a Meeting Startup Graphic Guide as people gathered.

The picture below shows Susan and Betsy suggesting key elements in the history that could be added to the chart in advance. These details served as a catalyst for the history storytelling. that would begin the meeting.

PREMEETING OPPORTUNITY CHECKLIST

Following are some of the things you should think about in regard to leveraging any event you might have that involves key players.

❏ **Briefing Executives:** Getting executive-level people to lead off the meeting provides an excuse to prep them, bring them along about the process, and strengthen their support.

❏ **Staging:** You may want certain information visible throughout your meeting. Focal murals provide chances to reinforce your goals and keep staff focused.

❏ **Facilitation Training:** Getting key people to help facilitate deepens their understanding and buy-in and increases collaborative leadership.

❏ **Consultant Training:** As a leader you need to know how to manage consultants. It's essential that you shape these kinds of events so that your organization benefits. Large consulting firms have a vested interest in selling time and aren't necessarily oriented to building capacity. Insist that your people get all the relevant experience they can and keep the consulting to just the bits you really can't do yourself.

❏ **Event-Driven Action:** In larger organizations many things compete for people's time. Having a commitment to hold a big event introduces some urgency and forces people to not only think things out in advance but also tidy things up if their work might be visible in the meeting. For many high-tech firms, managing toward new product releases is a way of life.

CEO	Director Leadership Development	Chief Medical Quality Officer	Chief Medical Officer
Tim Hanson	Betsy Stites	Craig Svendsen	Bob Beck

Leaders Frame the Opportunity

One of the most critical pieces of work for a leader is *framing* events and opportunities. This is, of course, a metaphor drawn from our experience with pictures in galleries and our homes. Just as picture frames are clues to value, the same is true for organizational events and processes. The HealthEast team did a model job of this. It's a practice you can put in your toolkit right now.

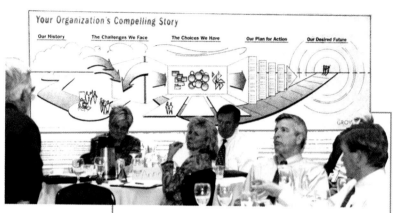

1. **CEO:** Tim Hanson, the CEO, opened the event and gave it his full blessing. This was an important endorsement. He'd become totally enrolled imagining using a map like this with his board.

2. **Director of Leadership Development:** Everyone knew Betsy was a driver and known for getting practical results on her prior projects. She told the story of how they got to this point and all the work that had been done behind the scenes.

3. **Chief Medical Quality Officer:** As a key stakeholder and key member of the project team, Craig Svendsen was the voice of the outcomes and goals for the meeting.

4. **Chief Medical Officer:** Bob Beck's endorsement was another essential signal that the doctors and nurses were behind the process. Bob introduced me as the facilitator of the event to make this perfectly clear. Bob was part of the project team and by this time was fully aware of how the meeting would be conducted and what they might expect.

5. **Facilitator:** I facilitated the meeting. One of the advantages of an external person in this situation was everyone knowing that my only stake was having the meeting work, with no position in the outcomes. Having a facilitator whose primary agenda was the success of the meeting itself allowed the key leaders to be full players in the event.

When you work with an outside professional, it's very important that you maintain complete control over the outcomes and intended results. The best way is to always have you and other leaders be the ones who give voice to what the meeting is about.

Panoramic Visualization

The next part of this meeting included three activities central to a big visual meeting aimed at visioning. It mirrors the three parts of the DVA > R formula talked about earlier. These elements would be very interactive and focused on the participants.

PROVIDING A PROCESS FRAMEWORK

You may have had experience with too much "process orientation" on the part of external consultants or internal facilitators and well-meaning human resources (HR) professionals. But organizational leaders are results focused and generally responsive to results-oriented visualization. The picture above is of me presenting a graphic framework to orient everyone to the key elements in a Storymap—The Grove's name for these large murals. It illustrates an integrated approach to visualizing the DVA > R framework. It is direct and results-oriented. It calls for clarity on:

1. Where are we now, and why change?

2. Where do we want to go in the future?

3. How will we get there?

The tangibility and results orientation of this framework are real advantages of visualization.

HEALTHEAST QUALITY HISTORY

This and the next page reproduce the entire history map created at the opening of the HealthEast leadership meeting. The detail will not be meaningful to those of you outside this system, but try to imagine what it must have been like to hear all these stories. St. Joseph's, the oldest hospital in the system and the oldest in Minnesota, was founded in 1853. Over the years five different organizations merged! Very seldom, if ever, had the leadership group had a chance to just celebrate its stories. "This meeting was so fun!" Betsy exclaimed when I talked with her about publishing this story. "The experience gave us a chance to celebrate who we are."

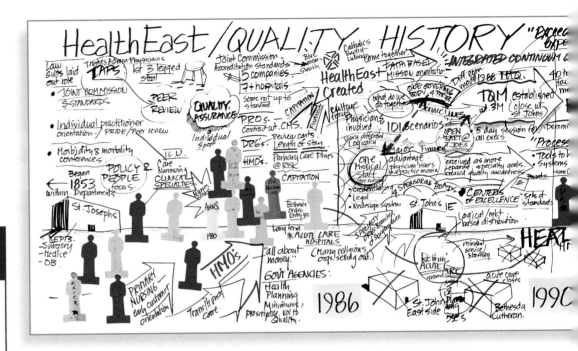

HOW TO DO YOUR OWN HISTORY

These are the steps to creating your own history:

1. Post a very long piece of paper on the wall and draw a horizon line.

2. Use sticky notes to write the years or months and space them out; give more to recent history.

3. Draw some key events/people/projects to anchor everyone's memory.

4. Have everyone put a sticker on the time he or she joined the organization.

5. Get the early folks to say what it was like when they joined and write down headlines and key points. Use circles for key meetings, arrows for projects, and simple images.

6. Ask, "When did that happen?" and keep going!

A History of Quality

Following the setup, the meeting sprang to life, with the first big session telling the quality story from a historical perspective. The entire history is included here so that you will get a visceral feeling of just how powerful an experience this can be. The details won't mean anything to you, the reader, but the little graphics and overall energy give you a sense of the kinetic quality of the process. Initially the history was a simple timeline with a couple of key drawings about events everyone knew about, such as when the different hospitals joined (shown as buildings). These were important anchors for everyone's memories. The second part was having everyone get up and post a little people sticky at the time he or she joined the organization. People milled around and talked, flooded with memories, and bumped up against cohorts who joined when they had.

It immediately, and graphically, demonstrated the wide range of experience at play.

The actually storytelling was done in the group as a whole, beginning with the earliest folks. This honored them and began to uncover some of the initiating elements that created the HealthEast culture. The story became dynamic, and very animated. As a facilitator you have to keep asking, "When did that happen?"

LOGGING IN: HealthEast leaders add their names to the history timeline at the beginning of the event.

GUIDING PRINCIPLES FOR A GRAPHIC HISTORY SESSION

If you are interested in doing a graphic history of your organization, following is a checklist that you can share with whomever you recruit to facilitate the session:

❏ **Leave plenty of time:** Once the stories start, it is very hard to slow the process down. A good history review can easily take two hours for a larger organization.

❏ **Create a simple framework:** Encourage your facilitators to have some of the anchoring events already added in, with clear demarcation of the years or months.

❏ **Use sticky notes to get engagement:** Having everyone get up and post things is a great energizer. It can be names, key products, or whatever you want to have pop out.

❏ **Encourage the facilitators to focus on writing quickly and simply:** Acknowledgment is the key in this process. If you want a refined graphic history, then work on it later and go through versions.

❏ **Call out people you know should be sharing stories:** There are always some people who are shy in group settings. The facilitator won't know as much as you do about who to draw out.

❏ **Follow with a break:** Let people continue talking. There are always more stories.

❏ **Take digital pictures:** People love to have records of these charts.

so you know where to write on the chart. It's fast, intentionally. Making the chart neat is a secondary concern. So what is really going on here, and why is this such a powerful process?

Interaction Is Key

The messiness of the history-telling process is one of its great virtues, and worked very well with HealthEast. In organizations everyone sooner or later crafts some sort of story about the past, about why this or that has come to be, and why certain things are valued and others aren't. For some people with long service, these stories can get quite developed. They become filters through which all new discussion must pass. How many times have you been in meetings where a person will chime in, "We can't do that. We tried it before, and it didn't work."

In a group storytelling session such as the one at HealthEast, it becomes clear very quickly that no one's story includes all the facts or all the important bits. People realize they've forgotten whole chunks. The process disturbs the entrenched stories and provides a chance to update them. No one loses face or has his or her individual stories challenged. In fact, the individual story elements that get shared are celebrated and recorded up where everyone can see.

One of the reasons for using simple graphics—like circles for meetings, arrows for big projects, and mostly bullet points—is because trying to reflect interpretations of what it all means is not the point. The point is to give people a chance to listen to each other. If anything, people should be watching the speakers.

But the graphics play an important role in creating a massive piece of evidence about the richness and complexity of the organization's experience, and in providing enough detail to allow people to start seeing bigger patterns. The primary value of this activity is community building and celebrating. But a strong secondary value is system-level insight. It is possible to follow a history session with an analytical activity that reflects on core values, for instance, or key operating principles, or traces back to key turning points. In HealthEast's case the purpose was celebration.

Continuing the Interaction around "Why Change?"

The next part of the Mapping Meeting began anchoring the emotion of the history session in the current realities of the quality effort at HealthEast. This part answered the question, "Why change?" We repeated the mapping experience the Quality Journey Team experienced, but on a much larger, self-managed scale. The chart shown here (twice as long) had a number of labels on it to begin with (see sidebar). Small groups were asked to identify quality activities that were happening now on hexagons and planned projects on circular sticky notes, mapping them into the categories.

The small groups had rousing discussions. It's not important to read this data but to appreciate that it was the real conversations and the overwhelming, incontrovertible evidence of the big display that made the case that everyone needed to align.

If you are a leader who doesn't normally facilitate, you should appreciate that this kind of exercise can be managed by anyone with some group experience. If you suggest it, and encourage whoever is conducting the meeting to work large scale, you would experience similar results. Panorama makes a difference. Everyone can feel the information as well as think about it. The advantage of sticky notes is you don't need a facilitator trying to write down everything. You do need to encourage people to write clearly.

MAPPING CURRENT REALITIES

The chart shown below is a simply structured context map. Small groups were asked to identify all current quality programs on hexagon sticky notes and all proposed and planned programs on circular ones. The colors were varied just to have a more colorful display. By lightly structuring the display, the groups could be asked to put their stickies in the relevant area of the organization. The labels were things such as:

CONSUMER	EMPLOYEES
INFRASTRUCTURE	PHYSICIANS
CULTURE	OPERATIONS
CLINICAL	CLINICS

(See Chapter 9 for more how-to advice.)

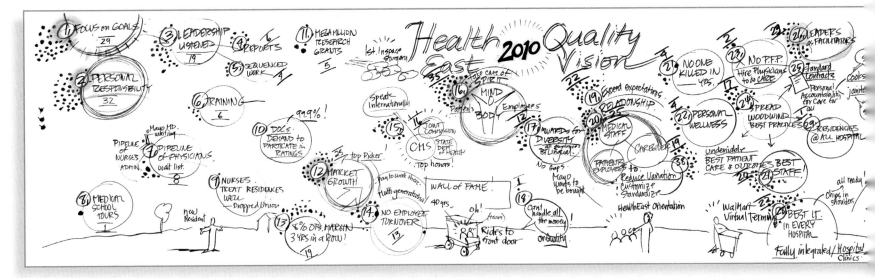

HEALTHEAST QUALITY VISION

After identifying all potential vision elements on a big cluster map, leadership participants marked dots on the elements they wanted at the heart of their vision moving forward.

Agreeing on a Quality Vision

The next part of the Mapping Meeting was as exciting and inspiring as the last part was sobering. Small groups were asked to think about the future and what results they would like to see. These

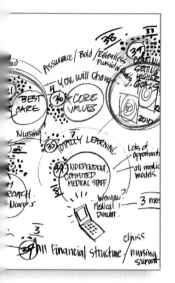

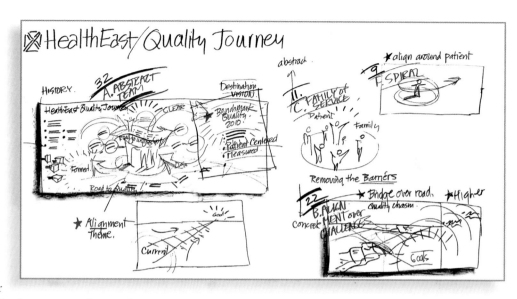

are called vision elements. Individuals at the tables were asked to be recorders of the key ideas. During the reporting process one group was asked to share an idea. It went up on the chart with a circle. Then other tables were asked if they had the same idea or additional thoughts. Then another table would volunteer a new idea and see it written down somewhere else. All the focus was on the people speaking and their visions of what was possible. No effort was made to organize the items. All the vision elements were just atoms of information at this point.

The exchange around these ideas was very inspiring. When all the ideas were posted, they were numbered. Everyone received one-third the total number to vote for. We used markers, not sticky dots, and asked people to cluster the dots around the number of the items. Within 15 minutes we could graphically see where the interest and passion lay. The top dotted items were circled to pop them out visually. This kind of process honors all individual ideas and the collective at the same time. It wraps the vision around everyone in a physically dramatic way that adds real excitement to the process. The dot voting is another chance to engage interactively with others outside of the table groups. The participation gives a chance for top leaders to see where everyone is focused and who is engaging whom. For Tim, the CEO, who wanted to have everyone enrolled, it was the evidence he needed to fully back moving to a more detailed plan of action.

FINDING AN INTEGRATING GRAPHIC METAPHOR

Several simple sketches illustrated metaphors suggested by the group for pulling the vision information together. Some wanted a picture centered on an abstract team; another suggested a family of service; another a journey image showing alignment going over a series of challenges; another a simple spiral. (There were four or five more on another chart.) Everyone voted for his or her top three choices, and two of these were picked for a smaller leadership core to consider the following day. These are the kinds of choices a designer would present to you based on the way you prefer to think about your organization.

INSTANT DECISION ROOMS

One of the essential tools explored later in Chapter 10 is the use of decision rooms for getting alignment on big decisions. This picture is an excellent example. The large charts created the day before at the HealthEast Quality Journey Mapping Meeting have been reposted here. The group did a walking review as a start for this second meeting. Big banners and charts allow for any room to be converted easily into a decision room. There is really no other medium that affords the power of panoramic display as directly as simple markers on large sheets. It is also completely affordable.

Quality Journey Project Team Meeting

The day after the big Mapping Meeting, the smaller project team (shown here) met at Health-East to refine the ideas and decide what would go into the final illustration of its Quality Vision. As a leader, you need to appreciate that there are roles for big group input, roles for smaller groups, and places where executive decision is needed. The big group gave everyone in the smaller group a sense of where the passion and general interest lay. Being inside the organization, the Quality Journey Team could also make sense out of the many different statements and interactions from the day before, noticing who was moving forward and who was resisting the contemplated change. All these understandings poured into this day's discussion.

This meeting would not be the last conversation, either. Visual mapping affords leaders the possibility to circulate versions and have many individual conversations that are required to align.

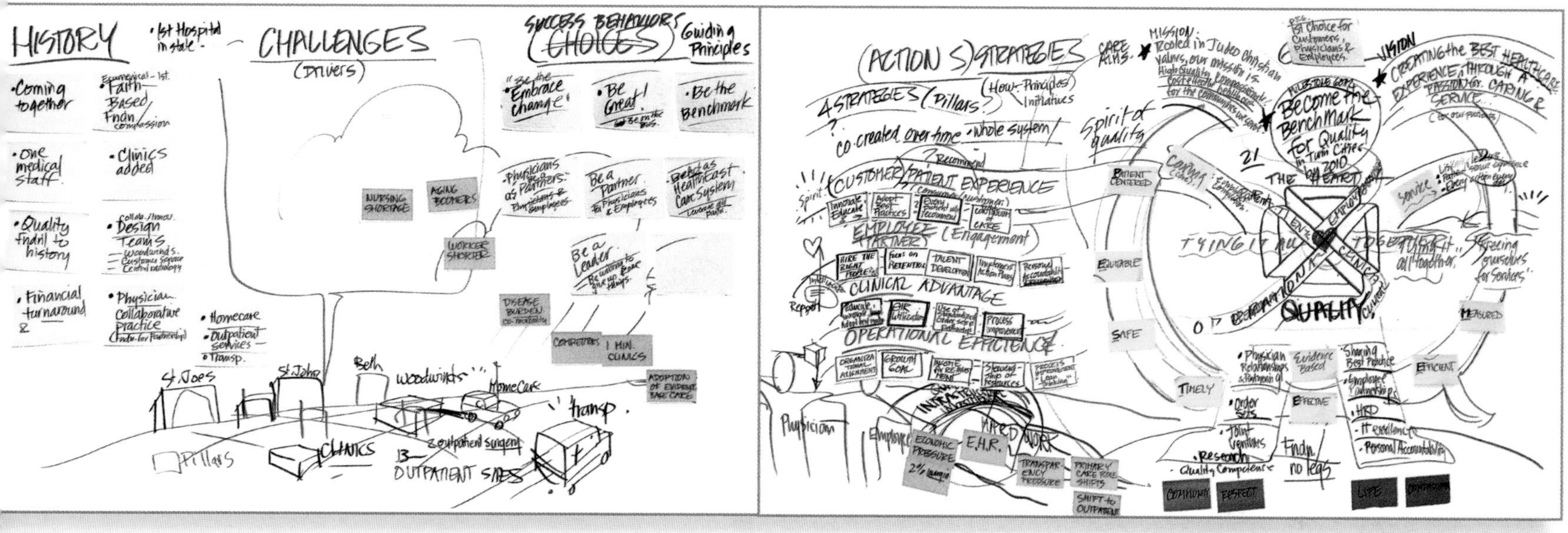

The chart above looks fairly organized, but it is the by-product of a very dynamic day of talk. There are some key process takeaways for visual leaders, apart from the content illustrated here.

1. **Use metaphors to support whole-systems thinking:** Having the group wrestle again with the integrating metaphor allowed everyone to think about the organization as a whole system in a very useful way. Seeing four strategies becoming the knot logo was exciting.

2. **Tag critical stories:** The content on the sticky notes was seen as headlines and talking points for critical stories that needed to be shared directly by leaders. They agreed that real change happens when leaders own the communication process, enrolling others personally, and staying aligned and using common language. Co-creating the chart made this possible.

3. **Use subgroups:** In this kind of meeting, smaller teams take a portion of the big idea and make a first pass at the language, then share and receive responses. Groups always have some who are better at the words than others. This small-to-big group process worked well.

INFORMATION ARCHITECTURE

The charts shown here are a great example of how an architectural design can facilitate detailed examination of elements. This is the "interior decorating" aspect of information design. The Quality Journey Team chose the journey-crossing-a-bridge-of-challenges framework, building on the metaphor embedded in their name. Subteams then developed the historic pieces that needed to be talked about, the challenges, the success behaviors, the action strategies, and the information on the far right about the end-state vision: their 2010 Quality Goal.

ABOUT THE HEALTHEAST QUALITY JOURNEY MAP

The Quality Journey map shown here is the sixth version of the large mural created to align all of the leadership and quality programs at HealthEast Care System in St. Paul, Minnesota. The content was distilled from the initial three meetings with over five dozen key stakeholders, refined by divisional leadership in many subsequent meetings, and vetted by the CEO. It served as a storytelling tool during implementation of new plans.

The full map allowed managers to explain where HealthEast began, where it was going, and how it intended to get there in regard to quality.

History: The left side of this map reflects the long-held mission of HealthEast and key points about the history, each of which is a story that leadership wanted to keep alive.

Context: The map shows, in a more literal way, the actual HealthEast Care System. There was a lot of discussion about the buildings and their size. Clinics were added in one of the versions. It's a simplified representation but had to be faithful to realities and respectful of all the stakeholders.

Challenges: Mapping these into the river that runs through St. Paul seemed perfect. Arguments about these factors ran well past the initial design meeting. They are arranged from oldest on the horizon to the newest in the foreground.

The concept and design were co-created by the HealthEast Quality Journey Team and The Grove Consultants International.

HealthEast Care System

MISSION

Rooted in Judeo Christian values, our mission is high quality, compassionate, cost effective health care for the communities we serve.

Quality Journey

HISTORY

1853
First hospital in Minn.

1980s
HealthEast formed
Faith-based principles
Coming together
ONE medical staff
Quality principles
3M TQM
One Board

1990s
Centers of excellence
Design teams
Physician collaborative practice
One system accreditation
IHI

2000s
EMR implementation
Transparency
External benchmarking
Nursing-magnet journey

Serving the Community ...all Faiths

WOODWINDS · MIDWAY CORPORATE SERVICES · CLINIC · HOME · OUTPATIENT · ST. JOSEPH'S · BETHESDA · ST. JOHN'S · CLINIC · OUTPATIENT SERVICES · SALUD · TRANSPORTATION

SUCCESS BEHAVIORS

★ BE the Change
★ BE a CARE System
★ BE Collaborative
★ BE a Learner
★ Embrace Legacy
★ BE a Steward
★ BE Accountable
★ BE in Service

STRATEGIES

Patient Experience
• Innovate, educate & adopt be
• Every patient will recommend

Employee
• Hire the right people • Rete
• Innovate, educate & adopt b

Clinical Advantag
• Standardized order sets • P
• Innovate, educate & adopt

Operational Efficie
• Growth goals • Organizationa
• Income for reinvestment • Ste

CHALLENGES
• Healthcare Reform
• Medicare Tsunami
• Aging Population
• Chronic Disease
• Workforce Shortages

Ver. 6.0 © 2008 HealthEast. Created by The Grove Consultants International

Creating the Final Quality Vision Map

During the next several weeks after the two meetings at HealthEast, The Grove created this graphic to reflect all the input. This is the kind of mural that a growing number of information designers can create for clients. At The Grove, we call them storymaps, because we want to keep the focus on the real power in the process, which is having leadership show up in an aligned way. This is, metaphorically speaking, a backdrop for management theater! Having co-created the map, everyone tells the same story because it reflects agreed-upon language and imagery, not

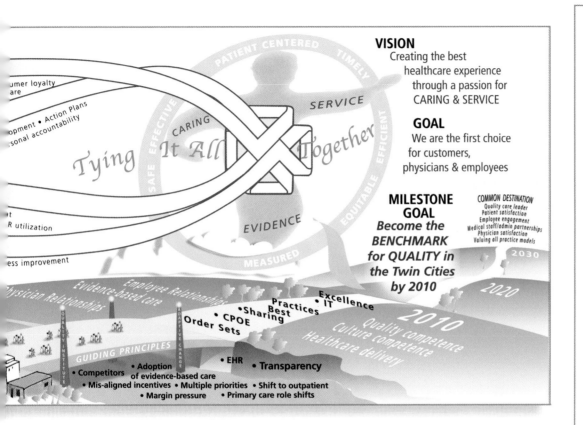

VISION
Creating the best
healthcare experience
through a passion for
CARING & SERVICE

GOAL
We are the first choice
for customers,
physicians & employees

**MILESTONE
GOAL**
Become the
**BENCHMARK
for QUALITY in
the Twin Cities
by 2010**

COMMON DESTINATION
Quality care leader
Patient satisfaction
Employee engagement
Medical staff/admin partnerships
Physician satisfaction
Valuing all practice models

2030

2020

2010

Quality competence
Culture competence
Healthcare delivery

Excellence
• IT
Best
Practices
• Sharing
• CPOE
Order Sets

• EHR • **Transparency**

GUIDING PRINCIPLES

• **Competitors** • **Adoption**
of evidence-based care
• **Mis-aligned incentives** • **Multiple priorities** • **Shift to outpatient**
• **Margin pressure** • **Primary care role shifts**

Employee Relationships
Evidence-based care
Physician Relationships

umer loyalty
care

opment • Action Plans
sonal accountability

R utilization

ess improvement

someone's independent artistic design. This map went through six versions with Betsy, Pam, and Susan involving all the critical stakeholders in dialogue over the best words to use. "We would go to each of the divisions and bring the Quality Journey map," Betsy said. "We'd say—this is a draft. We aren't changing direction. Can we all buy into the words? Are the barriers on the river really the ones? Is it correct? Are the four strategies where they should be?' We wanted ownership and wanted everyone to be really conversant with it so they could use it and speak to it."

TYING IT ALL TOGETHER

Your challenge as a leader is to help people in your organization see how everything you are doing fits together. A storymap process allows people to see the links that are sometimes obscured by isolated functions. Here are some more of the elements integrated in the HealthEast map.

Success Behaviors: Betsy, as head of the leadership development and cultural elements, wanted to make sure the work they had done on core values was integrated as "success behaviors."

Strategies & Action Plan: Pam, as the strategist, wanted to see the behaviors linked to the strategy. After many, many conversations about how they fit, everyone in the organization came to a mutual understanding. They also included specific action steps across the river on the ground.

Vision Image: It got a bit magical when they saw that the four big action areas could be seen as ribbons forming their knotted logo!

The story of the vision image on the left is instructive. The Quality Institute had a set of principles (shown in the big Q). Some other principles went beyond quality: caring, service, and evidence-based medicine. These seemed to compete, until the group realized that, mapped on the human body—in this case a figure representing the "spirit of nursing"—there wasn't a contradiction. People stand on their feet *and* have caring emotions.

Goals: The official strategic goals of the organization capped the map and put the quality vision in it's full context

VIP LEADERSHIP

A wonderfully simple leadership model came out of the Apple Leadership Experience in the 1980s when Jim Kouzes was just formulating his work in leadership. He talked about the success factors being vision, involvement, and persistence. This simple framework reflects Betsy and Pam's leadership style at HealthEast, and what you can take away as learning.

VISION
Use mapping to align leadership on 2010 Quality Goal and on how to implement it.

PERSISTENCE
They had it to spare, meeting twice with five hospitals, clinics, and the Quality group in 25 meetings!

INVOLVEMENT
They got totally involved and involved others as facilitative leaders.

This simple visual framework is a nice way to record ideas for each of these with groups you work with. It lightly suggests needing to connect the top-line aspirations with bottom-line realities. If you are interested in leadership, Jim Kouzes, in partnership with Barry Posner, has evolved the model into a well-researched and validated five-factor model described in *The Leadership Challenge*. It's a standard in the leadership development business.

Seeing the Results in Action

For Betsy and Pam, completing the storymap was only the beginning. Their first big step was developing the 2010 Quality Goal in HealthEast's strategy. But alignment in action is what they needed to actually see results. Their visual leadership provided this by sponsoring a big picture everyone agreed upon. From that process they reported these results:

1. Clarity, integration, and direction for HealthEast's quality strategy

2. Clarified language so that everyone was using the same terms

3. Leadership alignment

4. Crystallization and coalescing of ideas

5. Seeing how success behaviors link to core behaviors and the strategy

6. Building the Quality Vision into all new employee orientations

7. Using the Quality Vision at board meetings

8. Using the Quality Vision in HealthEast's Leadership Development Institute

9. Helping institutionalize visual practice at HealthEast

Betsy reports that they met the goals outlined in the map. Craig still uses it in his Quality Institute work. Pam's strategy work continues to be visual and template-guided. And a new CEO wants to repeat the process and get the current team aligned in this same way.

Let's turn our attention to how you can achieve these kinds of results yourself, in both little and big ways, no matter what kinds of organization you may be leading. In the last chapter, we'll return to HealthEast for a look at how visual leadership has evolved since the mapping project.

3. How to Run Visual Meetings
What Every Manager Should Know

Visual meetings are those face-to-face and virtual meetings that use active graphic recording, large displays, graphic templates, roadmaps, murals, and other visual media to support communications and interaction. Even though all these tools are part of the visual meeting tool set, this chapter focuses on how you as a leader can use interactive visualization, not a finished graphic of any sort, to support communications. In a time when presentation software seems to have dominated business meetings, it may seem retrograde to go back to simple visualization. However, experience suggests that less is more in this regard. If the goal of a leader is to get everyone engaged in focusing on the right things, and remembering them, visual meetings do this.

Regular and Special Meetings

Let's begin by thinking about all the meetings you hold. Bill Daniels, an influential consultant to organizations, makes an important distinction between "regular" and "special" meetings. He defines regular meetings as the kind that you as a leader or manager conduct with your direct reports as a way of regulating your organization. The special meetings are those workshops, planning off-sites, and special Web conferences where routine processes are set aside to engage in special activities. Let's look at the differences.

REGULAR MEETINGS	SPECIAL MEETINGS
1. Introduce new people	1. Step back to examine assumptions
2. Check progress	2. Explore visions and goals
3. Enforce discipline	3. Experience new ways to work
4. Make decisions	4. Focus on leadership development
5. Delegate work	5. Learn new strategies

Regular meetings are usually run by you and would reflect your style and the culture of your organization. They are probably highly individualized based on the way you like to run things. If you've

INTERACTION IS KING

People learn and remember when they are engaged and interact with new ideas and information. This illustration of a cycle of visual listening shows the different things going on. The elements happen with a bit of a time lag, stimulating participants to pay attention and understand the patterns. This interactive cross-checking and feedback makes visual meetings much more engaging than presentations with slide software.

THESE ARE
NICE AND BASIC

ever had an outsider try to run one of your staff meetings, then you will appreciate how tricky this is, unless he or she is, in effect, on the team..

Special meetings, on the other hand, are often facilitated by internal process people or external consultants, allowing you as the leader a chance to participate without derailing the meeting. Much of the methodology and tools used by facilitators and reviewed in *Visual Meetings* and in *Visual Teams* applies to these meetings. Visualization crosses this boundary. This and the next page list specific visual meeting tools you might use in both regular and special meetings.

REGULAR MEETING TOOLS

INTRODUCE NEW PEOPLE	CHECK PROGRESS	ENFORCE DISCIPLINE	MAKE DECISIONS	DELEGATE WORK
❏ **Share your history:** Tell the story of your unit visually.	❏ **Review roadmaps and special meeting reports:** Reorient to the big picture.	❏ **Review metrics:** Visualize measures that show progress against goals.	❏ **Review simple proposal sheets:** Have people describe things needing decision succinctly on handouts or flip charts (see Chapter 8).	❏ **Record action owners:** When you assign work, create a list and write the names of owners—better yet have them write their own names.
❏ **Review vision:** Share a printout of your vision.	❏ **Review progress lists:** Many managers use a simple matrix or list.	❏ **Acknowledge exemplary behavior:** Focus on positive reinforcement, if possible.	❏ **Create action lists:** Record agreements on flip charts. It strengthens commitments if you, the leader, do this.	❏ **Link to vision & goals:** Keep a clear line of sight to the bigger purposes of your work.
❏ **Summarize roles:** Lead a go-around with everyone identifying his or her role. (Someone could record this but it's not necessary.)	❏ **Record areas needing support:** Results come from everyone helping one another.	❏ **Explain personnel actions:** Get on top of interpretations if you have to let someone go.		

You'll recognize in the list of generic goals for special meetings the DVA > R formula shared in Chapter 2 (page 17). Special meetings are the times you as leader can step back and look at the bigger picture. This is where visualization is truly helpful. The outputs from special meetings then become reference documents in the regular meetings.

Scan through these choices and check off the ones you know. There are more tools than these, but these are some of the most common. In the rest of this chapter there are some regular meeting tools you can use yourself and suggestions for how to work with others in special meetings.

PANORAMAS

WOW!

"SPECIAL" MEETING TOOLS

EXAMINE ASSUMP-TIONS	EXPERIENCE NEW WAYS TO WORK	EXPLORE VISIONS/ GOALS	DEVELOP STRATEGIES & PLANS	DEVELOP LEADERS
❏ **Describe the relevant environ-ment:** Use context maps to under-stand the market, constituents, and stakeholders. ❏ **Identify drivers of change:** Identify reasons for change. ❏ **Summarize key presentations:** Record and keep posted.	❏ **Rapidly proto-type new ideas:** Use graphics to have small groups invent solutions to problems and report visually. ❏ **Make some videos:** Improvise some storytelling and shoot informal videos.	❏ **Create cover stories:** Stand in the future and imagine the big headlines. ❏ **Guided imagery:** Lead everyone into the future and imagine success. ❏ **Organize affinity charts:** Cover a wall with sticky notes and find ar-eas of agreement.	❏ **Prioritize vision elements and goals:** Use tem-plates and sticky notes to identify and sort priorities. ❏ **Create game-plans and road-maps:** Work a big wall until everyone clearly sees the way forward.	❏ **Explore meta-phors for orga-nization:** Identify and talk about the different answers to the question, "Our organization is like a . . . ?" ❏ **Create a Sto-rymap:** Explore how plans, cultural values, and norms support it.

OARRs METAPHOR

One of the most memorable frameworks for running a good meeting came from a client who asked what the simplest facilitation tool would be. The acronym for the four things to get right is OARRs and they map to the metaphor illustrated below. They suggest what you need to clarify to navigate the "river" of your meeting. This image is simple enough that you can get everyone to visualize these as a way to boost meeting productivity.

1. **Outcomes:** Clarify where you are heading.

2. **Agenda:** Get everyone in the same framework or "boat" to navigate the river of the meeting.

3. **Roles:** Define what you mean by leaders, facilitators, experts, and supporters before you begin.

4. **Rules:** Set any ground rules that will help you avoid capsizing.

Four Things to Get Right in Your Meetings

There are so many poorly run meetings that many people hate them. Considering their cost, it's worth improving them, especially if they are your meetings. An easy way is by getting four things right and visualizing them. This applies to any kind of meeting—regular, special, face-to-face, or virtual. They create the acronym OARRs. The metaphor should help you remember them. Let's look at each one briefly.

1. **Outcomes:** If you do nothing else, get these clear at the beginning of meetings. This is where you would express your expectations in a regular meeting and indicate the agreed-upon outcomes of a design team in a special meeting. They should describe what you want to have happen by the end of the meeting. Clarifying outcomes is the most effective action you can take to improve meetings. Writing them down visibly makes a big difference.

2. **Agendas:** A simple agenda is a list of the items that need to be covered, in the order you want to treat them. A graphic agenda would do this in a "time block" framework where graphics boxes around the items are sized to the amount of time you want to spend on them. Some simple agendas are illustrated in this chapter. Chapter 8 describes some ways to create larger agendas for guiding more complex processes.

3. **Roles:** Increase your flexibility by holding different roles and describing them clearly. Coach any facilitators or visual practitioners you work with to clearly indicate his or her role as well. Metaphors help. Are you the driver of the meeting, a coach, a referee, an evaluator, or designer? These are all leader roles but are very different from one another.

4. **Rules:** Make agreements about how you will handle known kinds of problems in advance of incidents. It can often prevent them from happening at all. How do you plan to handle people who are dominating? How will you deal with decisions? Are you going to make them? Will you accept input? Are you working by consensus? Can people use computers? Can they text during a meeting? All these things are better dealt with in advance.

CURES FOR SLIDE-O-MANIA

It's understandable that so many people get carried away creating slides. It's fun! It's visual. It makes your ideas look official and thought through. But like any quick fix, it has bad side effects, stemming largely from the assumption that people can consume pretty information just by having it presented to them. There are some cures, however.

❏ Take as long working with the ideas interactively as you did in getting them clear yourself.

❏ Stick to a few, simple, focal images, tell stories, and elicit discussion and dialogue.

❏ Use large murals for complex ideas that require study of connections and relationships.

❏ Hand illustrate ideas in their early stages so that people will be more willing to make suggestions.

The Problem with Presentation Software

If you are in the habit of making reports and reviewing work using decks of slides, you are already working visually, but not necessarily supporting good group interaction. The illustrations on this page visualize the problem. As the creator of a slide presentation, you or your direct reports get a good visual workout. This is what designers do—prototype ideas visually. So far, so good. But you have a problem if you assume that the slides can recreate the experience you had. So you send them out in advance. But people rarely spend much time studying things from e-mail unless it's mission critical. In meetings or Web conferences, long slide presentations are almost never at a pace where a person can absorb new ideas. And guess where the decks that are handed out end up—usually in a stack, and then … well you know the rest of the story. People put up with it because you are the boss. It doesn't mean it works.

If you want to really show you are listening, set up a flip chart and record yourself. You might do this for action items, adding names of owners of delegated projects, or outlining simple agendas for your regular meetings. Here are some basic tips.

❏ Use CAPS for titles and lowercase for supporting items.

❏ Write big enough for everyone to read easily.

❏ Capture key words; check with the speaker to make sure they are correct.

❏ Use earth colors for text—black, blue, green, and brown.

❏ Use bright colors for highlighting—orange and yellow.

❏ Use red for special emphasis.

❏ Draw thin lines between items in a list.

❏ Add consistent bullet points. (It's fun to develop a little set you can create easily—such as boxes, asterisks, and little arrows.)

❏ Line up all of your items on the left and leave some space for any annotations or comments.

For more detail along these lines, purchase Visual Meetings *and* Visual Teams. *They are available online at www.grove.com and loaded with help for visual practitioners. They are helpful if you like to use charts or to coach people who help you.*

Visual Listening Is at the Heart of Visual Meetings

What does work as an alternative to slide fixation is true engagement, interaction, and, most of all, real listening. All of the essential tools we will look at in Part III have at their heart visual listening—the act of reflecting what people say interactively with graphic visualization. Once this happens, then the pattern finding and planning that happen occur at an entirely different level of involvement and effectiveness. Putting person-to-person communication back at the center of your leadership, without sacrificing the quality of your thinking, is the goal of visual leadership.

Bob Horn, founder of Information Mapping in Boston, loved to record in his regular meetings. "It was so easy for me to dominate as the boss," he said. "Recording gave me something to do that was really effective—I was actually listening and everyone could see it in black and white."

With experience you will come to appreciate the power of visual listening as a leader. It's easy to think leadership is about "telling." But that is beginning leadership. The real art is bringing people along with you. In regular meetings, guiding everyone to review progress, flag issues, and ask for help is a continual process of asking key questions, then listening carefully. It's possible to do all this without recording, or course, but it's also very helpful for you to make notes of those things that everyone needs to remember, such as lists of issues and proposals for solution. Recording as the leader underlines the seriousness of your attention. If you do decide to use visuals actively as the leader, the following pages explain some basics about display making that will help you guide the process.

POWERS OF VISUAL MEETINGS

This graphic illustrates the four powers of visual meetings and was the framework that organized the book *Visual Meetings*. It applies to leadership and points to the predictable benefits of working this way. To break the presentation software orientation, you and your organization need to understand why it's important to work visually in an interactive way.

SPARKING IMAGINATION: Visuals of what success looks like, compelling metaphors, and visible mental models all stimulate your and your organization's imagination.

ENGAGING PEOPLE ACTIVELY:

Nothing is as engaging as acknowledging what people are saying by writing it down and drawing out the metaphors and models that shape their ideas. Sticky notes, group drawing, games, and other forms of interactive visualization all have this dividend.

SUPPORTING ENACTMENT & GROUP MEMORY:

Meeting notes, action steps, action plans, roadmaps, milestone charts, and large process maps that explain big changes are all most effective when they are visual, and big enough to be posted and referenced continually. These tools are critical to effective implementation and enactment of plans.

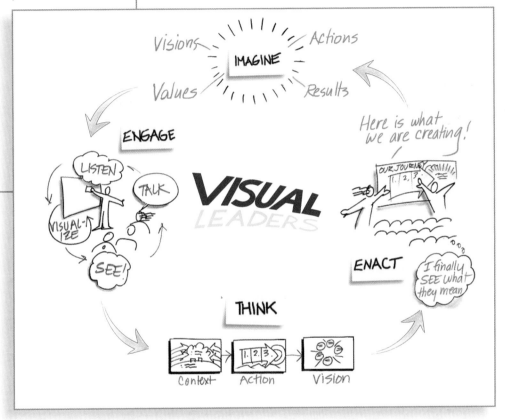

THINKING BIG PICTURE: Display making is the language of systems thinking. Doing it in groups vastly increases group intelligence and everyone's ability to see connections, find solutions, and understand how the big picture relates to specific elements of work.

THE STRUCTURE OF SPOKEN LANGUAGE

Our memories record sequences of experience. We live in time, one thing after the other. In fact, cognitive scientists have found that our memory is optimized to sense movement over time. It's no wonder that narrative or story structures are the most basic units of organization for words. There are some challenges stemming from this arrangement, however. Because the English language requires nouns, verbs, and objects to make a complete sentence, our minds are constantly sorting things out this way. This works if what we are thinking about is actually an object.

Visual versus Spoken Language

It's important to understand the word part of visual language. It begins with the spoken word, arranged in a linear format. It's sentences have a subject-verb-object structure biased toward action. This is one of the reasons that it is so hard to do problem solving with just talking. To compare different ideas and information you have to make a display somewhere. Since humans don't live only in linear time, and stories occur in contexts and environments, verbal language depends on words pointing at images we can imagine as it goes along. The listener creates the pictures in his or her imagination. Visual practice makes this process explicit, but spoken language does not.

This is the linear structure of the spoken word. It has subjects, which take action through verbs, which .

If whatever is selected as the subject (usually a noun) or the object (also a noun) is not actually a physically manifested phenomenon (such as an emotion or an intention), then this process of "objectifying" can result in some real errors in thinking. (See more on this in Chapter 6.)

Verbal Language Structure of English

- **Subject** (noun with modifiers)
- **Verb** (action words with modifying clauses)
- **Object** (that which is acted upon—a noun with modifiers)

Spoken languages in non-English cultures can have very difference structures. Japanese puts verbs at the end, which vastly increases the potential ambiguity of a spoken statement.

People make sense out of spoken language in four ways:

1. **Sequence in the sentence:** Position of the word in the sentence tells us if it is a subject, verb, object, or modifier. "Dog bites man," is a very different sentence from, "Man bites dog," even though both sentences have the same words.

2. **Definition:** There are official definitions of words as established by conventional use and recorded in dictionaries. But words accumulate many different meanings.

3. **Connotation:** A third element is not in the language itself but in our past experience with that word. This is called the "connotation." This aspect is a big part of what a leader needs to understand.

4. **Expression:** People emphasize key words and add emotional content with sound.

HOW CAN ONE WORD MAKE SUCH A DIFFERENCE?

BY BEING IN A DIFFERENT SEQUENCE.

GOOD / LEADERS   FIGHT   BIG   CRISIS   LOVE

Leaders Focus on Interpretations

Spoken language is not precise! The built-in complications of making sure people share similar interpretations of important communication, such as agreements regarding plans, is one of the big arguments for having listening be visual. This extra level of feedback, even if you are just recording things on a flip chart, opens up the possibility of correcting errors in interpretation. Events seldom have direct impact on you or your organization, but everyone's interpretation of what the events mean does! This is why leaders focus on interpretations. Becoming more conscious of metaphor and models will help provide you with some tools to help with this role.

. . . have impact on objects, described by modifiers.

One of the most useful guidebooks to thinking about language and its impact was written in the late 1960s by a French-Canadian Jesuit turned management consultant named Joseph Samuel Bois. It is called *The Art of Awareness* (and is well worth getting and studying if you want to become adept at the language side of leadership). It is a very accessible extension of the work of Alfred Korzybski, a Polish engineer and scientist who wrote *Science and Sanity*, a very influential, but challenging, book written in the 1930s. Korzybski contended that many issues in society flow from distortions introduced by our language and mental models and are probably a major factor in the wars people fight, which are often over sacred symbols and ideology. Korzybski cautioned against the trap of identifying with our language and symbols and is known as the originator of the maxim "the map is not the territory," a fundamental idea in visual leadership.

Bois makes all these ideas very accessible and wrote his book with the intention that it be a textbook for thinking about the relationship between thinking and action. He calls it epistemics or applied epistemology (for those of you who are interested in more abstract theory).

HERO WITH A THOUSAND FACES

Humans are hardwired for stories. Creating and telling them is a major part of any leader's job. You might be interested to know that there are some universal patterns for what makes up a good story.

Joseph Campbell in his seminal book, *The Hero with a Thousand Faces*, describes research that has uncovered one of the most basic story patterns—the hero's journey. He claims it is an archetypal story pattern that seems to be used worldwide. You'll recognize it from the following elements.

Hero's Journey Story Pattern

- A peaceful village gets threatened.
- An unlikely hero is selected to go find a solution.
- He or she ventures into the threatening wild, having to get past guardians.
- The hero encounters dangers and challenges.
- Then the hero receives magical help of some sort.
- He or she then returns to the village, again past various obstacles.
- The hero arrives and saves the day with the magical help he or she has received.

There are critiques of this story of stories, holding that not all of life is goal-oriented like this. But humans love to see an unlikely character rise above challenges and succeed. And regardless of the specific structure, stories provide a very central way through which we reduce the complexity of life to understandable, memorable pieces.

THE PATTERN ISN'T LINEAR! NOW WHERE DO WE PUT THE WORDS?

I GUESS IT DEPENDS ON HOW YOU DEFINE THE SPACE.

What Is Visual Language?

In the last century with the development of many sophisticating image-processing technologies, words, images, and shapes have come to be integrated into many different visual patterns. In previous centuries this kind of visual language was used for maps, diagrams, and illustrations for books, but not in the fluid, layered way it appears in contemporary media. Now all of us are visual thinkers, whether it's our preference or not. We work visually when we drive cars. Screens are all visual. Books are visual. Magazines, posters, billboards, and airline safety instructions are visual.

Even spoken language is visual, if you think about the way different words evoke images in a listener's imagination, or see gestures as graphic imagery without paper. This happens so naturally most of us don't think of this as visual thinking, but it is. The great value of working with visual displays and charts is the way it makes this integrated thinking visible and accessible. Active visualization opens the door to everyone becoming more conscious of the visual nature of all communication.

Visual Language Is Pattern Language

Pages 44 and 45 following this spread illustrate some archetypal visual-language structures that are the graphic equivalent of story structures. They are called display formats because they help shape and form the visual pattern that emerges. Like any structure, they highlight some things and obscure others. Helping pick the right display formats to support what you are talking about is the role of a visual leader. You don't have to actually be the one who does the writing and drawing to make a big difference in the clarity and impact of a discussion. In a way, what you are guiding people toward is appreciation of the patterns of thinking that are most likely to support you reaching your goals as an organization.

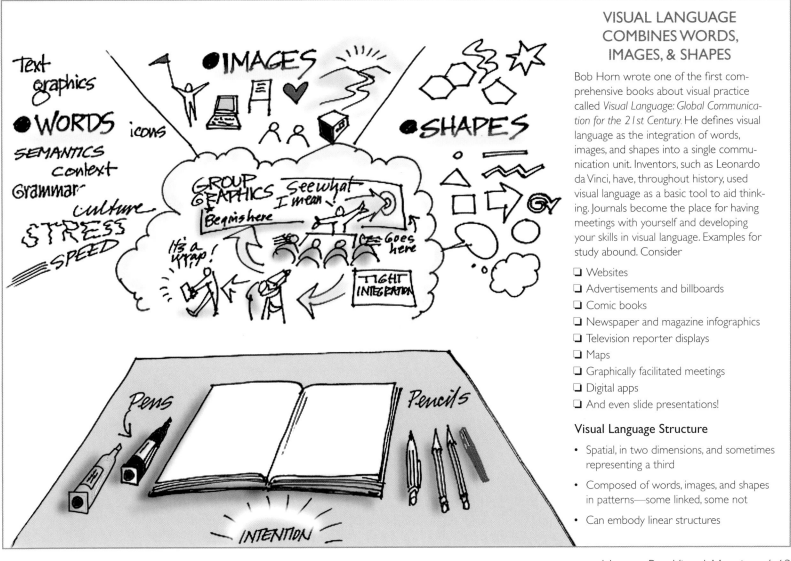

VISUAL LANGUAGE COMBINES WORDS, IMAGES, & SHAPES

Bob Horn wrote one of the first comprehensive books about visual practice called *Visual Language: Global Communication for the 21st Century.* He defines visual language as the integration of words, images, and shapes into a single communication unit. Inventors, such as Leonardo da Vinci, have, throughout history, used visual language as a basic tool to aid thinking. Journals become the place for having meetings with yourself and developing your skills in visual language. Examples for study abound. Consider

- ❏ Websites
- ❏ Advertisements and billboards
- ❏ Comic books
- ❏ Newspaper and magazine infographics
- ❏ Television reporter displays
- ❏ Maps
- ❏ Graphically facilitated meetings
- ❏ Digital apps
- ❏ And even slide presentations!

Visual Language Structure

- Spatial, in two dimensions, and sometimes representing a third
- Composed of words, images, and shapes in patterns—some linked, some not
- Can embody linear structures

The Importance of Picking the Right Format

When you decide to work visually in either a regular or a special meeting, you are adding displays to the give and take of the dialogue. As a leader, you need to pick the right formats. Here's how.

1. Focus on your chosen **outcomes.** Everything flows from this.
2. Pick a **display format** that supports seeing what you need to see (see the keyboard choices on this and the next page).
3. Record patterns of **key words** and **images.**
4. Pick a new format to get another perspective.

(See Chapter 8 for case examples.)

WE NEED TO WORK ON OUR NEW IDEA?

WHICH FORMAT SHOULD I SUGGEST?

THE GROUP GRAPHICS KEYBOARD

POSTERS	LISTS	CLUSTERS
Focus Attention	Energize the Flow	Activate Comparisons

VISIONING MEETING	PARKING LOT	CONTEXT • POSSIBLE ACTIONS
	☑ Schedule our next meeting	• RESOURCES
	☑ Rewrite the collateral materials for our guides	• CHALLENGES
	☑ Check on that long overdue invoice	
	☑ Clarify Margret and George's roles	

Differentiated	*Lined Up*	*Spaced Out*

BEST USE

- ❏ Meeting titles
- ❏ Themes
- ❏ Outcomes, agenda, roles, and rules
- ❏ Emphasizing visions, missions, or key principles

LIMITATIONS

- Can only make one point well
- Too many posters take away the effect

BEST USE

- ❏ Brainstorming
- ❏ General recording
- ❏ Agendas
- ❏ Expectations
- ❏ "Parking lots"
- ❏ Suggestions/options
- ❏ Inventories
- ❏ Minutes
- ❏ Agreements
- ❏ Next steps

LIMITATIONS

- Hard to compare
- Listing becomes a visual blur

BEST USE

- ❏ Context mapping
- ❏ Brainstorming options
- ❏ Recording open discussions
- ❏ Loose design
- ❏ Visioning
- ❏ Drawing out interests
- ❏ Identifying potential goals

LIMITATIONS

- Sacrifices sequencing to grouping.
- Chronology is hard to follow.
- Can seem messy

GRIDS
Build
Combinations

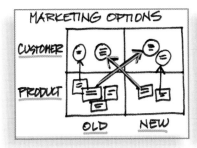

Crossed Categories

BEST USE

- ❏ Prioritizing
- ❏ Evaluation
- ❏ Project & agenda design
- ❏ Organizing tasks on a team
- ❏ Calendaring & roadmapping
- ❏ Mapping numeric data
- ❏ Mapping geographic info
- ❏ Perception stretching

LIMITATIONS

- Categories must be clear
- Doesn't reflect group process
- Hard to adjust
- Constrains improvisation if the discussion moves off topic

DIAGRAMS
Grow
Understanding

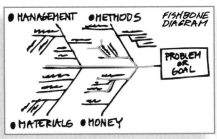

Branching

BEST USE

- ❏ Process mapping
- ❏ Mind mapping
- ❏ Systems analysis
- ❏ Finding root causes
- ❏ Decision trees
- ❏ Flow charting
- ❏ Organization charts
- ❏ Note taking

LIMITATIONS

- Slow and complex
- No natural stopping place
- Items must fit overall structure
- Hard to show multiple connections

DRAWINGS
Animate
Meaning

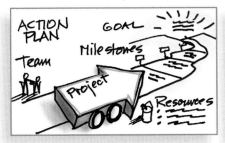

Analogy (Graphic Metaphor)

BEST USE

- ❏ Action plans & roadmaps
- ❏ Visions
- ❏ Understanding systems through a metaphor
- ❏ History charts
- ❏ Environmental scans
- ❏ Innovation sessions

LIMITATIONS

- Requires experience with the metaphor
- Can blindside thinking if the metaphor doesn't include an important element
- Maps are not the territory; metaphors are not reality

MANDALA
Show
Unity

Centered

BEST USE

- ❏ Introductions charts
- ❏ Visions
- ❏ Mental models
- ❏ Target charts to show unified focus
- ❏ Pie charts for financial data
- ❏ Radar diagrams for analysis
- ❏ Constellation maps

LIMITATIONS

- Complex and challenging to read
- Sometimes everything isn't unified
- Writing in a circular pattern can be difficult

1. **Focus the issue**: Have the group talk about the problem, and explore how they understand it. What are the underlying issues? You might list and circle the most important.

2. **Invite solution ideas:** Have pairs of people work on sticky notes, generating one idea per note.

3. **Group the sticky notes:** Post the notes and ask the group to organize them into clusters and label the headings.

4. **Discuss the proposals for understanding:** All of this wouldn't have to be recorded, but key points might be worth writing down.

5. **Vote on the most promising:** Take the number of items you are looking at (number them perhaps) and give everyone 1/3 that number of votes. Use dots or ask for hands up and record the votes.

6. **Discuss notes receiving the most attention:** Compare options. You might record each options advantage.

7. **Make a decision:** Either you, as the leader, make a call or, if you have agreed to work by consensus, ask the group to voice a consensus and work until you have one.

Describe, Then Decide

If you are determining how to work with large, visual display environments, especially in special meetings, a helpful principle is to separate describing what is going on from making decisions about what to do. Having different displays for each is helpful. You also handle this by using sticky notes to generate a picture of what you are working with and then sorting them to determine what to act on. Simply have everyone write whatever information you are seeking on the notes. Once these are written you can then analyze and prioritize, moving toward a decision. An example of where you personally might do some simple recording would be leading problem solving during a project review when your group seems stuck. You could take the series of steps described in the sidebar when you want to tap group intelligence around an issue:

If you do get up to record, there are some ways you can unintentionally get in your own way.

THINGS THAT GET IN THE WAY WHEN RECORDING

❏ Substituting your words for theirs

❏ Refusing to write because you don't agree; write first, then disagree!

❏ Writing so small or sloppily no one can read it

❏ Standing in front of what you write

❏ Taking over the conversation because an item triggers your interest

❏ Getting upset when people tell you what to record

❏ Going too slowly and getting behind; simply ask for time to finish the item you are working on

❏ Getting too involved in creating a cute drawing

Guide Your Team to Create Useful Documentation

It may seem like a small step, but as a leader you have the right to request how the work of the meeting gets communicated back to everyone. Here are some choices:

- ❏ Ask someone to take digital pictures of the charts and e-mail the results to everyone.
- ❏ Ask someone to type the agreements and send them out.
- ❏ Store the charts and bring them out at the next meeting.

In all these cases you are trying to keep the documentation and the experience of making the agreement in close connection.

Leveraging Visual Meetings in General Communications

One of the powerful things about beginning to work visually in meetings is having the chance to really tune in to the metaphors and symbols that have meaning for your direct reports. Explicitly working with images and words on paper invites an open discussion of how people relate to different ways of expressing things. Why does this matter? It's because to have communications be meaningful, people have to have a relationship to the concepts, words, and images. People are not empty minds waiting for wisdom. They are full of their own ideas. For you to connect with people and lead them effectively, you have to understand how imagery and metaphor actually work. A story from the past will help make this point.

In the Goldwater/Johnson campaign for president in 1964, the country was locked in a cold war. The United States and the Soviet Union had invested in extensive nuclear armaments, professedly to "deter" each other from going to war. The campaign rhetoric was charged, with a popular president challenged by Barry Goldwater, an extremely conservative hawk who even made his own party nervous. At one point, Johnson aired a now infamous "Daisy" ad that

SUPPORTING GROUP MEMORY

People remember things based on the impact that the original experience had on them. One of the reasons it is so hard to remember a slide presentation is that there is rarely a very engaging experience going along with it. Really great slide presenters know how to tell stories and link what they say to the experiences of their listeners, but most presenters do not have this skill.

Digital Capture Preserves Group Memory
One of the reasons visual practitioners use digital photography of actual meeting charts is to extend the experience and hence the group memory. Have you ever noticed how people will gesture at a corner of the room where some important thing was written down, even after the chart has moved? This is because we anchor our memory in the total experience—of the space, the colors, the form of the recording. It's a full pattern not just the data. Digital copies of charts play this role.

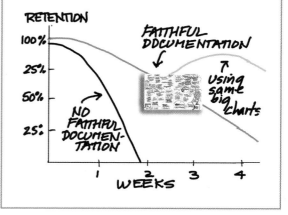

"TRANSPORTATION MODEL" OF COMMUNICATIONS

For many years this is the way people thought about communications. It drove the broadcast model. Package well. Reduce noise. Target the receiving people well. It's a seductive model but not supported by cognitive science.

"RESPONSIVE CHORD" MODEL OF COMMUNICATIONS

Tony Schwartz and many others believe that communication happens when words and imagery resonate with a person's already embodied values and interests. Establishing new values and interests requires new experiences, not slicker communications.

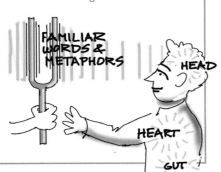

showed a young girl in a meadow picking petals off of a daisy, saying, "He loves me, he loves me not…" As she continues, a countdown begins quietly and then more loudly until an atom bomb fills the screen. There was no mention of either Goldwater or Johnson. The ad aired only a few days because it was so inflammatory. But in that short time it did its work, portraying Goldwater as a choice too risky to take. Why did this metaphor have such an impact?

Tony Schwartz, an experienced media professional, wrote a very influential book 10 years later, in 1974, called *The Responsive Chord: How Radio and TV Manipulate You…Who You Vote For…What You Buy…And How You Think*. It is a powerful lens into the world of communications. He centers his thesis on the Daisy ad and argues that the old transportation school of communication, which assumes the challenge in communications is packaging and getting messages through a channel without loss of signal, is not only outmoded but also incorrect. He prefigures much of today's cognitive science in asserting that people are actually filled with their own ideas and images, and don't decode messages as much as respond to those that "strike a responsive chord." This is why the Daisy ad was so inflammatory. It resonated with already established biases.

For leadership, understanding the biases of your people is essential to good communications. One of the best ways to develop this sensitivity and your own visual literacy is to begin using visual language in your own note taking—listening for the imagery and metaphors that your people use. Today, you can choose to do this on one of the many tablets and drawing programs that are available. If you happen to be someone who thinks out loud with others, then use your journal as a sketch pad while talking and watch the conversation come alive.

In the next chapters, you'll encounter a range of visuals and metaphors, all intended to strike a responsive chord with you, the reader. Notice what works and what doesn't as a way to get insight into your own biases. Wrestle with the ideas and see how *you* would visualize them.

Part Two:
Looking at Your Own Leadership

Part Two:
Looking at Your Own Leadership

4: What Is Your "Operating System"? Metaphors, analogies, and
mental models are the "sentences" in our brain's visual language. If you plan to help
your organization take advantage of the visualization revolution, you need to start with
yourself. This chapter establishes some critical definitions and perspectives that will be
used throughout the rest of the book.

5: What Kind of Organization Do You Lead? Of the mental
models of the world that you have in your brain, the ones you use to think about your
organization as a whole are most important to understand. This chapter introduces a
visual framework for thinking about organizations called the Sibbet/LeSaget Sustainable
Organizations Model, and the visual tools that are necessary in each stage of development.

6: Developing Your Visual IQ This chapter presents exercises that you can
do on your own to develop your visual intelligence. Some are imagination exercises, and
some will involve doing some drawing and diagramming. This chapter also explains some
of the generic meanings embedded in simple shapes that you might use to think about
organizational issues.

4. What Is Your "Operating System"?
The Power (& Peril) of Mental Models

Human awareness is a dance between what we are aware of in our thinking and what we are communicating and hearing from others. If you reflect on this continuum, you might observe that both ends are being processed through the same brain. We are never, in a literal sense, able to be outside our minds, however captivating the input from our senses, particularly our visual senses, seems to be. You've heard the old saying, "People remember 10% of what they hear, 20% of what they see, but 90% of what they participate in"? If you check out the accuracy of these numbers you'll discover a lot of argument about the percentages, but not about the general idea. It correlates with the fact that our brains respond to having rich sense data to work with. This dynamic is a fundamental principle behind the power of interactive visualization..

But it all is still being filtered through our metaphors, mental models, and paradigms—which function analogously to computer operating systems. What are these? If you are going to be stretching your and your team's visual thinking and using more innovative, participatory tools to support your regular and special meetings, you need to start by calibrating your own understanding of these concepts, and assessing your own bias in regard to making sense out of complexity.

What Does a Leader Need to Know about Metaphors and Models?

Let's define some terms as a way to get started. Here is a stack of words that all point to various aspects of our visual intelligence and that can be confused.

1. Image
2. Metaphor
3. Analogy
4. Mental model
5. Framework
6. Operating system

image

noun

1. a physical likeness or representation of a person, animal, or thing, photographed, painted, sculptured, or otherwise made visible.

2. an optical counterpart or appearance of an object.

3. psychology. a mental representation of something previously perceived.

4. form; appearance; semblance: We are all created in God's image.

5. counterpart; copy: That child is the image of his mother.

6. a symbol; emblem.

7. the general or public perception of a company, public figure, and so on, especially as achieved by careful calculation aimed at creating widespread goodwill.

8. rhetoric. a figure of speech, especially a metaphor or a simile.

—dictionary.com

metaphor A metaphor is a literary figure of speech that describes a subject by asserting that it is, on some point of comparison, the same as another otherwise unrelated object. Metaphor is a type of analogy and is closely related to other rhetorical figures of speech that achieve their effects via association, comparison or resemblance, including allegory, hyperbole, and simile. —Wikipedia

At the simplest level of visualization, we hold visual images in our minds. Think about your favorite vacation spot. You can probably see it in your *imag*ination (note the root word *image*). You may also notice a flood of feelings and maybe even hear some sounds. Our brains are able to record experiences in a very rich vocabulary that mixes sight, sound, and feeling. Poets and artists call these images. Graphic designers also call pictures images. The word is used in computing for exact copies. It covers so much ground (see sidebar) that it is a difficult word to use clearly. For this book think of *images* as a general word for the basic visual material we work with.

Metaphors Are Deeper Than Simple Comparisons

A metaphor is an image that has become a figure of speech in which one thing is held as similar to something else to which it is otherwise unrelated. If you listen with this in mind, you will hear many of them when people talk about your organization. Graphic recorders listen this way.

- We need to *leverage* our strengths (comparing strengths to machine).
- How can we *accelerate* sales (comparing sales with cars)?
- We have *clear sailing* on the project (comparing projects to a sailboat journey).
- Let's *harvest* our historic capability (comparing capabilities to an orchard or crop).
- If we don't *prune* our portfolio, we'll be in trouble (comparing portfolios to trees).
- We need to *rope up* (comparing teaming to mountain climbing).
- She's a *tiger* of a boss (comparing strong behavior with a strong animal).

Can you see images when you read these phrases? One result of being a visual practitioner is coming to appreciate how much of language is metaphoric. We are constantly comparing what we want to understand with things that are dissimilar in order to bring out one point or another.

In 1986 an English consultant and professor named Gareth Morgan wrote *Images of Organization*. It was a best seller and remains a very relevant book for visual thinkers and visual leaders. He begins by writing:

> Effective managers and professionals in all walks of life, whether they be business executives, public administrators, organizational consultants, politicians, or trade unionists, have to become skilled in the art of "reading" the situation that they are attempting to organize or manage… The basic premise on which the book builds is that our theories and explanations of organizational life are based on metaphors that lead us to see and understand organizations in distinctive yet partial ways … the use of metaphor implies *a way of thinking* and *a way of seeing* that pervade how we understand our world in general (*Morgan's italics*).

We'll return to this idea in Chapter 6, where you will find some explicit exercises you can do to apply this kind of metaphoric thinking to your organization in an explicit way. Because metaphors both illuminate and obscure (see sidebar), Morgan uses whole suites of them to analyze situations rather than getting stuck in one or the other.

Analogies Are Extended Metaphors: They Illuminate & Obscure

If you take a metaphor and explore it, in detail, you are making an analogy. In 2005 Giovanni Gavetti and Jan Rivkin wrote an article in the *Harvard Business Review* titled, "How Strategists Really Think: Tapping the Power of Analogy."

> Faced with an unfamiliar problem or opportunity, senior managers often think back to some similar situation they have seen or heard about, draw lessons from it, and apply those lessons to the current situation. Yet managers rarely realize that they're reasoning by analogy.

If metaphors can mislead, analogies compound the problem if you aren't aware of what they obscure. Gavetti and Rivkin argue that only 15 to 20 percent of the situations you face as a leader

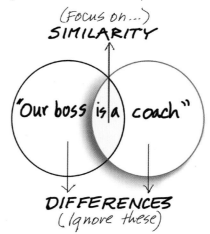

METAPHORS
HIGHLIGHT SIMILARITIES &
IGNORE DIFFERENCES

When we use metaphors, we are generally pointing at one aspect of the comparison and ignoring others. When metaphors are used unconsciously this can lead to much misinterpretation and even misguided action. Take this example.

A coach is a powerful influence in practice and on the sidelines but is not directly on the field of play. What if you as a leader are a critical element in a sales process? You are then "on the field," so to speak. Someone who takes this metaphor literally might not expect you to play on the field.

A METAPHOR WHERE STABILITY & FLEXIBILITY ARE PARTNERS

In America's Cup racing, the hull design is a critical competitive feature, precisely because it provides the stability needed for maximum flexibility in the sails. In single-hulled boats, this lifting keel is well below the waterline and not very visible. When the boats changed to multi-hulled designs, they achieved even more stability, less drag, and the boats were able to go even faster. The right metaphor can resolve contradictions and paradoxes, such as that between stability and flexibility.

AC90

23 ton   27.4 m.

Lifting keel.

are sufficiently information rich to be analyzed deductively—meaning reasoning from analysis of the facts. Most leadership decisions are made in situations that are too complex and dynamic to allow detailed analysis. So leaders resort to trial and error, guided by analogy with situations they understand. How many times have you heard, "How can we be more like Nordstrom in customer service?" or, "We need a *viral* campaign for these ideas," comparing with the Internet.

Analogies can fail in important ways. Gavetti and Rivkin point to leaders' tendency to rely on superficial similarities as the culprit, made worse by two other problems they call anchoring and confirmation bias. Anchoring is the phenomenon of an analogy taking root in a management team and sticking even in the face of changing conditions. Confirmation bias is the tendency of leaders to want to seek out facts that support his or her position and ignore others. On the other hand, analogies can be very energizing and resonant if they connect with experiences people have shared and can help resolve seeming paradoxes.

In the early 1990s, Levi Strauss faced challenges in the retail market and needed to change its organization and strategies. In a critical meeting with top management, a heated argument developed. On one side were people who were attached to the idea of Levi Strauss being a steady source of community-oriented values, getting involved in areas surrounding its factories, and treating internal employees with respect and consideration. The other group felt the company needed to become more competitive, streamlined, and contemporary, and not necessarily stick to the old ways. As the argument went on, it seemed polarized. As facilitator I asked a simple question, "How many of you understand the way America's Cup racers compete?" The conversation stopped. People were puzzled, because the question didn't seem to be connected. I went on. "From my understanding, one of the major points of competition is the hull design, the reliable part that facilitates the amount of sail you can put up or down. Looking through this analogy,

Levi Strauss' conservative culture might actually help with competitive flexibility." The conversation took a more engaged and productive turn at that point. Of course, Levi Strauss isn't an America's Cup racer. If you stretch any analogy it breaks down, but shifting to a different analogy can unstick the conversation and free up energy as you highlight some different factors.

Mental Models Are Highly Developed Analogies

When analogies become a habitual way of seeing things, they should more appropriately be called mental models. If these models become widely accepted, supported in their validity by repetition and evidence, they become culturally embedded operating systems for thinking (another analogy of course). All of the generalizations of science are different mental models of this type—abstract assumptions about the rules that govern our world—expressed in text, numbers, and graphic images.

Everyone's thinking about organization and leadership is shaped by these models. When they become the standard way our brain processes information, they function in a way that is analogous to the way operating systems manage computer software. Your general mental models literally guide your behavior as you seek to get predictable results in different specific situations. Becoming conscious of your mental models is a first step toward upgrading them and becoming more able to work with people who have different ways of thinking. This assumption is one of the drivers behind this book. Interactive visualization is one of the most direct and powerful ways to both become conscious of these models and also to upgrade them. It's one of the five disciplines of a learning organization according to Peter Senge. In Chapter 7 we'll look at some examples of how to visualize the more useful models. As you look at the sidebar here and the different metaphors Gareth Morgan explores, imagine looking at your organization systematically through several of these metaphors. Rather than getting caught up in any one of them, harvest all of them for gifts of insight. Helping your team do this would be a great example of visual leadership.

MORGAN'S METAPHORS

In *Images of Organization*, Gareth Morgan analyzes organizations with a series of metaphors that have widespread applicability. Here is a graphic summary of questions raised by each one.

ORGANIZATIONS AS MACHINES
Is scientific management, which drove thinking in the early 1990s, still possible?

ORGANIZATIONS AS ORGANISMS
Organizational development in the 1950s and 1960s wondered if organizations weren't like botanical systems.

ORGANIZATIONS AS BRAINS
Cybernetics depicts organizations as brains processing information.

ORGANIZATIONS AS CULTURES
Maybe we should understand social systems, subcultures, norms, and shared realities.

ORGANIZATIONS AS POLITICAL SYSTEMS
Aren't interests, conflicts, power, and different forms of governance important?

ORGANIZATIONS AS PSYCHIC PRISONS
What about repressed sexuality, patriarchy, family systems, and the shadow?

ORGANIZATIONS AS FLUX & TRANSFORMATION
Let's remember dialectics, morphogenic fields, and organizational evolution.

ORGANIZATIONS AS INSTRUMENTS OF DOMINATION
What about class, control, global reach, and exploitation of workers?

PAPER IS BRAIN INTERFACE

Paul Saffo, a professional forecaster and insight maven, claims paper is the way we see our own thinking. This, of course, applies to screens we can draw on, as well as journal pages like this one from my early days in consulting.

Why Visualize Our Metaphors and Models?

When you as a leader are adept at visualization, you can encourage your people to talk about the metaphors, analogies, and mental models they are using to make choices about strategy and operations. This is the terrain of conscious decision making. The beauty of visual meetings is that they make the exploration of metaphors and models fun and nonthreatening (mostly). If everyone can argue about the graphics that are going into a key piece of communication, then they can, in effect, challenge each others' central metaphors and models without directly challenging the person who is using them.

On this page is a copy of a journal page created in the early days of my consulting. I was sitting in an airport, ready to fly to Europe, sketching my thinking. Working visually allowed me to include all different kinds of things, mixing personal and business elements, all sitting on a big map of organization process. Everyone's mind works this way, blending many levels of awareness. Display making and drawing support seeing patterns in our thinking in one place.

Visual Frameworks Are Special Kinds of Conceptual Models

The model shown on the journal page reproduced here suggests that organizational development is a process of evolution interrupted by revolutions. Perhaps it would be more appropriate to call this a framework than a model. (It is an integration of Arthur M. Young's arc of process and Larry Greiner's evolution/revolution graphic.) Frames are the structures that hold paintings, or perhaps the skeletal parts that define a wall in carpentry. In either case the frame is not the principal content, but a means of bounding what you are thinking about so you can see something through it. It does influence how important we think a painting is. But it is the content we load into these frameworks that generates ideas and insights. Graphic templates used in visual planning (see Chapter 9) are, for the most part, frameworks. They may reflect some underlying assumptions about what is relevant to look at, but they are not intended to be models of the real thing, like a blueprint for a house.

The next chapter shares one of these frameworks—illustrating seven ways of looking at different organizations that you might be leading. Each of the seven can be seen as "stages" of one organization as it develops, or as subpatterns in more complex organizations. The differences among them are carefully drawn to sharpen your thinking. By being simple, these little frames allow you to look *through* them, as if they were a kind of window frame, and then appreciate the complexity in the real-life situation you are thinking about. From an analytic perspective, it helps to appreciate that metaphors, visual models, and frameworks always have four associated features when you put them into use (see sidebar). They spell GIFT if you want to use a mnemonic to remember.

1. **Graphic (Metaphor):** This is the drawing or graphic template itself—a visual design that abstractly indicates a few basic features in what you are supposed to think about.

2. **Intention (Goals):** Refers to the purpose and goal you have in using the metaphor, model, or framework. Consider the sidebar about maps. They have limited utility if you aren't looking to find something on the map.

3. **Feelings (Experience):** This refers to your personal experience with the metaphor, model, or framework. In verbal language this would be called the connotation. It's the memory you have of past associations thinking this way. On a map it is your personal experience with the scale of the map and what a mile over a certain type of terrain actually means in practice. With a graphic template it's knowing from experience how much you can write in it.

4. **Territory (Facts):** This refers to the actual, factual situation you are considering. You may love a certain management framework, such as the Tuchmann Model for team development, with its catchy "forming," "storming," "norming," and "performing" stages. But the team you are looking at may be struggling with implementation, which isn't really dealt with in this model, so you might need a more comprehensive map to your territory.

FOUR ASPECTS OF A MAP

Arthur M. Young would use a map analogy to get people to understand how fourfold analysis works in his Theory of Process. He contends that any situation we need to understand has four aspects we can pay attention to.

1. **Graphic Design:** Clearly there is a graphic design to the map. It's on paper or a screen, and has a distinct pattern. But we need to understand 2-4 to truly use a map.

2. **Intention/Goals:** To use a map you need to know where you are on the map and where you want to go.

3. **Experience with Scale:** The mile or kilometer markers on a geographic map are critical to understanding how to use it—but the scale does not tell you anything without your *experience* with what a mile or a kilometer means in practice.

4. **Territory:** There is usually something very real to which the map is referring. In geographic maps the symbols are abstract. The actual land might be very different, in fact.

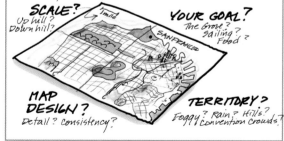

How Can You Identify Your Operating System?

In *Visual Teams* a chapter called "Shared Visual Language, Toward an Operating System for Visual Teams," includes a guide to mental models that Kenneth Boulding outlined in his seminal book *The Image: Knowledge in Life and Society*. It is an elegant map to this territory of metaphors and mental models (which he calls images). Follow the exercise below to see where you come out.

1. Read the seven "frameworks for thinking" that Boulding describes as basic ways of understanding. Study the pictures and descriptive bullets.

2. Think about what you are trying to understand or communicate as a leader in your organization. Substitute your own intentions for the examples.

3. Think about your own experiences with each of these models. Which do you understand the most? Rate yourself on the scales 0 to 10, with 10 being "10+ years of experience."

4. Look at which models attract you on this basis. Rank the frameworks 1 to 7.

5. Now think about your own organization. Which framework is the mostly commonly used with your leadership team when you think about organizational matters?

6. Think about what might happen if you explored looking at your own leaders and organization through a different framework.

	NONLIVING MENTAL MODELS		
FRAMEWORK NAME	**1.** STATIC	**2.** MECHANICAL	**3.** SELF-REGULATING
GRAPHIC & DESCRIPTION	**FRAMEWORKS** Parts **connect** • Parts seem relatively permanent • Held by inertia • Hierarchical, classification-oriented Includes buildings, scaffolding, bridges, banks, and static structures of all kinds.	**CLOCK WORKS** Parts connect and **move** • Energy from outside • Works as a whole • Every part necessary • Action and reaction; cause and effect Includes clocks, engines, cars, boats, airplanes, and mechanical machines of all kinds.	**CYBERNETIC SYSTEMS** Parts connect, move, & **adapt** • Feedback is critical • Moves in and out of homeostasis—balance • Limits to how fast it changes Includes thermostats, regulators, computer systems, and intelligent software.
YOUR INTENTION	Think about structure? Think about hierarchy?	Think about action and maximizing results?	Think about flexibility and adjustment?
YOUR EXPERIENCE	1-2-3-4-5-6-7-8-9-10	1-2-3-4-5-6-7-8-9-10	1-2-3-4-5-6-7-8-9-10
YOUR PREFERENCE	RANK 1-7	RANK 1-7	RANK 1-7

LOW——————————— COMPLEXITY ———————————HIGHER

LIVING SYSTEMS MENTAL MODELS

FRAMEWORK NAME	4. SELF-REPRODUCING	5. SELF-EXPANDING	6. SELF-MOVING	7. SELF-REFLEXIVE
GRAPHIC & DESCRIPTION	**CELLS** Parts connect, move, adapt, & **reproduce** • Self-maintaining • Can replicate itself • Parts' existence depend on existence of cell itself • Change is fundamental Includes living cells, viruses, single-celled plants.	**PLANTS** Parts connect, move, adapt, reproduce, & **grow** • Live in ecosystems • Can transform basic elements into life • Seeding, cloning, regrowth all allow for growth Includes flowers, vegetables, bushes, trees, and plant ecosystems.	**ANIMALS** Parts connect, move, adapt, reproduce, grow, & **self-move** • Can modify outside environmental conditions • Move in packs, gaggles, herds, flocks, schools and swarms • Can express moods and needs Includes birds, mammals, insects, and fish.	**HUMANS** Parts connect, move, adapt, reproduce, grow, self-move, & are **self-aware** • Can think about time • Can abstract with symbols • Exercise free will • Can invent and adapt Includes families, gangs, teams, performers, organizations, communities, and civilizations.
YOUR INTENTION	Think about regeneration and replication?	Think about context and interdependencies?	Think about collaboration and network effects?	Think about awareness, ethics, and social dynamics?
YOUR EXPERIENCE	1-2-3-4-5-6-7-8-9-10	1-2-3-4-5-6-7-8-9-10	1-2-3-4-5-6-7-8-9-10	1-2-3-4-5-6-7-8-9-10
YOUR PREFERENCE	RANK 1-7 ☐	RANK 1-7 ☐	RANK 1-7 ☐	RANK 1-7 ☐

LOWER ——————————— COMPLEXITY ——————————— HIGHER

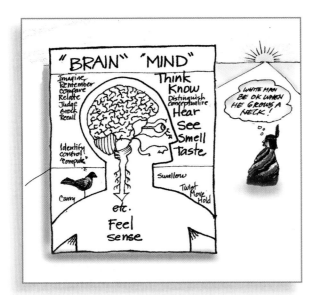

CAN WE RECLAIM EARTH WISDOM?

One consequence of being raised on the eastern side of the Sierra Nevada in California is having a very intimate relationship with nature writ large. A steady interest has been to observe how humans have steadily disconnected from a deep connection with living systems. It's understandable if we spend most of our time in our heads and on screens, but there are consequences that are beginning to pile up as a legacy we might not be proud of generations from now. This issue of how we change our deep patterns of thinking is fundamental to transformation and to our very continuation. A picture from the 1980s reflects my thinking about all this.

Can You Change Your Operating System?

Ways of thinking about organizations, and therefore about leadership in organization, become deeply rooted as we grow older. The most formative influences are those experiences in which we have spent many years directly experiencing this or that organization. Few people have more than one or two they have experienced deeply in a direct way. These become embedded experiential metaphors and can influence a large part of our understanding of the world.

My being raised in a Protestant church environment led to a deep understanding of how organizations can be guided by deep values. First, jobs in agribusiness, starting with gardening as a teenager, made thinking in agricultural terms easy and nuanced. Then working in communication led to understandings about media, writing, and visualization. Founding and running a business evolved models of leadership. Living in the San Francisco Bay Area near Silicon Valley included immersion in new technologies of all kinds, the attendant tools, and its ways of thinking. These metaphors and models are now embedded ways of viewing things, as reflected in this book.

Ask yourself about your own formative experiences. Where did you learn about how people cooperate in groups? What is your experience-based template for thinking about large organizational systems? What is your mental model about leadership? The places where you have spent considerable time will surely have shaped your thinking.

The next two chapters in this section will ask you to stretch a little beyond your place of central comfort. First we are going to look at a number of generic ways of thinking about the stages of organizational development so that you can experience visualizing about the kind of organization you are leading. Then you can read about some exercises that you can use to begin building your personal visual literacy. In Part Three we'll focus back on the essential tools for visual leadership, with many useful stories about what other organizations and leaders are doing.

5. What Kind of Organization Do You Lead?
Linking Tools to Stages of Development

We are now going to look at how organizations develop and the kind of organization you are leading. We'll stay at a big-picture level and focus on what kinds of tools are helpful. This will also be an introduction to how to use visuals to think about organization itself. The visual models are meant to stimulate your thinking. You should fill in the details.

What Does It Mean to Be Organized?

People will say, "That leader has his unit well organized," or "That project is very well organized." What do you think this means? The root metaphor of the word *organization* is "organ," drawing comparisons with the human body and how the different parts work together. But how do the parts connect in an organization? At the physical infrastructure level, different machines and mechanisms do connect literally in order to work properly. But at the levels of organizational communication and interaction, it's more a matter of people holding a common mental model of how things fit together and hoping all the different activities come together to support a result. Can you see how this is a visual perception? As the previous chapter explains, metaphor and mental models are the way human brains understand complex systems: by finding patterns in all our specific experiences of any given territory. The seven generic frameworks of thinking are, in a sense, also ways of understanding organization. But they are a bit static. Let's look at some that reflect more of the dynamics of real-life organizations.

Purpose and Goals Drive Organizational Choices

A pattern of organization comes into being to serve a purpose. These patterns, sometimes called concepts, function in relation to thinking about organization the way formats do for display making, only at a more macro level. Both are visualizations that serve a purpose. Eli Goldratt wrote a very popular book about how to improve organizations called *The Goal: A Process of Ongoing Improvement*. It's a novel about a young manager who has to regain profitability in a

COULD THESE ALL REPRESENT COMMON PATTERNS OF ORGANIZATION?

THEY ARE COMMON METAPHORS, FOR SURE. DID YOU READ THE PREVIOUS CHAPTER?

failing plant or it will be closed by the owners in six months. He's confused about his challenge, but happens to run into a management consultant friend in the airport one day. He describes his problem, and the consultant asks, "Do you know the goal of your company?" The young manager isn't sure what this means and begins to ask questions. "I'm sorry, but I have to catch my plane," his friend says and leaves. Goldratt's literary device was fun, because it left me, the reader, wondering along with the young manager how to determine the goal of an organization.

The young manager finally realizes the real goal of his particular plant was to make money for the larger organization. He thinks about other goals, like providing work for people or contributing to the community, but after thinking about it he knew the real reason the plant was created in the first place was to turn a profit for the owners. The young manager calls his friend and excitedly shared his insight. "Very good!" his friend answers. "Do you know if you are making money right now?"

Well he didn't, and, of course, the friend had to hang up, leaving the young manager again puzzling out the story. You should read the book if you are interested in how to apply total quality management tools, because the manager learns to think about end-to-end processes, inventories, bottlenecks, and so forth. By putting these ideas into a novel format, Goldratt created powerful, memorable images that allowed the ideas to stick in my memory. Telling stories about how things should be organized is one of the central roles of an organizational leader.

But turning a profit isn't the only kind of goal an organization can have. The sidebar here has a whole list of different aspirations. They reflect different goals for different stages an organization goes through as it develops. But goals are only the top-line consideration. Once you have some purpose or goal in mind, you immediately face current realities and constraints. The situation you are in might not support what you want to do. The people might not have the right skills. Your organizational processes and procedures might be inadequate. Your cultural norms and values might not support the right kind of behavior. So how can you think about all of this complexity?

Organizational Forms Are Dynamic—Like a River

It is seductive to think about organizations in a static way, by focusing on the structure and the arrangements of roles as reflected in an organization chart. This is the lure of the nonliving mental models we know so well, living, as we do, among so many machines of all kinds. But if you've spent any time in organization, you know that the organization chart is a convenient simplification that does not really explain how the organization works. Students of living systems know that structures grow up along flows of energy. In nature these are sources of water, sunlight, and animal and plant life. In human organizations the flows of information, money, and attention give rise to different organizations. Your goals determine which you embrace at any given time.

Perhaps you have rafted down a river or seen movies of a rafting trip. The river is constantly moving. It is, of course, constrained by the terrain it moves through, but it is equally shaped by the amount of water in the river and the force it presents. As dynamic as it is, an experienced river rafter comes to identify certain repeating elements in the river. Knowing these is invaluable if you want to be a river guide. Experienced guides can identify these patterns of organization:

1. **Put-Ins:** These are places calm enough to get your rafts in the water.
2. **Heavy and Light Rapids:** Rapids actually have number ratings 1 through 5.
3. **Waterfalls:** These have a range, but are the names of drops that you can't raft over.
4. **Pullouts:** These are quiet areas with beaches where you can have lunch.
5. **Holes:** These are places where the water spirals around a rock. They also have grades.

It's obvious that different tools and methods are needed for each of these. The same is true for organizations. Let's look at the stages of organizations through this metaphor.

STAGES OF A RIVER RUN

A river is one continuous flow of water, but various stages have characteristics that become named. There is a constancy to the phenomenon, despite the fact it's quite dynamic and changes in detail with different levels of water flow. This is a very useful way to think about organizations—as being in constant motion but having repeating features that change in detail with different flows of energy and resource.

TYPES OF SUSTAINABLE ORGANIZATIONS

The graphics in this chart illustrate seven sustainable stages of organization, from simple to complex. Each can be stable and successful as long as people share one of the driving aspirations and are willing to deal with accompanying constraints. Jumps to new patterns happen when internal or external conditions change this focus.

Check off the characteristics that apply to your organization
Where are you focused now? Do you need to jump to a new form? Is your current stage sustainable?

Here is a sketch that shows some of the dynamism you will have to imagine in each graphic. The discs change size to reflect more and less bulk.

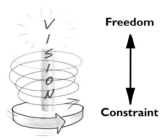

Freedom

Constraint

1.

Bright Idea

STARTUP

Opportunity

STARTUPS need little more than a strong idea and an opportunity to try it out. Attention is focused on:

❑ Creating a vision and story
❑ Finding initial clients
❑ Finding a name and brand that points at the vision
❑ Hiring people who can implement the idea
❑ Setting up a beginning communications and delivery infrastructure

2.

Strong Leadership

GROWTH

Cash Flow & Staff

GROWTH ORGANIZATIONS focus on lead products and services that generate the cash flow or constituents needed to grow. Attention is focused on:

❑ Identifying the strongest offering and marketing it heavily
❑ Getting everyone "on the bus" of the central effort
❑ Keeping momentum
❑ Stopping activity that doesn't serve the primary focus

3.

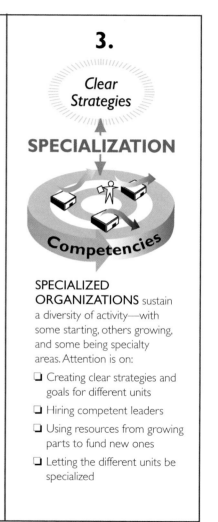

Clear Strategies

SPECIALIZATION

Competencies

SPECIALIZED ORGANIZATIONS sustain a diversity of activity—with some starting, others growing, and some being specialty areas. Attention is on:

❑ Creating clear strategies and goals for different units
❑ Hiring competent leaders
❑ Using resources from growing parts to fund new ones
❑ Letting the different units be specialized

4.

Reliable Returns

INSTITUTIONALIZATION

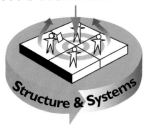

Structure & Systems

INSTITUTIONS rely more on structures, systems, and processes for constancy than on one set of leaders. Attention is focused on:

❏ Creating systems and structures that are reliable

❏ Planning longer-term investments and profit centers

❏ Formalizing reporting

❏ Creating robust infrastructures for accounting and communication

5.

New Growth

REGENERATION

Adaptable Processes

REGENERATING ORGANIZATIONS focus on growing into new geographies and new markets. They've learned how to replicate their processes and systems, like living plants. They focus on:

❏ Clear, replicable processes

❏ Streamlining end-to-end flows of resources

❏ Integrating communications

❏ Developing process-oriented leaders

6.

Agility & Innovation

CO-CREATION

Trusted Alliances

CO-CREATIVE ORGANIZATIONS are interested in innovating and leading with new products and services. This requires continual new input from alliances and partners. These organizations focus on:

❏ Creating trusted alliances

❏ Sustaining a strong brand and culture

❏ Networking within value webs

❏ Creating platforms for collaboration and crowdsourcing

7.

Lasting Impact

TRANSFORMATION

Shared Intention

TRANSFORMATIVE ORGANIZATIONS care about lasting impact and supporting new paradigms of thinking and possibility. They focus on:

❏ Raising awareness, and aligning on shared intentions

❏ Articulating a compelling vision

❏ Encouraging individual acts that embody the new principles

❏ Renewing commitments

WHICH OF THESE
SHOULD WE USE?

DO YOU KNOW
WHAT PART OF
THE RIVER WE ARE
RUNNING?

OARRS

ROADMAP

GRAPHIC
VISION

FLIP
CHARTS

Seven Kinds of Organizations and the Tools They Use

Each of the patterns of organization have a name and a core structure illustrated in the graphics on the blue discs on the previous pages. Graphics like this work as simple conceptual frameworks through which you can look at your own organization. It also helps to see the patterns described in words, which is where we turn now. Different parts of your brain are activated by images and words. Full understanding usually involves integrating the two. (This is why using simple images on slides and then talking about them works. Your word side and your visual side synchronize.)

There is one aspect of this graphic depiction that can't be shown well on paper, which is the way things nest together in real life. In nature, simpler systems become subsystems in more complex ones. This is true of organizations. The simpler forms become subelements in the larger organization. You'll have to imagine that the tools and some of the capability learned in first-stage organizations will carry forward and be used in later stages. For this reason the tools mentioned in earlier forms of organization are not repeated.

I. STARTUPS

The simplest kind of coherent organization arises from combining a bright idea with someone who will pay you to realize it. To enable this, an entrepreneur needs a good story, often described in a business plan. A nonprofit needs a strong grant proposal or key donor. Venture capitalists and foundations don't really think a startup will follow these plans precisely. But the plans are a way to assess the level of competency of the leaders. Thus the most important thing is to have a really credible story and the personal ability to win the confidence of whomever you are talking with. The process of working out your business plan is what can lead to this kind of presence, because you know you've thought it through. Evidence helps. This is why startups need names, business cards, websites, and leave-behind materials that tell their story in a compelling way.

Here are some visual tools that a startup might use:

- ❏ Logos
- ❏ Graphic visions
- ❏ Visual business plans
- ❏ Introductory videos
- ❏ Marketing-oriented websites

2. GROWTH ORGANIZATIONS

Sooner or later you will want to have some steady income or flow of constituents if you are a nonprofit dependent on volunteers. This usually requires focusing on lead products and services, and channeling the "anything goes" energy of the startup into a focused, aligned effort. You need good strategy tools at this point, because you need to understand your market on one hand and your own capabilities on the other and make a good match. Growth-stage organizations are often lean and action-oriented and focus on new product releases and letting key events drive organizational activity. Momentum, commitment, and drive are valued. Success often flows from catching a wave of interest and paddling hard, to use a surfing metaphor.

These tools help organizations that are aiming at rapid growth:

- ❏ Basic strategic visioning processes and graphic templates
- ❏ Visualization of environmental factors in context maps
- ❏ Market segmentation maps
- ❏ Visualization of sales processes
- ❏ The "S" curve as an explanatory framework (see sidebar)

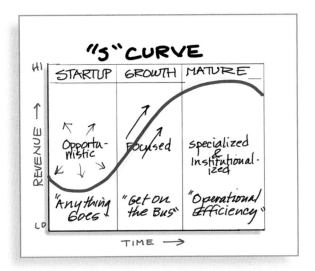

THE "S" CURVE

A simple way to understand the stages of organization is to appreciate the "S" curve pattern. This is mapped on traditional *x* and *y* axes in which *x* is time and *y* is revenue. Startups cost money. Growth organizations should be making steady money. Mature organizations experience less growth but need to continue bringing in revenue. Each stage needs a different kind of leader, culture, and organizational tools to be completely effective. You can see that this framework, in essence, describes the first several types of sustainable organizations.

Robert Fritz writes in *The Path of Least Resistance* that organizational systems change when they have to resolve structural tensions between visions and current realities. This is what drives the jump from one organizational form to another, as either end changes. You can experience this if you take a rubber band and stretch it out. The rubber molecules want to pull back to their rest position. If you imagine the upper finger as your vision or aspirations and the lower finger as current realities, how will you resolve this tension? Structural tension always seeks resolution, according to Fritz.

❏ Lower your vision?

❏ Change current reality?

❏ Don't connect the two?

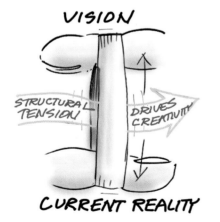

VISION

STRUCTURAL TENSION

DRIVES CREATIVITY

CURRENT REALITY

3. SPECIALIZED ORGANIZATIONS

As your organization matures, it will develop strong leaders who want to have their own areas of creativity. Successful growth will also attract competitors who will push you into diversifying. Collegial organizations, such as professional services firms and colleges, are often organized this way. Decentralized organizations, such as Hewlett-Packard in the 1990s, worked this way. At this stage of organization, executives set strategies for their units and count on really competent managers to run the suborganizations, some of which might be startups and some of which might be high-growth elements. The central structures are often minimal. Tools that help here, in addition to the ones mentioned before, are:

❏ Strategic vision maps for the organization as a whole

❏ Graphic templates for annual business planning in different units

❏ Visual meetings that clarify roles and synergies

❏ Organizational concept maps for guiding alignment (more on this later)

❏ Accessible navigation on websites

❏ Problem-solving tools for helping with organizational efficiency

4. INSTITUTIONS

Any of the prior organizational forms can develop into institutions if they figure out how to have regular returns on investments. This requires having strong information systems, legal and financial arrangements, leadership development pipelines, talent management programs, succession planning and a host of other processes. If your organization is a government agency, then it may have a mandate that ensures its continuation, but even these have to be maintained. Some institutions have monopolies on a key resource, such as a desirable location, and can slack off on the systems. Visualization usually becomes essential as things get more complex. Institutions develop a great deal of inertia and require creative effort to challenge thinking and create spaces for fresh ideas. Visual meeting methods do this. Visualization can also help leaders conceptualize critical infrastructure services in which stability and quality are more important than creativity.

Tools that help institutions in addition to the ones mentioned for earlier types are:

- ❏ Visual meetings to improve engagement, systems thinking, and group memory
- ❏ Graphic histories to renew everyone's sense of purpose
- ❏ Strategic planning templates identifying drivers of change
- ❏ Visual investment portfolios illustrating resource allocation
- ❏ Decision rooms for supporting alignment
- ❏ Business model templates illustrating how the organization makes money or grows constituents

5. REGENERATIVE ORGANIZATIONS

At some point, people may want to bring growth energy back into the organization, tackling new markets and bringing forward new products and services. Although some might think that organizations get big, bureaucratic, and die, humans are capable of renewal and regeneration. An organization that learns how to replicate its processes and throw off new enterprises, much the way a living plant would seed itself, is one that can move beyond just being a stable institution. A regenerative organization is more like an ecosystem than a large machine. It will retain elements of each of the other kinds of organizations in different functions, but add the ability to replicate itself in other areas. The total quality movement is all about helping organizations become aware of their processes so that they could streamline and transfer them to new units.

Although some might think that organizations get big, bureaucratic, and die, humans are capable of renewal and regeneration. An organization that learns how to replicate its processes and throw off new enterprises, much the way a living plant would seed itself, is one that can move beyond just being a stable institution.

TOTAL QUALITY MANAGEMENT CHARTS

Regenerative organizations get very good at streamlining and replicating processes. The majority of total quality management tools are visual. Here are some common ones that will increase your ability to understand your processes.

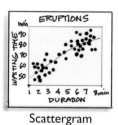
Frequency Checklists

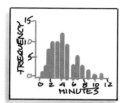
Histogram

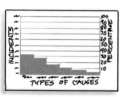
Scattergram

Pareto Chart

Flow Chart

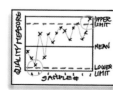
Fishbone Diagram

Control Chart

Regenerative organizations use the following kinds of tools in addition to the ones mentioned:

- ❏ Total quality management tools (see sidebar examples)
- ❏ Process maps that illustrate key steps and stages
- ❏ Project management tools for project review and improvement
- ❏ Video sharing internally to spread organizational know-how
- ❏ Communication platforms that allow visualization at a distance
- ❏ Graphic case studies
- ❏ Mental models that help everyone think in process-oriented ways

6. CO-CREATIVE ORGANIZATIONS

People need fresh input to stay creative. It's very hard to do this within a single organization. The most vital organizations are often in industrial clusters such as Silicon Valley and Hong Kong. Co-creative organizations work in webs of collaborating organizations—such as the RE-AMP network in the upper Midwest that is cleaning up global warming pollutants with 140 nonprofit organizations and 15 foundations. Being able to form critical alliances and have a network of partners is the key to this kind of organization. To maintain its identity and direction in this environment, an organization has to be strong in its own culture. The tools that help are:

- ❏ Robust Web conference platforms and mobile communications
- ❏ Special meetings with partners to do joint strategic visioning
- ❏ Co-branding
- ❏ Links in social networks
- ❏ Video exchanges

- ❏ Storymaps showing links between strategy and culture
- ❏ Special meetings to identify cultural values and guiding principles

7. TRANSFORMATIVE ORGANIZATIONS

A final form of organization is one that is interdependent with the prior forms in that it needs their functionality to operate but has a different aspiration, which is to bring about lasting, paradigmatic change. These organizations are more networks and movements and do work with visualization. Because shared awareness is really the bottom-line constraint of a real movement, aligning this is a continual issue, and compelling visual metaphors and visions help. Here are some of the tools that are distinctive in addition to the ones mentioned earlier:

- ❏ Compelling mental models of new ways of being and working
- ❏ Graphic visions and videos that tell stories of possibility
- ❏ Graphic articulation of guiding principles
- ❏ Symbols and icons of change

Freedom and Constraint

The seven examples of organizations just described are integrated in a model co-developed with Meryem LeSaget, a colleague of The Grove and a leadership expert. It illustrates organizations as seven archetypes arranged from simplest to most complex (see following page). If you can imagine the Four Flows model running behind this framework, you can see that the path of organizational development is one of increasing materialization, as organizations add structures and processes. But a turn comes when organizations begin to operate more like plants, animal systems, and conscious human systems. Knowledge, not more mass, is what carries organizations into the more complex arrangements.

SIBBET/LESAGET SUSTAINABLE ORGANIZATIONS MODEL

On the following page is an integrated picture of the Sustainable Organizations Model (SOM). It suggests a general path of development for any organization. Larger ones are usually combinations of the earlier forms.

This model is, as readers of the earlier books on visualization will recognize, animated by Arthur M. Young's Theory of Process, a framework for thinking about evolutionary processes in nature. Larry Greiner's popular *Harvard Business Review* article in 1998 on organization evolution and revolution (see resources for links), and Henry Mintzberg's organizational archetypes described in *Mintzberg on Management* added validation and research anchored in business practice. Meryem LeSaget, a longtime colleague in Paris and syndicated writer about leadership and organizations, helped refine the framework over these years and tested it with European managers.

There is now wide agreement that organization development happens in fits and starts, through periods of revolution and evolution. The full SOM indicates the types of crises that can disrupt each phase.

This book is not primarily about organizational development, but about visual leadership. However, this visual would be an example of a carefully designed visual model that can become shared language for leadership teams making big organizational decisions. See where you think you are in terms of this model.

An exercise you can do with yourself or with your direct reports is to engage in a dialogue about where you are in your organizational evolution. Each of the stages of organization depicted on this model are potentially viable, if you are aligned on one of the overarching goals shown in the yellow circles and willing to work at mastering the constraints shown in the blue medallions. Here's how you can conduct that dialogue.

1. Share a picture of this model and explain that a coherent organization is one aligned on connecting aspirational intentions to current realities.

2. Have everyone look over the red labels that indicate the types of crises that can disrupt a stable form of organization. Which are you experiencing?

3. See if you can agree on where your organization is right now. Are you in a crisis? Are you simply needing to get better at one of the stages? Are you needing to leap to another form of organization? Remember these stage depictions are like lenses you look through. No organization "fits" one of these precisely.

Sibbet/Le Saget
SUSTAINABLE ORGANIZATIONS MODEL

1. *Bright Idea*
STARTUP
Opportunity
TRUST? WILL TO LEAD? RESOURCES?

2. *Strong Leadership*
GROWTH
Cash Flow & Staff
SUSTAINABILITY? POSITIONAL POWER? IDENTITY?

3. *Clear Strategies*
SPECIALIZATION
Competencies
CAPITAL? CONTROL? SUCCESSION?

4. *Reliable Returns*
INSTITUTIONALIZATION
Structure & Systems
COMPETITION? STAGNATION? PRODUCTIVITY?

5. *New Growth*
REGENERATION
Adaptable Processes
FLEXIBILITY? ARROGANCE? RED TAPE?

6. *Agility & Innovation*
CO-CREATION
Trusted Alliances
COMPLEXITY? MISTRUST? POLITICS?

7. *Lasting Impact*
TRANSFORMATION
Shared Intention
UNCERTAINTY? LOSS OF FAITH? TRANSPARENCY?

KEY
Freedom
Intentions/Drivers
STAGE NAME
Icon
Constraints
Constraint
Cumulative Complexity
Typical Values
EXTERNAL OR INTERNAL CRISIS?

16.0 SOModel ©1998–2012 The Grove Consultants International

6. Developing Your Visual IQ
How Visualizing Makes You Smarter

So far in this book you've had a chance to think in rather sweeping terms about visualization and your role as a leader. Some of it may already be familiar to you. Other ideas might seem a bit off to the side in terms of your interests. Ultimately what is going to make the biggest difference for you is the extent to which you, yourself, begin to practice being more conscious of your visual communications. That means using visuals actively.

What Is a Visual Practice?

When visual facilitation began in the 1970s, working this way was something designers did, not everyday managers. But today is a different time. Computers and phones are highly visual. Most are moving to touch screens. Drawing and visualization applications are too numerous to count. There really is no technical barrier now for playing with visuals.

But you may be a busy executive or a new young manager up to your ears trying to learn how to lead others. How in the world can you take time to learn, for instance, to take visual notes? Well, you won't if you don't think you'll get something from it, so carefully read over the list of the benefits on the next page.

Getting Success from the Start

Earlier we looked at the metaphor of learning to play a musical instrument. It's challenging, but the great news is it can be fun from the very beginning if your teacher knows how to pace things. This is why you should treat yourself to a well-paced progression of activity that gives you results all the way along. In the following pages are a series of activities that you can undertake that will build your visual IQ. It's like any other faculty or muscle. Practicing makes it stronger.

Keep firmly in mind that the act of drawing and diagramming is itself a way of thinking, regardless of what the result looks like. If you are doing this just for yourself, why hold back?

Technology makes it possible to not only interact with information but also create it. Visual notes can be saved to the cloud, sent to friends, or just saved as think pieces for yourself and others. If you love working on a paper journal, digital photography using your phone allows you to share these notes the same way.

EXAMPLE OF VISUAL NOTES

Below is a page of notes from a recent tele-conference recorded in a journal. They reflect a simple "magazine format" in two columns, with breakouts for visuals. Here are the benefits of such a practice:

❏ Important items pop out with pictures.

❏ The seating diagram is memorable.

❏ Interesting patterns emerge. It helps you pay attention, listen for imagery, and remember.

❏ Information is chunked into logical types.

❏ Color emphasizes points.

Visual Notes

NOTE TAKING PRACTICES

Taking visual notes for yourself is far and away the best method for practicing visualization. Here are some tested beginning exercises.

TAKE NOTES ON CALLS AND WEB CONFERENCES

1. If you are using a tablet, set up your pages in advance so you don't have to worry about saving files.

2. Make a little seating chart when you record everyone's names.

3. Use a listing style at first, adding little graphics and shapes to help you remember the parts that jump out at you.

4. Highlight items you want to return to.

5. Develop an icon for actions, such as little arrows.

6. Include your own ideas and reactions in little clouds (like the one at the bottom of these notes).

DEVELOP A VOCABULARY OF SEED SHAPES

On the next page are some pictographic images that have the property of allowing you to add to them if you wish. Practice drawing them until they are second nature. (Some diagramming shapes are on page 82.)

1. Draw the basic star person.

2. Vary the width of the arms and legs.

3. Vary the length of the arms and legs.

4. Make the first arm go up, then down.

5. Put two together and have them interact.

6. Draw little shadows.

BRAINSTORM WITH YOURSELF

1. Put a topic in the middle of your paper, and then take notes all around, using words and graphics.

2. You can branch these in a mind map diagramming style if you like, or just cluster them in little groups. Using icons will help you remember the ideas.

Start with Simple Graphics

The graphics on this page are a fun set of starter graphics. These kinds of figures are called pictographs, or ideographs, and function like icons or graphic words in your note taking. The Grove calls the ones that are designed for improvisation seed shapes. Designers distinguish two types:

1. **Pictographs:** These are little pictures of real things in a simplified format. The examples here are all pictographs.

2. **Ideographs:** These are graphic symbols that don't look like the real thing. For instance, money doesn't look like the dollar sign; love doesn't look like a heart.

You can also develop several varieties of handwriting so that you can show differences in types information, such as explanations versus actions. Following are some things you can practice:

3. **Titles:** It helps to have an "all CAPS" style of lettering for headings. You can add lines over and under or colors to mark off a meeting or call attention in your journal.

4. **Bullet Points:** Little stars or circles for bullets indicate items in a list or where to start reading a line of text. If you shift to a lowercase style of writing, you can show subpoints under the major categories of information.

5. **Borders:** It's easier to remember information that is grouped or chunked. Use cartoon conventions—talk balloons for things people say, clouds for thoughts, glow lines for bright ideas, and boxes of various kinds to simply group information.

USE SIMPLE SEED SHAPES

Taking visual notes primarily starts with words and a few simple drawings. Above is how you would draw three useful kinds of pictographs (technical name for little pictures of real things). They are called seed shapes because you can improvise with them by adding features without changing the underlying drawing. The star person is the first you can have fun with. Because they are in our own notes, it doesn't matter how skilled you are—it's the idea. The little cube is also fun. Many objects in cities, offices, and homes can be represented with combinations of this cube.

Here are some simple ways you can raise your awareness of metaphors. A more thorough exercise is on the next page.

Listen for the metaphors your direct reports use in meetings and write them down.

❏ Better yet, draw sketches of them!

❏ Read a magazine article and underline all the metaphors.

❏ Explore a magazine and tear out pictures that you like. Can you see what they are associated with in your imagination?

ALL THESE COULD
BE ORGANIZATION
METAPHORS, BUT
I DON'T GET THIS ONE

Exploring Metaphors

When it comes to thinking about your own organization, which is likely complex and dynamic, metaphors are an important way to get perspective. Bear in mind these basic principles:

- Pick a metaphor you understand fully (or you'll have two things you don't know about).
- Remember that the metaphor is *not* the thing itself (the map is not the territory).
- Pay attention to the similarities and ignore the differences.
- Think of the metaphor as a type of lens or window.
- Look through more than one metaphor.
- Listen for resonance.

Pay Attention to What Resonates

Resonance is a word that describes how one thing can vibrate in the presence of another. You can hear this in the piano when a bass string vibrates even though you aren't playing it. It happens in your psyche when an idea suddenly seems magnified. Maybe you are walking through a city and smell a pizza. Your entire attention starts "resonating" with the idea of eating a piece! After a while you can learn to sense in your body and mind when an image or metaphor has this effect.

Free association works on this principle. It's how psychologists explore dreams. In a recent dream a troublesome charismatic character needed to be managed in a meeting. An attractive girl in the group sought the fellow out and they were gone long enough to be up to something. The girl reappeared and reported the fellow was "amazing" and a healer. The shift in feeling about this man woke me up. Assuming all these parts of the dream were me, I asked, "What troublesome part am I trying to manage?" Perhaps it was a side that could be helpful in a healing situation. This kind of exploration is metaphoric thinking. Using graphics to illustrate the metaphor can help you with this kind of analysis. See the next page for suggestions on how to do this.

Follow these steps to exercise thinking about a problem or organizational situation using metaphoric analysis.

1. Write down the problem or situation you want to analyze.

2. Identify a sports team, a type of performing arts group, and an organization or business team that you understand fairly well.

3. Create a drawing of all the elements in each of the three metaphors (see examples here).

4. Start with one and map your problem or situation onto the metaphor by associating different aspects of your situation with the elements you have identified.

5. Identify yourself with one of the elements in each metaphor.

6. List what, as that element, you are doing about the problem or situation you picked.

7. Pay attention to any idea that crosses your mind. Pay attention to what resonates.

8. Now repeat this process with a second metaphor.

9. Stay with each metaphor long enough to get at least a few ideas.

10. Make sure you do more than one thoroughly. The real benefit is taking multiple points of view.

SOCCER TEAM

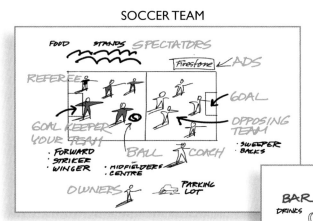

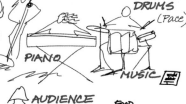

YOUR PROBLEM OR SITUATION

TIP

- Work on a large sheet of paper and write down your associated ideas in a separate color around the graphic.

JAZZ ENSEMBLE

PARAMEDIC TEAM

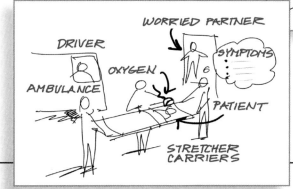

*I PREFER TAKING OFF &
LANDING TO THAT PEAK AND
VALLEY METAPHOR.*

Personal Visioning

Doing personal visioning with yourself using simple templates will help you understand the value this activity could have for your leadership team and larger organization. These exercises can be very rich and take a number of hours of reflective time, or they can be done quickly, in a sketch fashion, to get some quick insights.

History and Vision Go Together

People's sense of the future is filtered through their sense of the past. If you begin visioning with your career history, this will stretch your imagination well beyond the two- to five-year horizon most organizations consider. Even if your career is just starting, you'll have a number of decades to consider. Your career might be long and rich. In either case the peak-and-valley template is a quick way to begin. Apple used this to orient leaders to one another at leadership off-site work-shops. Each participant would create his or her picture in advance and spend some time sharing at the event. You can do this, too, if you feel comfortable sharing the drawings afterward. Telling the story to someone else might be another way you could stir up some personal insights.

The SWOT template is a tried-and-true planning framework that is used to be clear about strengths, weaknesses, opportunities, and threats during strategic planning. The value of harvesting your ideas on a graphic template is to see the interconnections. Opportunities are those things in which you have a related strength, or can reverse a weakness. Threats are sufficiently big that you might consider dealing with them when they are just smaller problems.

Visioning requires that you imagine yourself in the future. A trick you can play on your mind is to think entirely in the past tense, as though everything has already happened and you know all about it. You might get someone to partner with you. After you brainstorm some ideas, tell that person the story in the past tense, saying "I did this, and I did that." Chapter 9 will show you how to use graphic templates such as this to create an organizational strategy.

Here is a simple way to spend time visually reflecting on your personal aspirations as a leader.

1. Find three sheets of 11" x 17" paper (or a computer tablet).

2. Label the first sheet My Personal History and draw a time line along the bottom.

3. Intuitively draw a peak and valley line representing the ups and downs in your career. Then label the turns. Brainstorm some of the other events that surrounded the ups and downs.

4. On a second sheet, draw a four-box grid and label the left-hand cells Strengths and Weaknesses and the two right-hand ones Opportunities and Threats.

5. List your strengths, using the history as a stimulus. List weaknesses. You can think of these as gaps or problems, if you wish.

6. On the right draw some circles and fill them with opportunities. These are situations in the near-future you could take advantage of.

7. List threats. These are problems that could end or significantly diminish your career or life.

8. Take a third sheet and draw yourself on a mountain peak. Imagine you are in a future time, at the peak of your career. What can you imagine is part of your life and capability at that future time? Use words and simple images to make a circular map of your vision.

PEAK AND VALLEY TEMPLATE

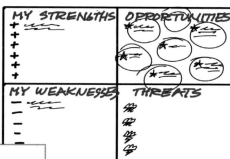

VISION MANDALA

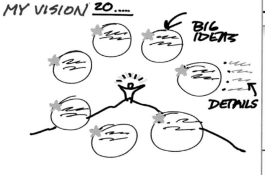

TIPS

- *If you have a long history, begin with your different homes and moves. This will help anchor your memory.*

- *Don't worry about being neat. Just jot stuff down.*

SWOT GRID

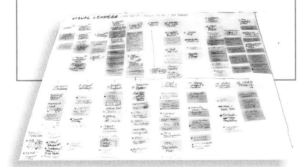
Personal Decision Wall

Decision making is all about context and choices. The main challenge is keeping in mind the full range of options and criteria for success while you are zooming in on specific options and thinking them through. It's easy to get stuck on one or the other option for reasons that may not be entirely obvious. Creating a decision wall is an enormous help. It is the personal equivalent of the decision room tools we will talk about in Chapter 10.

Making Big Displays

It's easy to underestimate the power of making a really big display. You might think, "I'll just pop things around on my computer to do this." However, when you work on a wall, you must stand up and move around. It literally broadens your perspective and gets more of your intelligence into the process. It's worth figuring out how to get a space that is at least as big as an average whiteboard. Most offices have a conference room that is big enough. If you work on paper rather than the board itself, you can roll everything up and even take it home to continue working.

The work you did in the personal strategic visioning might precede a decision process like this. There are many contextual perspectives to understand when you make big decisions. Mapping these in addition to the options themselves is quite helpful.

What about Intuition?

It is tempting to think that rational thinking will always result in a good decision. That is not the case in many situations involving a great deal of complexity and numerous variables. Intuition is that part of our selves that at some level can compare everything we know and register if it "feels right." Some might call this checking their gut or their heart. Combine analysis and intuition by preparing yourself with a visual display, and then sleeping on the decision and inviting yourself to wake up with the answer. You may well wake up knowing just where you need to be.

A decision wall encourages you to keep a big picture in mind while working on your options. Here's the general process:

1. Hang up a large sheet of paper in a conference room or lay one out on a big table.

2. Get some sticky notes and pens.

3. Begin by thinking about the decision you need to make and the criteria that would make it a successful one (some general ones are suggested here).

4. Identify the different choices you have, one per sticky note.

5. Draw out a large four-by-four grid and label it as shown here.

6. Arrange the sticky notes based on your best judgment about what the consequence would be. Then ask yourself:

   • *Is this apt to result in a high reward or low reward?*

   • *Will it be easier or more difficult to implement?*

7. You can add notes around the stickies, recording what you like about each choice and what you don't like about each choice.

8. Eventually you will have to decide, but this exercise will help you gain some perspective.

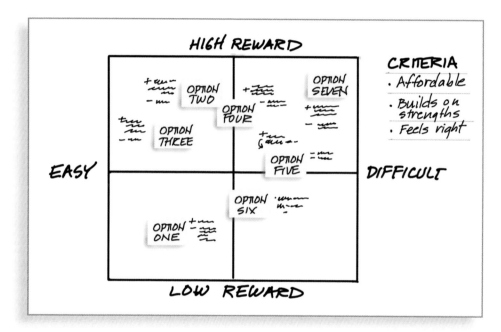

MEANING OF SHAPES

These seven shapes are sufficient to diagram almost anything. Points and lines are not technically shapes, but they do make for a full vocabulary of graphics. The meanings arise from what it feels like to draw the shapes. The diagram on the following page shows how they work together.

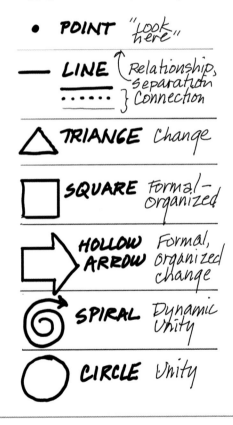

- **POINT** "look here"
- **LINE** } Relationship, separation Connection
- **TRIANGE** Change
- **SQUARE** Formal—organized
- **HOLLOW ARROW** Formal, organized change
- **SPIRAL** Dynamic Unity
- **CIRCLE** Unity

Diagram a Process

Diagramming is the language of systems thinking, and understanding your core processes as a leader is the most relevant place to have a reliable big picture of what is happening. There are many processes that make up an organization. Diagramming one is a superb visual exercise.

Types of Organizational Processes

Following are some of the repeating process that may be a good focus for your practice session:

- New business startup process
- Major project sales process
- Strategic and annual business planning process
- Talent management processes for hiring, development, and firing
- Website development process
- Infrastructure development processes (such as putting in a large customer relationship management computer system)
- New office acquisition and startup
- Training program development process
- Process improvement process—making something more efficient

If you list all the processes that your organization depends on, then you would be in the hundreds for organizations of any size. When you set out to improve things, it's important to understand which are core processes that drive the others.

You also might want to diagram a process from your personal life, perhaps a community, extracurricular, or family activity—such as taking a vacation. Sometimes when the content is less critical, you can focus more on learning the new skill—in this case, diagramming.

1. Pick a project or process that you know well, preferably one in which you were a leader.

2. Draw out a time line for the duration you want to diagram.

3. Pencil in the major meetings and project deadlines as a framework.

4. Add smaller meetings, Web conferences, and other group engagements.

5. Add document pictographs for the deliverables (paper or digital).

6. Add star people here and there where appropriate—perhaps to indicate project leads on subprojects or persons in oversight roles.

7. Draw pictures of anything physical that is relevant, such as opening a new office, or getting some new equipment that was critical.

8. Use lists of bullet point items to remember the details.

TIPS

- *Don't worry if you can't remember everything. The point of the exercise is to identify gaps and think about the process at a big-picture level.*

- *Share the drawing with someone else who knows about the process.*

- *Use sticky notes to get started.*

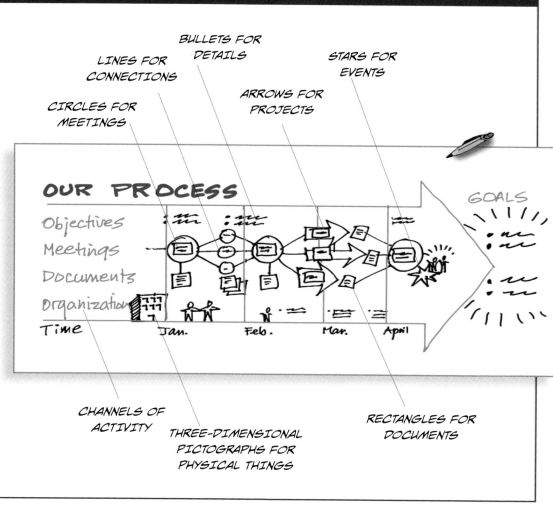

LINES FOR CONNECTIONS

BULLETS FOR DETAILS

STARS FOR EVENTS

CIRCLES FOR MEETINGS

ARROWS FOR PROJECTS

CHANNELS OF ACTIVITY

THREE-DIMENSIONAL PICTOGRAPHS FOR PHYSICAL THINGS

RECTANGLES FOR DOCUMENTS

Scenario Mapping

People expect leaders to provide direction and have vision. But you know full well that many times the future is very murky and uncertain, and you don't really know the best way to go. It's possible to be a learning-leader as well as a confident strategic one. The learning-oriented leader gets everyone involved in exploring what is possible—guiding people into learning and exploring new opportunities. You are going to be much better at this if you are comfortable doing this speculation yourself. That is the reason for doing some personal workouts when no one is watching or criticizing. You can be as daring a thinker as you want to be!

The Importance of Working Backward

If you are competent enough to be a leader, you are probably fairly practical and results-oriented. The part of your brain that is oriented this way needs to be tricked in order to think differently. One of the easiest ways is to work backward from the future. If you imagine purchasing a new home, for instance, you can probably imagine a really great house—a dream house perhaps. You could also imagine actually moving in and the help you would need from a mover or friends. To do that you would need to imagine having the time to do the move. Then you would need to be far enough ahead on other projects to have this time. You would also need to have made arrangements with a bank, and have the ability to get financing. If you work backward like this, you can plot out a path that would take you to your dream result.

At first, this way of working might feel unfamiliar, but with practice, you can begin to do it more easily. Once you are confident, you can then lead your leadership team in this same process.

One consulting firm that specialized in scenario planning collected hundreds of potential event cards and had teams of people sort the cards into a sequenced story, working backward from an imagined future, making a plausible sequence of the events. You could make up your own cards and do this with your team if you find that working this way is yielding good insights.

Scenarios are stories of *plausible,* not provable futures. You can explore them with visualization by combining drawing and sticky notes in the following way:

1. Focus on something about which you want to imagine the future. It could be work, family, or your own career.

2. Pick a time in the future and make up what an incredibly great result would look like. Use simple icons and words to draw a picture of it.

3. Do the same for a horribly bad result, and for one that would be just so-so.

4. Then, working backward, ask, "What has to happen to end up with this result?"

5. Then ask what has to happen to have that event take place. Continue until you are back at the present.

6. Do this for each story line. Use the sticky notes to refine your story.

7. The visual patterns in the three scenarios will begin to reveal some of the patterns of assumptions you are making.

TIPS

• *Stay loose and imaginative. You are making up a likely story, not a factual one. You are exploring for insights that you wouldn't have otherwise.*

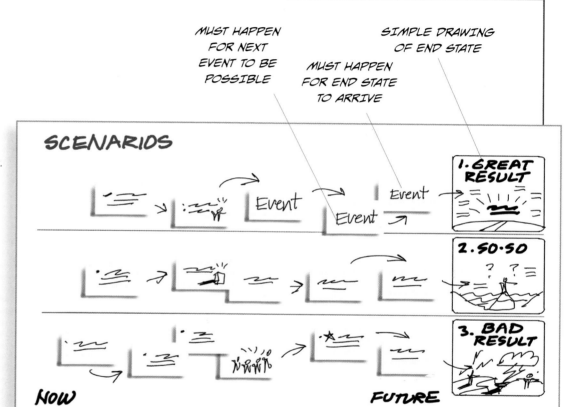

Truth Tracking

Arnold Mindell, a trained Jungian therapist and practicing Buddhist, wrote a great book called *Working on Yourself Alone* that describes a way to track down your deep personal truths. Mindell observes that humans can be aware on a wide range of "channels," borrowing a metaphor from television and radio, but awareness gets blocked when our protective selves (egos) don't want us to see something. Our deeper life process continues: It just moves to another channel. Mindell suggests to either amplify your attention in a stuck channel, or go with the switch and pay attention to what comes up on the new channel. Then craft a story that threads together the flow.

Channels of Awareness

Following are some of the channels of awareness Mindell identifies:

- Seeing images and pictures in our minds
- Hearing sounds and imagining conversations
- Feeling our emotions
- Noticing movement in our bodies (shifting postures, urges to stretch)
- Having "proprioceptive" feelings—little itches, aches, and pains inside your body
- Dreaming and daytime reveries
- Receiving medicine gifts—the appearance of animals, winds, things in the world that are symbolic (native people work on this channel a good deal)
- Opening to the gift of strangers (having someone appear and tell you something just when you need to hear it)
- Serendipity—the chance occurrence of something meaningful

Mindell suggests this "going with the flow" process as a way to discover your personal truth, much like a hunter would track an elusive deer through the forest by following subtle signs.

One way to "track" your subconscious is to work with little three-dimensional objects. Jungian psychologists call this sand tray work and literally use trays of sand and figurines, asking people to create arrangements out of them to explore topics. Following is how you can play with imagery of this sort as a way of gaining insight into a problem or situation.

1. Identify some problem or situation about which you want insight.

2. Find a toy store that has many little animals and figurines (most larger toy stores have sections with these items).

3. Think about your situation and rapidly pick out as many different items as you think might relate in some way.

4. Buy them and take them home with you.

5. Make an arrangement of the items that represents how you think about the situation you are considering. Work rapidly.

6. Next make up a story about the arrangement. Speak it out or write it up.

7. Take the part of one of the items and, out loud, give voice to what it sees and might say. Then take another and do the same.

8. If you have a hard time doing this alone, do it with someone you trust. The more you can imagine that you are the symbol the more surprising associations will appear.

AT LEAST WE CAN FIGHT THE BAD GUYS. MAYBE WE'LL SAVE THE IMPORTANT THINGS.

I HAVE TO SWIM CLEAR ACROSS THIS OCEAN AND CAN'T BELIEVE ALL THE CRAP THAT'S FLOATING IN IT! IS SOMEONE TRYING TO KILL US ALL?

I THINK HELPING PEOPLE APPRECIATE THE INTERCONNECTION OF THINGS IS A LEGACY I WANT TO LEAVE FOR MY GRANDKIDS!

DON'T COMPLAIN! I DON'T EVEN EXIST ANY MORE.

YOU THINK YOU KNOW WHAT'S HAPPENING--YOU HAVE NO IDEA!

AT 2,860 LBS, HOW LONG CAN I LAST?.

How Does All This Help Your Visual IQ?

Alan Kay, one of the true pioneers of Silicon Valley, is famous for imagining the Dynabook, the first truly portable computer, when he worked at Xerox. As a practiced innovator and inventor, he loves to say, "Point of view is worth 80 IQ points." Of course, he is using IQ as a metaphor, but his message is that the way you look at something makes a really, *BIG* difference in the quality of your thinking. All of the exercises suggested in this chapter come down to different ways to shift your point of view with visualization. It will have that impact if you actually practice them.

Wouldn't it be wonderful if we could just take in new information and change right away. Well you can, if the information is a green traffic light and you are completely competent at driving and know that green means go. But that kind of change isn't why you need to work at visualization. If you go to a country where people drive on the other side of the road, you will have to work hard to rework your automatic responses. Even then you are apt to make mistakes just crossing the street. You'll have to practice imagining traffic on the opposite side of the road.

If you need to take your thinking to a whole new level and really develop a new "operating system," you can expect it to take years. Folk wisdom asserts it takes 10,000 hours of practice to become masterful at a musical instrument. To master a new way of thinking you will need to do a lot of visual note taking and playing around with the ideas, and it may take years. But it is possible to "reprogram" your brain. Writing, drawing, diagramming, and visualizing are direct ways to do that. The process literally creates new neural networks, which lead to new levels of awareness and upgraded mental models, and then to more effective responses to situations.

We're going to move now to the seven essential tools. These are the ones that are most likely to help you raise the IQ of your entire leadership group and from there your organization. Enjoy!

Point of view is worth 80 IQ points.

—Alan Kay, Inventor of the Dynabook, Silicon Valley pioneer

Part Three: Power Tools for Visual Leaders

PEOPLE WILL REMEMBER THIS STORY!

WE CAN GET OUR WHOLE VISION ON THIS TEMPLATE!

JOURNEY VISION

- MISSION
- GUIDING PRINCIPLES/VALUES
- HISTORY
- CRITICAL ISSUES
- ORGANIZATION
- CORE COMPETENCIES
- ENVIRONMENT

VISUAL MEETINGS

Part Three:
Power Tools for Visual Leaders

7: Metaphors & Models This chapter shares stories of organizations that successfully connected their visions with compelling imagery and mental models that leaders can use to keep their organizations focused on the big picture while working on the details.

8: Visual Meetings How do you really engage people and create an environment where your people feel comfortable working visually? This chapter includes more real-life stories of how visual leaders use these tools.

9: Graphic Templates Providing light, intellectual scaffolding for critical planning meetings, reports, and other visual communications gives visual leaders a chance to guide the attention of the organization in productive ways without having to draw themselves.

10: Decision Rooms When decisions need aligned commitment it helps to have everyone understand the big picture as well as the choices being made. Staging panoramic meetings is a direct path, online as well.

11: Roadmaps & Visual Plans Visual time lines are as useful in organizational work as itineraries are on vacations. People need to know the big milestones and channels of activity, especially the ones you are managing!

12: Graphic Storymaps Leaders who show up and communicate authentically are the drivers of effective, aligned organizations. Visual maps and murals make it much easier to do this and provide ways you can stand out from the deluge of information everyone is trying to deal with in contemporary organizations. Storymaps uniquely link plans to culture.

13: Video & Virtual Visuals Video is as common as e-mail for young people and many organizations that are keeping pace with technology. This and other communication tools are allowing organizations to work effectively in distributed formats. This chapter outlines what to get right.

7. Metaphors & Models
Helping People See What You Mean

The first set of essential tools for visual leaders includes the visual metaphors and mental models that help you communicate your stories of direction and purpose. We've already addressed this idea in the previous section. Here we'll look at three specific examples of where metaphor played a big role in leadership. We'll also look a little more closely at some very useful models for communicating how your people can think about your organization as a whole system.

Otis Spunkmeyer Fires Up Sales

Otis Spunkmeyer is a leading fresh-baked goods company, begun in 1977 by Ken Rawlings, a charismatic leader whose innovations in frozen cookie dough opened up new opportunities in fresh baked cookies. Otis had double-digit growth for many years, but in the mid-1990s sales flattened and for three years there was little growth. The company needed new leadership, and Ken finally convinced John Schiavo, senior vice president at J&J Snackfoods in charge of the west, to move up from Southern California and take over as chief executive officer (CEO). It was 1996.

John is a very personable man. He loves people, loved Otis's products, and understood the industry, but he knew he had to do something beyond one-on-one meetings to get sales going again. "We had an antique DC-3 that we flew on tour around San Francisco with Otis printed on the bottom," John remembers. "We had pictures of it in the hall. But we were a nationwide company and this wasn't paying off. But the poster lit a spark in my mind. I decided to take the plane on a tour national." In the next few months John crafted a campaign called Cleared for Takeoff. He had the marketing department create new materials with the theme. And importantly, he staged a big takeoff event.

Cleared for Takeoff

"We had all our salespeople go to a hangar at the Oakland airport for our annual meeting," John said. "Our salespeople were dying for new materials. They were at that point photocopying their

A CAMPAIGN WITH REAL VISUAL IMPACT

John Schiavo's Cleared for Takeoff campaign began when he took over as CEO of Otis Spunkmeyer in 1996. It is a classic example of using the full power of visual symbols and visible actions to get people excited and aligned. Sales went from flat to double-digit growth in five months after the campaign began!

own materials. Customers were complaining. We announced our goal of doubling sales in five years and passed out the new materials. Then we opened the hangar doors and Ken Rawlings and I climbed into the DC-3 and literally took off. People were rocked!"

Sales went from flat to double-digit growth in the next five months! It was so successful that John kept at the campaign for three years. "We went to the National Restaurant school with the nose of a DC-3, cockpit and let people take pictures in it. We also set up games and made the show fun and airplane-oriented. One game was a target with a hole in the center. The object was to fly a paper airplane through the hole and win a prize. It was simple and yet a real attention getter."

Connecting Medium with the Message

Let's step back and look at what was working in this Otis example. First off all, John was abso-lutely focused in his intention to boost sales rapidly. He was clear that he'd been hired to fuel high growth. "I knew a lot of Otis's customers from my prior job," he said. "They were pretty frustrated at Otis's lack of support and decided to give me a pass. I knew I had one chance to get it right."

The role of strong intention is a feature in all great leaders. Jim Collins makes this very clear in the research that backs up his best-selling book *Good to Great.* Great leaders are committed people.

But John needed a way to reach everyone nationally. He had to get beyond his own personal im-pact and energize the entire organization. Everyone needed something they could talk about and be proud of. It was important that John was sparked by something already in the Otis environ-ment. People knew about the plane, and it was part of the organization's self-image already. John simply took the idea and made it really *BIG* and visible.

John also didn't slack off after the initial event, although he's convinced the launch itself was criti-cal in jolting the sales force into action. The campaign was reinforced after that with media, fliers, other events, and continual messaging on his and leadership's part. "We ended up taking it to all the air shows around the country and giving away free cookies. Our customers were thrilled. Everywhere that DC-3 went around the country, people would notice and remember."

National Tool & Die's Refrigerator Award

Let's look at a second example of how a simple metaphor can become a meaningful leadership symbol. This is a story Tom Melohn, CEO of North American Tool & Die (NATD), shared repeatedly at Apple's Leadership Experience during the 1980s to inspire that company's emerging leaders. Tom spent the first 25 years of his career working for a nationally known, consumer packaged-goods company. After losing his job, he purchased NATD and successfully revolutionized the company by partnering with his employees at a whole new level of seriousness. The company was recognized in the highly acclaimed PBS television series *In Search of Excellence*, as well as in the *Harvard Business Review* and *Inc.* magazines. Apple wanted Tom to share his inspiring ideas with their young leaders.

One of the things Tom needed to turn things around was having everyone contribute their all to the effort. He didn't want to fire people (and didn't). He just worked in every way possible to make it clear that he truly valued everyone's participation and contribution. As he told the story, he managed a complete turnaround in quality, taking it from a low rating to 99.9 percent error-free production, without big changes in personnel. What he changed was everyone's understanding of the importance of a partnership relationship with employees. What he gained was trust.

A visible symbol of this orientation was the periodic "refrigerator award." He would gather everyone in the middle of the main factory around an old refrigerator. He would then open it up, pull out an envelope, and name the latest recipient. It would be a person or team who had contributed something yet again to the improvement of quality at NATD. The refrigerator

NORTH AMERICAN TOOL & DIE'S REFRIGERATOR AWARD

Tom Melohn, CEO of NATD, underlined his "partnership" approach to employees by acknowledging contributions with a refrigerator award, created for a young employee who put a part in the refrigerator to shrink it and eliminate damage during a closely fitted assembly process.

JAN, IT HAS YOUR NAME ON IT THIS TIME!

HEADLANDS CENTER
FOR THE ARTS

HCA's 13-building campus is located in the old Fort Barry site in the Marin Headlands portion of the Golden Gate National Recreation Area. It is 10 minutes from San Francisco and yet is situated in the Rodeo Valley, which, except for the old Army facilities, has been restored to its natural state of wildness. This artist-in-residence center is unique in inviting artists from around the world to come and explore the edges of their work and do basic research on the relationship between the natural and human creative processes.

became a symbol of his partnership orientation because of a young man who had solved a persistent quality problem. It was caused by a part that fit into another part at such close tolerance it was regularly getting damaged during assembly. The young man improvised by putting the part into the refrigerator. As it cooled it got slightly smaller, just enough that it would fit right into the other part without damage! That became Tom's symbol! This example, like Otis, is a case where something real and meaningful to people was elevated to a symbolic status by a leader who knew how to work with visible manifestations of his point of view.

Envisioning a New Art Center

Let's look at a final example in the nonprofit sector, in which a mental model became a visual symbol of a vision, and highly visible symbolic enactments became a path to funding. In the early 1980s a planning effort began to determine how an art center could be created in an old fort in the Marin Headlands, just north of San Francisco across the Golden Gate Bridge. In 1976, at the peak of the environmental movement at the time, several forts in Marin County became the Golden Gate National Recreation Area (GGNRA) by an act of Congress. It created one of the largest national parks by area in the country, and it included an odd assortment of old Army barracks, rifle ranges, Nike missile sites, and acres of relatively wild coastal land. Many public workshops were held to figure out what to do, and meeting after meeting imagined having an art center in Fort Barry, halfway between Sausalito and the ocean in an area called Rodeo Valley.

Fort Barry contained more than a dozen buildings, all constructed in the early 1900s. Redwood and other materials were in plentiful supply, and they were built to last. But they'd been boarded up for many years and had become a place for young people to break in and have parties.

A board of trustees inherited a plan for the art center and was given a small barracks building out near the ocean in Fort Cronkhite as a temporary base of operations. But the GGNRA wasn't about to let a tiny startup take over 13 buildings at Fort Barry unless it proved itself. How could this happen? To the board it felt like a chicken-and-egg problem. Everyone loved the Fort Barry site, but they couldn't occupy it without funding and some momentum.

Taking Two Years to Craft a Vision

In the case of the Headlands Center for the Arts (HCA), getting clear on a compelling vision took two years. The board realized that it was challenged in that Marin County itself had a stereotyped image nationally. Everyone assumed that the art center needed to be a national organization to hope to afford renovating a dozen buildings. There were pieces of a vision that had grown out of the workshops. People could easily imagine an artist in residence center. It was in the wild but only 10 minutes from San Francisco. This was a huge and nearly unique asset. People could also imagine famous artists working with apprentices. A less clear idea, but one with real commitment on the part of several board members, was creating a dialogue between creative artists and environmentalists about the relationship between the natural and human creative processes. But when it came to answering the question "What are we?" the board couldn't agree.

If the art center championed one kind of art or another at this stage, it would be running a huge risk. Fashions change. If it operated too locally it could get branded as a amateur operation. To operate nationally it needed major funding and a very compelling story.

Crisis Is Opportunity

An old adage states that in crisis there is opportunity. In the case of HCA it came as a spark of insight one meeting when the directors realized that the central question they were trying to answer was in fact the answer. The art center would focus on being a place of research on this

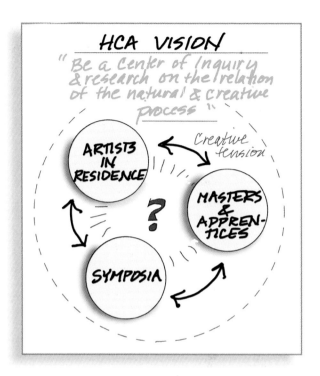

HEADLANDS CENTER FOR THE ARTS VISION

This diagram summed up the vision of the board of the Headlands Center for the Arts during its startup years. By making its inquiry about the nature of the arts that would be created there the very center of its mission, it resolved an issue of how to make the program areas "fit." Visuals can easily show things that are in tension by illustrated them right next to each other!

question of the relationship between the natural and the human creative process. The diagram on the previous page captured the vision. It is an example of a simple mental model, not a branding image like the Otis airplane, but a clear, memorable framework. The important idea was that the art center would keep the center open and focused on a question and not an answer. The diagram reminded everyone that the three program areas would be in creative tension with one another and that in and of itself it would generate continuing energy and interest.

Making the Vision Visible

As with Otis, it wasn't enough for the board to have a clear vision. Many people needed to become aware of the HCA's plans. The board decided that the only way to accomplish this was to do something symbolical in each program area to demonstrate commitment to the vision.

1. **Artists in Residence:** To manifest that part of the vision, HCA made a deal with the Art Institute in San Francisco to take over one of the Fort Cronkhite barracks. It became the artist-in-residence program overnight. The Art Institute was hungry for studio space for students, so it was a win-win.

2. **Symposium:** The board organized a conference between GGNRA park partners and the Headlands artists to explore the new theme. This would be documented and published.

3. **Master/Apprentice Program:** To demonstrate that HCA was serious, it managed to convince William Wiley, a famous local artist, to create a "piece" in the park itself, designed by him and executed by apprentices. This would be launched with a show including other artists such as Gyongy Laky, a well-known fiber artist also working with apprentices, and a gallery show in the Fort Cronkhite offices.

The first two actions were very successful at showing that the HCA board was serious. The third was helped out by some lucky circumstances. Bill Wiley, it turned out, was rather well-known for his parties, and decided to come and throw one at the launch event. This attracted an audience

It wasn't enough to have a clear idea on the board. Many people needed to become aware of the Headlands Center for the Arts' plans. The board decided that the only way to accomplish this was to do something symbolically in each program area to demonstrate commitment to the vision.

of other well-known artists and importantly an article in *Art Week*, which heralded HCA as a welcome, edgy new art center—just the evidence it needed to show it could operate nationally.

Persistence Pays

Lest you are left with the idea that having messages with meaning is *all* you have to do to be successful, the HCA story required a lot of follow-through. Bill Wiley's art piece ended up being a Burma-shave-style set of murals painted on the sides of three old, square, concrete septic tanks dotted along Rodeo Valley (which have since been removed). The first at the beach read "IS THERE" in 5-foot tall, green letters with Druidic symbols. A little farther up by a lagoon a second read "ANOTHER." A third at the rifle range read "PRESENT?" Wiley's idea was to engage the park community in a dialogue around HCA's central idea. Well, engage the public it did. The GGNRA received more mail than it could handle, much of it angry and contemptuous. "How could you defile this sacred area!" It turns out people go to parks for refuge, not engagement with artists! But of more concern to the park management was the firestorm of graffiti that erupted on all the gun emplacements and bunkers through the park! The young people got the message. Yes, *we* are present! And, of course, they had no problem being graphic about it!

The HCA board had agreed that if the outdoor show presented any problems it would take it down right away, and that is what happened. The Wiley murals were painted over within two weeks. But the statement had been made. HCA was launched. The arts community was impressed. Funders were impressed. And shortly thereafter the center received a large, three-year grant that allowed it to hire Jennifer Dowley, a very experienced arts administrator, who, along with a very aligned board, built the center into a viable and funded national organization. For years the metaphor of "keeping the center an open question and focusing on inquiry" was its guiding light.

HEADLAND CENTER FOR THE ARTS—LANDMARKS EXHIBITION

William Wiley and Gyongy Laky "marked" the land at the inaugural exhibition of the Headlands Center for the Arts in the Golden Gate National Recreation Area. Bill's installation is described on this page. Gyongy, working with dozens of other fiber artists, wove triangles of blue and yellow plastic ribbons near the road approaching the building that HCA hoped to occupy some day.

This little drawing is from my journal after the event, which I curated as a member of the board. I had no experience with art shows but a great deal with the power of visualization and organizational development. We did make a mark on everyone's memories.

CONCEPTUAL TOOLS

Mental models that work as shared visual language often have a focal visual icon. You might recognize some here, starting on the top left with Larry Greiner's graph of the stages of organization evolution and revolution, then Arthur M. Young's arc of process, the structure that informs the Drexler/Sibbet Team Performance Model.

Visual Mental Models

If metaphors link your communications to the experiences of the people to whom you are communicating, mental models can be appreciated as a lens that help you focus in the right places. Some of these are worth using as a standard visual language for thinking about organizations as whole systems, and are definitely important to share as a leadership team. Many mental models that have stood the test of time have a visual graphic or diagram illustrating the central ideas. Is it possible that there is an integrating, visual, process language across all these choices? You can see from these journal pages how vast this territory is, and my early work establishing primary symbols.

When a visual framework such as any of these becomes a standard visual language for your communications, it's like getting a broadband connection to your computer. It can help communicate complex ideas. The Headlands' vision is an example. Its model does not represent an underlying philosophy, but a simple depiction of the three program areas. The common denominator is providing an image that reminds everyone of how the big pieces of your organizations work together. Sometimes these models can be comprehensive. *Visual Meetings* explains the Group Graphic Keyboard, the fruit of the explorations visualized here and the first application of Process Theory to groups. *Visual Teams* explores the Drexler/Sibbet Team Performance Model in equal detail. This book focuses on the Sustainable Organizations Model. Their common basis provides a powerful, integrating language for leaders.

TOOLS "OPERATING SYSTEM MAPS"

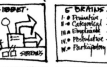

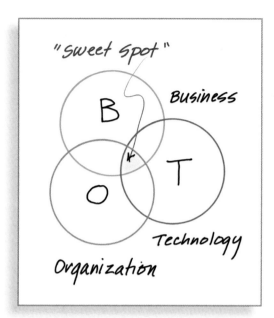

BOT MODEL

In its technology functions in the 1990s, Procter & Gamble wanted to balance its focus on business (finance), organization (people), and technology (infrastructure and tools), and not get overly focused on technology. Leaders used this graphic (technically called a Venn diagram) to make that point.

Integrating Business, Organization, and Technology

Procter & Gamble (P&G) provides an example of a mental model in action. In the 1990s the information technology group was expanding rapidly. P&G was at the forefront of using computer networks to integrate its business. But it was important to keep in mind that the real win was in integrating with business operations, which focused on financial results, portfolios, and the like, and the organizational side, which focused on people. To do this, leadership developed a very simple three-circle diagram illustrated here. By consistently using this visualization, P&G kept the idea front and center for the technology folks. It functioned like the HCA vision diagram.

Seven S Model

A more comprehensive mental model of a whole organization is the Seven S Model, developed by McKinsey & Company and used as a criteria screen by Robert Waterman Jr. and Tom Peters in writing *In Search of Excellence* (a book credited with igniting the business publishing genre in the early 1980s). Their book did not include any graphics of this model, but it has been visualized many times since (as illustrated on the next page). Richard Pascale, another McKinsey colleague who helped develop the original model, subsequently wrote *Managing on the Edge* and did include a very interesting visualization of the model, which is one of the most complete to describe all the aspects of an organization that need to integrate and align.

Pascale was convinced that it is more helpful to think of organizations as dynamic, organic entities than fixed machines. He appreciated that each of the seven Ss could manifest as an inward oriented, centripetal, orientation or be more outward-oriented and centrifugal. For instance, strategy could be highly centralized and controlled, or it could be outward-oriented and opportunistic. To support more holistic, systems-oriented thinking during strategy implementation, The Grove translated Pascale's work into the Seven P Organization Process model and created

SEVEN S MODEL

This model developed at McKinsey & Company guided the authors of *In Search of Excellence* in the 1980s. It has remained a very popular way to think about organizations as whole systems.

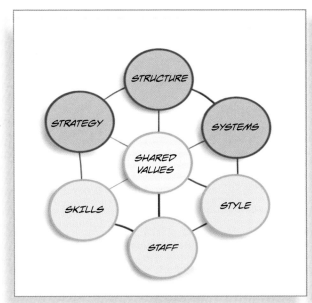

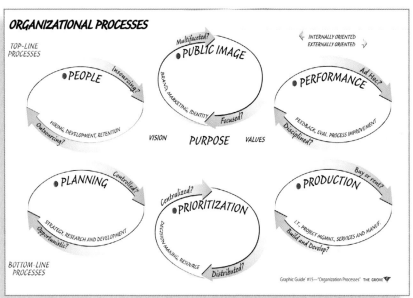

a template that organizations could work with interactively to diagnose where they are on the inward/outward continuums. Unlike the Pascale diagram, which had "overcontrol" at the center and "chaos" on the edges, we put purpose in the middle, with its manifestation as vision, and values as the glue between the "hard" and "soft" elements.

Understanding Comes from Using Models

Just giving people frameworks such as the ones on this page won't help your people think more systemically. You need to guide people to work with them by mapping your own organization with these as a guide. At National Semiconductor, during one of their reengineering efforts, one group added a 1/10 scale on each of the arrows in the Organization Process Graphic Guide, with 0 to 10 on each arrow. Then everyone on the management team, with sticky notes, indicated where they thought they were on each of the 12 arrows. It took awhile to do the assessment, but the conversation afterward was engaged at an unusual level of depth and insight.

ORGANIZATION PROCESSES GRAPHIC GUIDE

This Graphic Guide is an adaptation of Richard Pascale's version of the Seven S Model. It shifts from describing parts to describing processes. Mapping the elements to human's natural orientation, bottom-line being the "hard" elements and top-line being the more aspirational, this guide flips the orientation of the Seven S Model. It reflects Pascale's observation that each element has an inward-looking and an outward-looking manifestation and that most organizations sustain some of both, with changes over time. Descriptors are in the arrows.

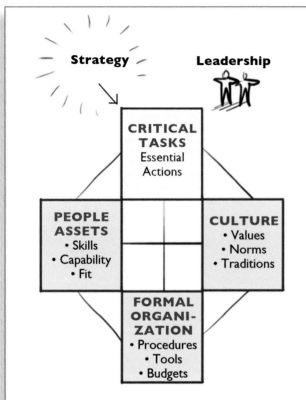

ORG ELEMENTS MODEL

Charles A. O'Reilly uses this model to show how people, formal organization, and culture need to align with and support the critical tasks needed to implement whichever strategy leaders set.

Organization Alignment Model

If you do not want to engage yourself or your team in as much complexity as the Organization Process template provides, a middle-ground framework might work better. One of the most effective was created by Charles O'Reilly, one of the most popular business school professors at Stanford. In both corporate and government agency settings it is pitched at just the right level of detail to quickly become a useful kind of visual language for a management team. Charles's book, *Winning Through Innovation*, (co-authored with Michael Tushman), is a terrific example of using this model as a thread of visual language to make quite complex ideas very accessible. Let's appreciate how he visualizes the organization as a whole.

Bill's assumption is that leadership and its strategies drive identification of specific "critical tasks" that are essential to actually achieving the goals that are being set out. He defines them simply as the "essential actions." In your organization you might call them priority initiatives, or they could be the bold steps that come out of a strategic visioning process with leadership (see Chapter 9 for a description of a full process).

According to Charles, implementation difficulties arise when three additional organizational elements are not aligned to support these actions. He names them the people assets, with all their skills and competencies; the formal organization, representing the budgets, formal policies and procedures, and technical infrastructures; and culture, which includes the values, traditions, and what psychologists call "norms"—the acceptable behavior that is simply understood.

While working on the one hand with leadership at Agilent Technologies—the spin-off from Hewlett-Packard that is a leader in instrumentation— and on the other with the National Park Services executive-leadership program, Charles consistently worked to help people understand that when it comes to strategy implementation, culture trumps all the rest. By simplifying his model and making culture one of the big, three areas needing alignment, he makes this point very visibly and keeps leadership focused on its importance. Charles provides example after example of companies that succeed and then fail because a deeply rooted culture can't change fast enough to adapt to new conditions. His newest book with Tushman, *Ambidextrous Organizations: Resolving the Innovator's Dilemma*, continues with many more examples.

Meaning Is a Function of Personal Experience

Charles O'Reilly's contention that culture trumps strategy gives another edge of insight to what lies behind skillful use of metaphors and models. It underlines Schwartz's conclusions that people's personal experiences and personal relationships with symbols—be they metaphors or models—is what truly gives them meaning. This is why, if you are going to introduce a new vision or a new way of thinking about your organization, you need to simultaneously think about how to create experiences through which people can begin making them meaningful. Just because they are meaningful to you does not translate into impact on others.

If you want to delve a little deeper into these ideas, read a wonderful book called *The Poetics of Space*, by Gaston Bachelard. He was a well-known philosopher of science at the Sorbonne in Paris during the 1900s. He turned to aesthetics in his later years and speculated on the origins of meaning in poetry and architecture. He wrote *The Poetics* in 1958 and invites the reader to think about how words first become meaningful. He believed that it is our first experiences in whatever home we were raised that are the grains of sand around which we pearl our sense of what words mean. *Submerge*, for instance, is rooted in the first time you were ever completely under water. *Closed in* is embedded in the first dark closet you found yourself in with the door closed. It doesn't matter if your home was big or small, rich or poor. First experiences have the power of the first marks on the blank canvas of meaning.

Charles O'Reilly's contention that culture trumps strategy gives another edge of insight to what lies behind skillful use of metaphors and models. It underlines Schwartz's conclusions that people's personal experiences and personal relationships with symbols—be they metaphors or models—is what truly gives them meaning.

More contemporary evidence can be found in George Lakoff's work. He is a cognitive scientist from University of California, Berkeley, and well-known author of such books as *Metaphors We Live By* and *Philosophy in the Flesh*. He began his professional life assuming that computers would allow humans to finally figure out the underlying logic and grammar of language and support the development of real artificial intelligence. He found, however, that at the bottom of his inquiries into the origins of meaning was the same conclusion that animated Bachelard. Meaning is rooted in unique, personal experiences! It is our first associations that drive our attraction and repulsions and are a big factor in filtering our interests. They are inherently unique and personal.

Understanding Comes from Linking to Direct Experiences

The implications for leaders who work with visual metaphors and visual models is that the first order of business is to truly get to know your audience and your followers. It is their native understandings that will be your channels for connection. Second, if you want to introduce something truly new, you need to design experiences that allow people to develop new personal connections that result in real understanding.

It is this conclusion that lies at the root of wanting you to understand just how ineffective "push"-style communications, supported by massive slide decks, are. You might as well just spray people with a firehose. Not much sinks in. For people to come to new understandings, they need to *experience* something new.

- They need to see John Schiavo and Otis founder Ken Rawlings physically get on the airplane, together, and take off, together. There's no question about that kind of commitment.

- They need to actually see artists in residence, experience an edgy art event, and participate in a symposium to bring to life the HCA vision model of being a center of research.

- They need to see John Melohn give out several refrigerator awards to move to deep trust that they too might be honored if they stretch a little at work.
- They need to actually use a framework like National Semiconductor did with the Organizational Processes Graphic Guide and map how their actual organization shows up when viewed through this framework.

Leading by Learning and Questioning

In Chapter 12 we'll return to this theme of how metaphors and models can help you communicate by taking a look at Grove Storymaps—large murals that use rich graphic imagery to communicate plans, linking them to cultural icons and values. Storymaps use rich graphic metaphors. Visualized mental models are more diagrammatic. But the models we've been exploring here can provide the underlying architectures for these more graphic depictions. It helps if graphics are supported by widely understood frameworks that can function like the base maps in a geographic map. Keeping in mind that, like geographic maps, conceptual models are not the territory; clean, well-organized frameworks such as those explored in this chapter can operate like fine lenses and help you explore the real-world messiness in an orderly way.

But well-organized visuals are powerful enough that it is possible to get seduced by them. When you think about their power and how they illuminate remember they also blindside (see Pascale's comments in the sidebar). Remember this story about Peter Senge at a Leadership and Mastery workshop in San Francisco. He stood at the board and began to ask the participants what the different elements of an organization were and how they interacted. He started with customers, who make orders, which result in deliveries, which are affected by inventories. He went on and on until he had created the chart shown on page 106 (a faithful copy of his wall drawing). Peter

Perceived patterns over time form a mental infrastructure—or mind-set. Scientists call it a paradigm. Danger arises when our mental maps cease to fit the territory. The problem with mind-sets or paradigms is that we tend to see through them, and so the degree to which they filter our perception goes unrecognized. To counter this threat, individuals and organizations must build mechanisms (i.e. checks and balances) that cause them to question and update their mental maps.

Richard Pascale
Managing on the Edge,
page 13

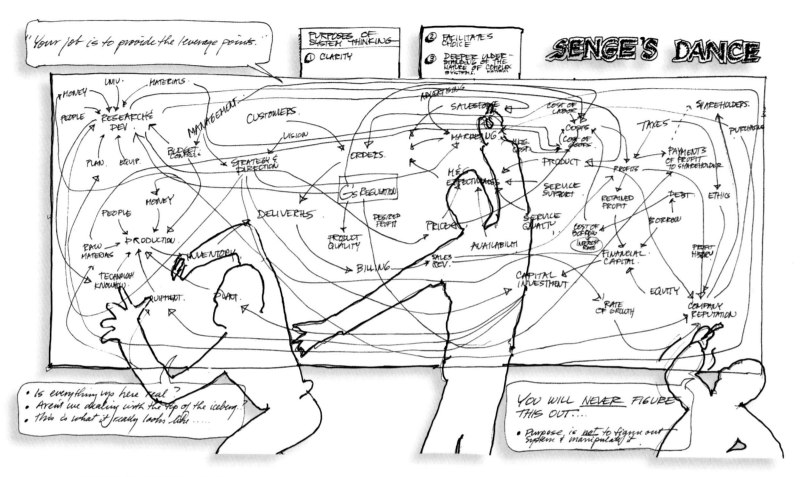

SYSTEMS MODELLING

In *The Fifth Discipline: The Art and Practice of the Learning Organization* Peter Senge identifies systems thinking and mental modelling as two of the five disciplines. Here he is demonstrating (and cautioning).

then turned and asked everyone, "What is the point?" It wasn't to figure all of this out and then manipulate the organization. It was to raise awareness and provide a context for decision making, which ultimately needs to draw on the sum total of your experience, including values, intuition, and gut feel, as well as analysis.

8. Visual Meetings
Stimulating Engagement & Creative Contribution

A second essential tool set for visual leadership includes the practices of visual meetings. This involves the routine use of interactive visualization in regular and special meetings, both face-to-face and virtual. An earlier book, *Visual Meetings: How Graphics, Sticky Notes, & Idea Mapping Can Transform Group Productivity*, was written for visual practitioners who don't necessarily draw but want to lead visual meetings as practitioners. This chapter is for you leaders who won't necessarily work visually yourself but who want to support this way of working in your organization. The possibilities will come to life with stories from several organizations. The chapter also offers an activity you can use to become more aware of how to ask for the kind of visualization you require.

In Startups, Seeing Is Believing

Lana Homes has started more than 30 different companies. She's an expert in leading organizations in their beginning phases. "The first thing I do is gather everyone around a whiteboard and get all our ideas up on the wall," she said without hesitating when asked if visual meetings played any part in her work. She knows startups have to get a good story going and that this is a group effort.

Luke Hohmann is a great example. He is growing Innovation Games, a company using "gamification" to help organizations do strategy. His first years happened in an office with his team around a table next to the huge whiteboard wall covered with sticky notes (shown here). This wall guided them at the big-picture level. (Games, by the way, are hugely visual.)

Another Silicon Valley startup called S3 decided to use six big murals to brief Wall Street analysts on its intentions and results to stand out from the crowd and allow everyone to see the big picture. Creating the murals involved everyone on the management team in a number of engaged conversations and achieved alignment from everyone as a by-product.

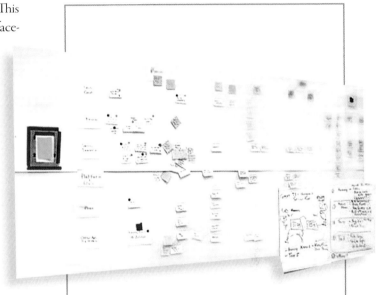

STARTUP STICKY NOTE WALL

Innovation Games, a startup company in Silicon Valley, navigates with the help of a big wall like this. It sits right behind the big table where the programming team works. Just as blackboards are an essential tool for teachers, sticky note walls are a prime tool for the beginning stages of thinking about anything that has many elements—such as a new game.

FORMAT FOR OPERATION DECISION MAKING

The flip chart format shown illustrates a format used by the San Francisco Foundation executive director Martin Paley to support operational decision making on the part of his distribution committee—the formal board of directors for the foundation. It's a simple list format that was very helpful. Here were the benefits:

❑ In creating the charts staff got aligned on the potential actions and its recommendations.

❑ The distribution committee could see at a glance the full range of decision needed and help Martin manage through the decisions.

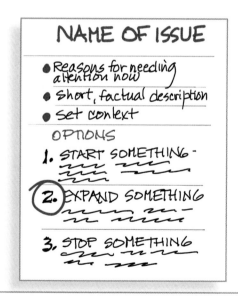

People in startups want to contribute, and because so many questions are unanswered, everyone's point of view is helpful as problem after problem rears up, begging for solution. The problem-solving process suggested in Chapter 3 is just the kind of visual meeting practice that you might use frequently. The sticky note wall is another example. Visual meetings are a clear power tool for the beginning phases of anything when contribution from everyone is at a premium.

Visualizing Choices in Philanthropy

More established institutions also benefit. Martin Paley was, in the 1980s, an innovative executive director of the San Francisco Foundation (SFF), a community foundation that, with the help of dozens of special trusts that it managed, supported the larger San Francisco Bay Area with about $7 million in grant money annually. He loved to work visually and regularly involved graphic recorders and special visualization strategies in both regular and special meetings. When his organization was thrown into a whirlwind with the receipt of a bequest that would triple its annual giving, he supported the many changes required with visual meetings.

Martin also improvised in his regular meetings with his board, which were very formal affairs that were not facilitated meetings and were chaired in very particular ways. Martin had a challenge. The distribution committee only met once a quarter to review the grant proposals being suggested by foundation staff. This involved producing a large book of material that needed to be studied in advance. The board had the formal power of actually making the grants, and this work was a priority. But given the new challenges at the foundation organizationally, Martin also needed the board to give him operational advice in critical areas where it retained oversight. How could he do this? Adding this material to the grant binders risked losing the decisions in a sea of other information. Martin and his key staff devised a visual meeting strategy. It was simple, and something that could apply to any of your regular leadership meetings. In advance of the meeting they summarized each operational decision on one flip chart (see example on the prior page). On the chart was a clear title in capital letters that named the issue. Under that were three to four bullet points about why the issue needed to be dealt with. Under that were listed three choices about what to do. These were intentionally kept short and sweet so that no chart was longer than one page. One of the three potential actions was the one being recommended by staff.

In the first meeting where Martin used this method, the distribution committee was able to review and decide on the operation items in less than a half hour! Staff was thrilled. This approach was used in subsequent meetings. They could handle a dozen or more issues quite quickly.

Using Visual Meetings on a Regular Basis

Sticky note walls and pop-up flip chart recording are pretty basic to supporting problem solving-thinking in meetings and recording commitments. But you might also want to support you and your team's taking a big-picture look at something that deserves bringing in a graphic recorder or graphic facilitator and working at a large scale. Graphic recorders are people who can document what is happening while you conduct the meeting. They work like secretaries, except the notes are visible and can be challenged and improved on the spot. A graphic facilitator is someone you might ask to lead the meeting as well as create the graphics so that you can participate fully without unintentionally shutting down participation from others.

The picture on this page shows a typical recorded meeting. In a few pages we'll review the different formats you can use for this kind of visual meeting. It's important that you have a good sense of what you want as a result so that you can ensure that the most useful information is

GRAPHIC FACILITATION

As a leader you may want to recruit a graphic recorder or graphic facilitator to support meetings that have to deal with information that you want people to look at as a whole, or where you want to encourage input and creativity. This picture illustrates a typical team meeting where recording is happening on a large chart. The graphic facilitator is using a cluster pattern to record, grouping information without explicit connections in order to stimulate more thinking.

being captured and emphasized. If you simply want documentation, then advise that the graphic recorder be off to the side. But if you want to support real group thinking and co-creation, have the graphic wall as an integral part of the meeting, with the facilitator acting like a human cursor for the display of your and the group's thinking. More advanced formats, such as grids, diagrams, and graphic metaphor mapping, all benefit from having a single graphic facilitator working the chart under the group's direction. Let's look at an example where visual meeting methods were able to handle a fairly large group.

Council on Foundation Conference Planning

Visual meetings worked so well for Martin Paley that he advised using the approach at a special meeting of the Council on Foundation's conference planning group on which he sat. The program committee was composed of some two dozen up-and-coming philanthropists around the country who were being introduced to national leadership through this involvement, part of an intentional leadership development strategy. Community foundations, private foundations, and big nonprofits, such as Ford and Rockefeller Foundations, all have different interests and ways of working. The value of combining them in program planning was the wide-ranging dialogue that emerged as everyone worked to decided on keynoters, special workshops, and other elements needed that year. Everyone learned a lot about the field and its current challenges and approaches to funding.

You would be right in guessing that this type of committee can be a political nightmare. How in the world can a large, diverse group get convergence on something as complicated as an annual convention? Better to let power players propose and others come along for the ride—unless you understand how to run a good visual meeting, which Martin did. He wanted it graphically facilitated with him working as a participant. Martin and a meeting design team decided that trying a big, "one-wall" approach might work. This consisted of creating a 30-foot long representation of the entire conference, with AM and PM columns for the four days of the meeting (see illustration on the previous page). Every hour was indicated graphically so that you could easily see how much time was available for different sessions. (This tool is called a time-block agenda.)

The meeting began with a round of dialogue about what success might look like generally. This brought up everyone's assessment of the current drivers in the foundation world and what various people felt a really good conference should look like. This was recorded as people brought up their ideas, and out of this were harvested some criteria. The meeting then shifted to the big, time-block agenda. There were, of course, some things that had already been decided, such as the venue (which had to be booked years in advance) and some other items. These were added to the big agenda right on the paper. But all the other items were handled with 8.5" by 11" pieces of paper, using tape loops to facilitate movement. (The letter-sized paper was necessary for legibility in a big group.) Everyone was invited to start making suggestions, and all of the ideas were recorded on these sheets, which were then either put onto the board in certain time slots or off to the side.

As the program began to take on some form, more engaged debate began occurring over the overall architecture. Several shifts took place to make it possible for key resources to be involved. The facilitator mirrored every suggestion with a move of the sheets of paper. When the group reached consensus, the item was taped down. Standoffs remained stuck on the board at a slant.

The chair of the committee had never seen a facilitated meeting, and although initially skeptical, she got very excited as she saw the process actually working. They were getting a real design, *and* they were having the great conversations that were at the heart of their leadership training goal.

MATCH A CHALLENGE TO A VISUAL MEETING TOOL

The nine different challenges listed below can all be addressed by one of the nine visual meeting tools illustrated on the next page. See if you can match challenges with a tool.

1. You have some new members on your team who need to be brought up to speed.

2. You have a tight time frame for a meeting and want to avoid unrelated topics.

3. You need to establish some basic meeting discipline in your leadership team.

4. Your people are hunkered down and working too hard to think anything could change.

5. You have some stakeholders you'd like to involve in the design of a critical offsite meeting.

6. You have an initiative in mind and need a group to take ownership and get busy implementing.

7. Your people have many ideas, but they aren't organized.

8. You'd like an honest, open discussion of what your organization is facing right now.

9. You have to narrow down a whole set of choices to a critical three or four.

Matching Practice to Purpose

There are as many different possible ways to support dialogue with displays as there are people who can wield a marker. So how do you begin to know what to do? We've looked at three different cases so far, but there are hundreds more, of course. The best approach is to start with a simple repertoire of things you know work and build out from there. It's the way performers in any medium, such as music or sports, become proficient.

HE SUGGESTS THAT DIFFERENT FORMATS WORK BETTER FOR DIFFERENT GOALS.

WHAT TOOL WILL WORK FOR ME?

On the next page are illustrated nine tried-and-true visual meeting tools that are specific versions of the seven archetypal formats described in Chapter 3. Then, on this page, is a list of generic challenges that would generate different goals for your meeting. The exercise is to match the tool with one of the challenges. The next page shares the matches.

This type of thinking is what you would be doing as a visual leader, because you know that the pattern that everyone sees develop in the charts will have some sticking power. It needs to be focused on the right things. As you read the recommendations, don't feel overly constrained by them. Any tool can have multiple uses, and you may well think of ones not listed here. That's the fun of this way of working. If you want to explore the full breadth of choices, consult the book *Visual Meetings*. It's loaded with examples of what you can do in meetings to tap the full power of visualization.

VISUAL MEETINGS

A OARRs CHART

Create flip charts or slides that clearly visualize your desired outcomes, agenda, roles, and rules for a meeting.

B SUCCESS LOOKS LIKE MANDALA

Use a large, blank sheet, flip charts, or Web whiteboard to record everyone's thinking about what success would look like.

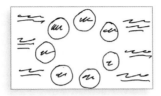

C GRAPHIC RECORDING

Have someone takes notes on flip charts or large paper using simple list and cluster formats. Use colored chalks for emphasis and highlighting..

D PARKING LOT FLIP CHART

Record issues needing discussion outside the meeting on a flip chart or an online whiteboard page.

E AFFINITY CHART

Brainstorm with sticky notes and then arrange them in clusters that have an affinity for one another. Label the categories.

F GRAPHIC HISTORY

Visualize your team history on a long time line by using sticky notes and simple recording. Keep the focus on the storytelling and accept a lively chart.

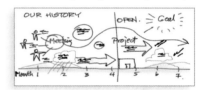

G BIG AGENDA FRAMEWORK

Use a large agenda framework with the times illustrated in boxes whose size indicates time to support a sticky note design session.

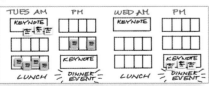

H HI-LO GRID

Create a four-box grid labeled "high reward" on top, "low reward" on the bottom, "easy" on the left and "difficult" on the right. Sort options on stickies.

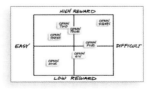

I GRAPHIC ACTION PLAN

Use a graphic template to agree on goals, roles, and key channels of activity around a specific project.

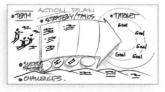

RECOMMENDED TOOLS

Here are recommendations for the nine different challenges listed below. The text explains the reasons for these choices.

1. You have some new members on your team who need to be brought up to speed.

2. You have a tight time frame for a meeting and want to avoid unrelated topics.

3. You need to establish some basic meeting discipline in your leadership team.

4. Your people are hunkered down and working too hard to think anything could change.

5. You have some stakeholders you'd like to involve in the design of a critical offsite meeting.

6. You have an initiative in mind and need a group to take ownership and get busy implementing.

7. Your people have many ideas, but they aren't organized.

8. You'd like an honest, open discussion of what your organization is facing right now.

9. You have to narrow down a whole set of choices to a critical three or four.

F
D
A
B
G
I
E
C
H

Following is the line of reasoning for matching tools to the challenges:

1. New team members need to hear stories and history. Using a **graphic history** to visualize how you got to your current situation is the most fun and direct way to accomplish this.

2. Meetings with limited time can easily get off course with important but unrelated items being introduced. Create a **parking lot** and note the item and agree to deal with it later. Advocates of these topics can usually let go of their concerns if they see them written down.

3. The **OARRs** model is basic. Be clear on outcomes, agenda, roles, and rules, and your meetings will crackle with productivity.

4. When people are too caught up in the day to day, they can get discouraged. A "**what does success look like**" session can invite some future thinking. Writing down everyone's ideas lets people feel connected and engaged.

5. A large **agenda-planning framework** and sticky notes allows you to do with agenda planning what financial folks do with spreadsheets. It creates a dynamic "what-if" environment. You can always come back and refine your first versions, but the big wall technique lets everyone wrap his or her imagination around the big picture.

6. If you need action from a team, assign it the task of doing a **graphic action plan**. Answer these key questions: What is my target? What is our team? What are our tasks? What challenges do we have to navigate? What are the success factors? Do it graphically, and you have a great way of reviewing the work after the team does its initial planning.

7. If you have a lot of ideas bubbling to get out, use a big wall to create an **affinity chart**. Generate the data and then find patterns and clusters. It's a great bottoms-up way to work.

8. Simple **graphic recording** of what everyone says is just right when you want to get a general sense of what everyone thinks about a topic. Recording lets people know they've been heard.

9. A **hi-low grid** is a perfect way to do an initial sort of a wide range of choices. Have the whole team move the sticky notes around without talking and see what happens.

9. Graphic Templates
Visuals for Any Kind of Planning

We've looked at the importance of compelling visual metaphors for communication and visual meeting practices for engagement. When you want your team to really think deeply about a subject and grapple intelligently with planning choices, graphic templates become an essential tool. Graphic templates are large worksheets designed to be used by small groups. Their purpose is to visualize everyone's information in a format that optimizes the chances of everyone seeing important relationships in the information. It helps to provide some light structure for whatever aspect of the planning process you are addressing. The Group Graphics Keyboard explained in Chapter 3 reflects the underlying archetypes in templates, but in actual use these are tailored to the specific purposes of your planning process.

Graphic Templates Support Large Group Processes

Predrawing and preprinting graphic templates bring a level of standardization to visual practice that is especially helpful with large groups. When break-out groups work with the same format, it empowers cross-group comparison of the content. When groups draw their own charts from scratch there is a great deal of visual "noise" reflected in the different drawing capability that isn't necessarily relevant to the content you are exploring. Working with preprinted graphic templates is increasingly appealing to organizations wanting to save the time it would take to create them.

This chapter will introduce you to some of the most useful graphic templates for planning and a process for integrating these in a full planning process. We'll look at some examples of The Grove's formal Strategic Visioning templates called Graphic Guides. Working with sequences of graphic templates such as these results in a whole new level of group insight and understanding.

I'LL MAKE A NOTE FOR US TO COME BACK AND REPLACE THIS ARROW WITH A GRAPHIC METAPHOR THAT REPRESENTS OUR DESIRED ORGANIZATION.

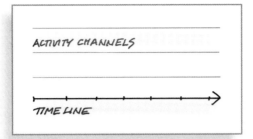

SIMPLE TIME LINE & SUPPLIES

ACTIVITY CHANNELS

TIME LINE

The key tools for doing time lines are long sheets of paper, sticky notes, and pens. Often you will want to see multiple flows of activity over time.

Paper
Use plotter paper, the kind that is used on large ink-jet printers. Most large stationary stores have it in both 3/4-foot-wide roles. You want paper that is *not* highly absorbent.

Tape
Art stores also sell white artist's tape that is a bit kinder on walls than masking tape.

Pens
Use water color markers to avoid bleeding.

Chalk
If you really want to encourage some creativity, suggest that people use chalk pastels for coloring. When you burnish the chalk with a tissue, it looks like you used an airbrush.

Sticky Notes
These are very helpful for any template work. Both 3" by 5" and 5" by 8" sizes are useful.

Basic Template Types Sort into Time Lines and Grids

At the most general level, no matter what you are planning, some of your work will be about how things work over *time* and some of your work will be about how elements fit together in some *spatial* structure (such as a priorities grid). Thinking about time is best supported by time lines, surprise, surprise! Thinking about space and structure has a wider range of possibilities, all derived from gridlike spaces. Some graphic templates combine the two formats, as we shall see.

In regular meetings, you probably won't be using more than one or two templates. For instance you might choose a time line to tell the history of your group to new members or have your action plan reflected in a roadmap of some sort (see Chapter 11). If you are working virtually, you would be focusing on one template or another during different parts of the meeting. If you decide to do a history, then guide your staff to use as big a piece of paper as the wall allows. People really like to reflect on the past, and most of the time, people are not getting nearly enough acknowledgment for all the hard work they are doing. The space fills up quickly.

In your special planning meetings you can use a series of templates. Starting with the history is a perfect way to get everyone's imaginations stretched out into a longer time frame. Apple's Leadership Experience in the 1980s used to cite the research of Omar El Salway at the University of Southern California as a reason for starting with history. Salway gave two groups of 15 executives an assignment. Each person in one group was to describe his or her career history. The others were to describe career futures. On average the group that began with the history went back 15 years. The future group on average went forward five years. But when the groups switched assignments, the results were different. The futures group now doing the history went back 15 years as well. But the history group now doing the future went forward 15 years! Clearly stretching their imagination prepared them to think more boldly. This is the value of starting with history.

You then might follow with a SWOT grid, looking at strengths, weaknesses, opportunities, and threats. Four-box grids are good tools for guiding people to get beyond simplistic thinking. It is the doorway into systems thinking and understanding how parts connect in your organization. There are dozens and dozens depending on what you want to examine. As a leader, getting your team to sort things out this way counters getting stuck in one-quadrant thinking.

Your Role Is to Shape the Categories

Visualizing as a group on a display, either in face-to-face meetings or Web conferences, engages everyone experientially in making sense of information. What makes a graphic template work is the light structuring of the categories. The categories are really questions you are posing. What goes here? What goes there? Questions are what stimulate inquiry and exploration.

The categories on graphic templates are really questions you are posing. What goes here? What goes there? Questions are what stimulate inquiry and exploration.

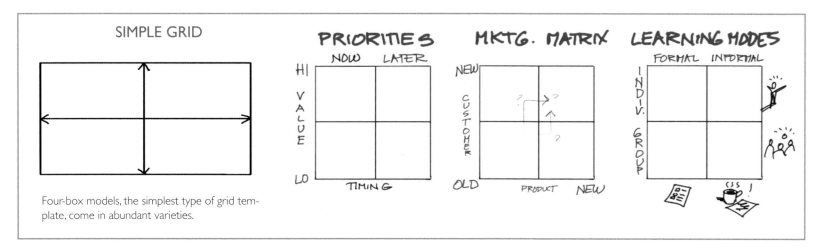

Four-box models, the simplest type of grid template, come in abundant varieties.

TIME-BLOCK AGENDA	LOOSE CLUSTER TEMPLATE	NINE-BOX MATRIX	MIND MAP TEMPLATE
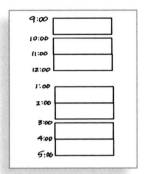	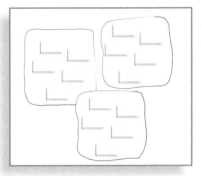	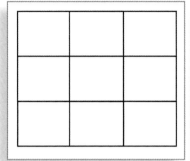	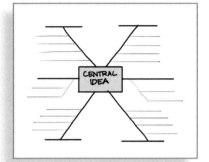
Graphic boxes represent fixed amounts of time so that when you plan your agenda, you can think about how long things are taking.	Sometimes you might want to use predetermined categories and have people brainstorm into them.	Separating things into nine boxes refines everyone's distinctions. Getting the categories clear is the secret to success with matrices.	Diagrams branch in organic patterns. You might want to prename the main branches to guide the exploration.

Uses

❏ Regular meeting agendas	❏ Brainstorming issues	❏ Calendars	❏ Analyzing a field of ideas
❏ Special meeting agendas	❏ Identifying goals	❏ Segmentation of markets	❏ Identifying root problems
❏ Design team meetings	❏ Clustering vision themes	❏ Criteria matrices	❏ Organizing a presentation

OPEN-SOURCE GRAPHIC TEMPLATES

All of the templates on this page are common, generic graphic templates that you can easily reproduce yourself. They are all variants of the archetypal patterns represented in the Group Graphics Keyboard in Chapter 3.

How to Use Graphic Templates in Practice

The graphic templates illustrated on this and the next page are tools you, as a leader, can use to stimulate your people to improve the quality of their insights in any planning process. Any time you are meeting with your staff or external consultants to plan a special meeting, you should be familiar enough with your range of options to match the display formats to your overall purposes. If you are working virtually, these simple graphic templates work best on the whiteboards that are available in almost all Webconference software. Presentation software often incudes graphic

LANDSCAPE METAPHOR TEMPLATE

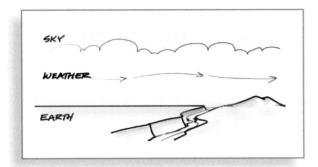

People are so familiar with landscapes that they constitute one of the truly universal metaphors. Mapping your information by sorting the tangible, physical elements from the intangible things such as strategy and intention helps people see their thinking as a complete phenomenon, integrated the way nature connects its different elements.

Uses

❏ Environmental scans

❏ Roadmaps and visions

❏ Drivers of change charts

MANDALA TEMPLATE

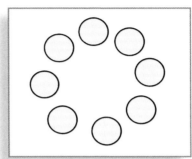

A simple circle template like this provides spaces for people to identify sub-elements as well as the central unifying idea.

Uses

❏ Team introductions

❏ Visioning

❏ Prioritization of ideas

TARGET TEMPLATE

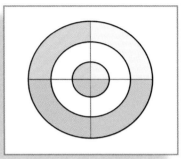

Targets can be simple or more complex, depending on what you decide the quadrants will represent.

Uses

❏ Mental models

❏ Operating systems

❏ Goals and visions

---

templates and diagrams (except maybe the landscape template shown above). One way to generate templates for group use is to mock them up in presentation software and then print them out big on a plotter. However, presentation software isn't really designed to support large-scale printing, so you might have to consult with your technical staff to get a good result. You can also show your meeting staff what you are looking for and have them draw up the templates in advance of your meeting or get them preprinted from a source such as The Grove. In Web conferences with whiteboard capability, it is possible to draw a simple template on the spot.

ONLINE VISUALIZATION

Many new software platforms are emerging that allow groups to work together on a common graphic. These collaborative visualization tools usually have graphic templates included. They are mostly cloud-based, and allow a user to invite others to help co-create the graphic or presentation.

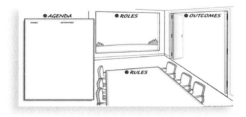
Put Templates Together in an Integrated Planning Process

The Grove's Strategic Visioning (SV) process is an example of how to integrate templates into a full process. It evolved during the booming 1990s, when organizations were expanding rapidly and many were jumping into reengineering processes to adapt to new technologies. The core intention of SV was to overcome the analytic bias of traditional strategic planning, which emphasizes hindsight by looking at historical data. Innovative organizations need to balance hindsight with aspirational thinking and the kind of foresight that comes from envisioning a different future. Both of these perspectives need to converge and support insight in action in the present.

The SV process model is itself a kind of template, although designed for guiding process design, not for recording group content. (See Chapter 7 for more on models.) The figure-eight image in the SV graphic suggests the need to integrate hindsight and foresight into insight in action and to go through repeated cycles at different levels of the organization to get full understanding and buy-in. The primary aim of such a process is to develop strategic, visionary thinking capability in the general system through regular rounds of visual planning. The plan and related graphic templates are devices to drive the development of this strategic thinking capability.

You might notice the small graphic symbols on the far left of the model on the next page. These represent the four flows leaders need to manage and the different kinds of intelligence that you as a leader need to tap into in your organization. The light burst at the top points toward top-line intentions and the need to involve your intuitive thinkers. The small yin/yang-like symbol represents the feeling body of the organization, the energetic, experiential aspects of the culture. Human resources staff and facilitators focus on these aspects. The small diamond represents the technical, thinking part of the organization. The cube represents the operational, bottom-line, hands-on-the-work aspects. These four levels are represented as symbols because different orga-

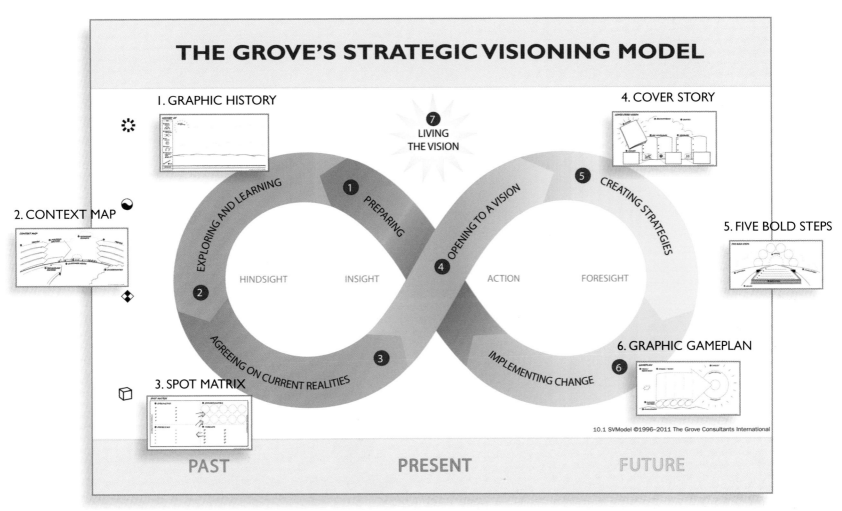

THE GROVE'S STRATEGIC VISIONING MODEL

1. GRAPHIC HISTORY

7 LIVING THE VISION

4. COVER STORY

2. CONTEXT MAP

5. FIVE BOLD STEPS

3. SPOT MATRIX

6. GRAPHIC GAMEPLAN

EXPLORING AND LEARNING

1 PREPARING

OPENING TO A VISION

5 CREATING STRATEGIES

HINDSIGHT   INSIGHT   ACTION   FORESIGHT

2

4

AGREEING ON CURRENT REALITIES

3

IMPLEMENTING CHANGE

6

10.1 SVModel ©1996–2011 The Grove Consultants International

PAST   PRESENT   FUTURE

See larger versions of these Graphic Guides on the next page.

nizations have many different words for these distinctions. The point is to integrate these levels in a process that optimizes everyone coming to key insights and seeing key relationships.

Integrate Intuition, Feeling, Thinking, and Sensing

The figure-eight pattern integrates top-line and bottom-line thinking. When the SV process was developing, Meryem LeSaget, a Grove associate in Paris, pointed out that the real value of the large-scale graphic history telling was the way it tapped the group intuition and feelings. Although the exercise can be led in an analytic way, most of the time it releases storytelling and

1. GRAPHIC HISTORY

Use a landscape metaphor to visualize the key events in your organization's time line.

2. CONTEXT MAP

Mapping trends and factors as clusters of environmental features stimulates seeing relationships.

3. SPOT MATRIX

Use a grid to show how opportunities build on strengths and flip the energy tied up in problems (sometimes called weaknesses).

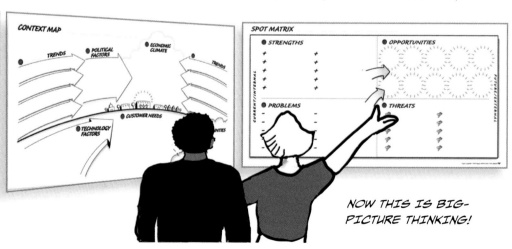

NOW THIS IS BIG-PICTURE THINKING!

a celebration of community. On the other hand, working in the matrix of the SPOT template tends to ground everyone's attention on the specific, concrete problems faced in the operational part of the organization. Asking everyone to imagine the future as if the organization were on the cover of an important magazine shifts attention back to the future and a more intuitive modality, whereas grounding things in the Five Bold Steps requires prioritization and agreement—a much more constrained and operational mode again. This cycle of work and the changes in point of view on each template ensure that you optimize the chance of the full spectrum of the group's embedded wisdom emerging.

4. COVER STORY VISION

Imagine being on the cover of an important magazine. Have everyone write the future story!

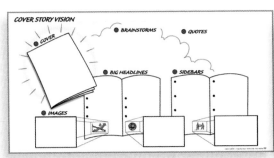

See www.grove.com for more on Graphic Guides

5. FIVE BOLD STEPS

Identify shared elements of your vision and match them with key initiatives in the present.

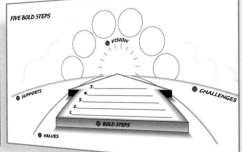

6. GRAPHIC GAMEPLAN

Assign action teams to develop plans for each of the key initiatives or bold steps.

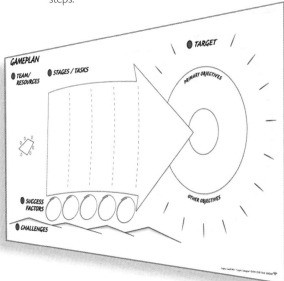

OBJECTIVE	GOALS	STRATEGIES	MEASURES
~~	• ~~~ • ~~~ • ~~~	1. ~~~ 2. ~~~	• ~~~ • ~~~ • ~~~
~~	• ~~~ • ~~~ • ~~~	1. ~~~ 2. ~~~	• ~~~ • ~~~ • ~~~
~~	• ~~~ • ~~~ • ~~~	1. ~~~ 2. ~~~	• ~~~ • ~~~ • ~~~

OGSM TEMPLATE

A format that many businesses use for planning at the functional level is an OGSM chart. It stands for objective, goals, strategies, and measures. The graphic above illustrates using a standard grid. You could also use a computer spreadsheet. This is often the format used for this kind of planning. The advantage of spreadsheets are their familiarity. They are easy to create on your computer. The downside is that it doesn't provide any visual anchors for remembering all of the information.

What about Regular Business Planning?

Strategic processes happen less frequently than annual business planning. Although many organizations simply roll up numbers from each division, some actually support functional groups to think through their plans visually using some of the same templates described earlier. As the next chapter will explain, there are some very productive ways you as a leader can ask for functional plans to be presented to you so that you can compare and prioritize their activity and look at your organization as a whole system. These types of environments are called decision rooms, project rooms, or rapid decision support centers.

At Otis Spunkmeyer, following a successful visualization of the overall company strategy, John Schiavo asked his functional groups to conduct planning workshops to determine what their objectives, goals, strategies, and measures (OGSMs) would be for the coming year, aligned with overall Otis Strategy that had been visualized in a large mural. He selected three templates to have each team complete—a history, a context map, and a Five Bold Steps template adapted to the OGSM model (see sidebar next page). Each functional group then brought these into one room, and they had a company-wide review of all the plans. There is a description and pictures of this process in the next chapter on decision rooms. The point to appreciate here is how John guided his functional directors in not only what kind of information they should consider but how he wanted them to report on it. In the process he created an environment supporting more engagement and insight than normal "roll-up-your-numbers" annual business planning.

Because all of The Grove charts are also available in PowerPoint format, each group was able to carry this work forward to the following year, thereby creating a real sense of continuity.

Planning for Reorganization

The Grove's work with templates grew out of an extensive organization-change process with National Semiconductor (NSC) in the early 1990s. The chief executive officer, Gil Amelio, had formulated an overall vision and strategy with his top team and empowered an internal change staff to begin implementation. This team created a visual Storymap that was very successful (see page 156). It was a large-scale graphic mural to depict its vision, and it included a bit about its history and some more about values and challenges. The change team subsequently led nearly two dozen internal planning processes, many of which were to create the framework for what at the time was called reengineering. This usually involved streamlining priorities and upgrading technical infrastructures. The leadership at NSC wanted these plans to integrate, so they encouraged a standard approach to the presentation. This resulted in a graphic template called the Journey Vision, which is illustrated on the following page. It was one of the first that begged for being preprinted so that it didn't have to be drawn time after time. This evolved into a standard framework that built on the near-universal experience of taking a journey.

Using Graphic Templates as Agendas and Reporting Formats

The NSC process usually involved putting up the template and using it as a visual agenda for the workshop. Each piece would be developed on flip charts and other paper, and then formalized as an element on the Journey Vision. The completed graphic was the overview of the plan that the team could share with others in the company, and provided a type of graphical user interface to the more detailed, conventionally depicted plans that underpinned them.

GRAPHIC OGSM TEMPLATE

Above is a way to visualize the OGSM chart borrowing a design from The Grove's Five Bold Steps Graphic Guide. The metaphor of an action arrow heading toward the sunrise of your primary objective provides a memorable visual image to anchor the same information that in a spreadsheet format might be harder to remember.

JOURNEY VISION

The template illustrated below is one of the first to emerge from a large turnaround project at National Semiconductor.

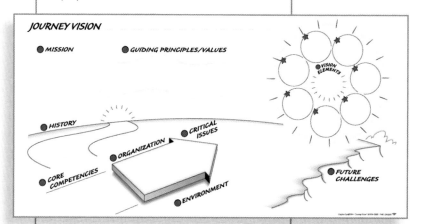

When training internal facilitators to work visually became a priority at NSC, The Grove designed an agenda for a Strategic Visioning workshop that used the Journey Vision Graphic Guides as a format.

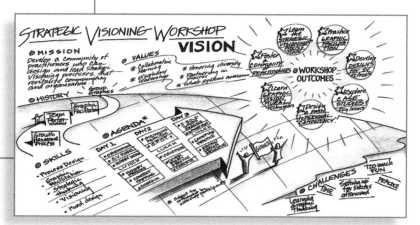

During the NSC change process, The Grove developed a training approach to strategic visioning, and used the same template to illustrate the workshop outcomes, agenda, mission, values, skills, and challenges. It was a way of having the medium be the message. It is reproduced here to show you what a completed graphic template might look like.

In this instance the arrow format in the original template was retained. In many of the NSC visions, some of which will be shared in Chapter 12, the arrow would be replaced by a graphic metaphor that the functional unit chose as representing the type of organization they would like to be. The leaders of each unit were very active in finding just the right compelling metaphor for this purpose, putting into practice the metaphor tool described in Chapter 7.

Templates of any sort are simply a starting point. As a leader, you need to take ownership not only for the content categories but also for the overall format. Language of any kind shapes perception, and visual language shapes our appreciation of the bigger picture.

Business Model Redesign

At the heart of your organization is the concept of how you actually survive. In a business it's how you make a profit. In a nonprofit it is how you will attract enough contributors and supporters. In government it is how to ensure that the laws and taxes provide sufficient revenue. Understanding what these are becomes important if you want everyone in the organization to see how his or her work relates to the success of the organization.

Alexander Osterwalder wrote his PhD thesis on this subject, and then he began a process of creating a template-based tool called the Business Model Canvas, which would help leaders clarify and change their business models. It is a customized grid using sticky notes to play with different business models. Alexander and four other colleagues wrote a book about it called *Business Model Generation*, and in the process they involved more than 400 colleagues in an online network to review and respond to the ideas. Patrick van der Pijl, a Dutch consultant with experience at PriceWaterhouseCoopers, was on the core team and attended a VizThink conference in Berlin, where The Grove was presenting a workshop on visual thinking and making the case that visualization is the language of systems thinking. The ideas took hold and the business model group invested heavily in visual meetings methods in their work.

Business Model Generation includes an entire chapter on visual facilitation, and the book itself is a testimony to how visuals can be used in publishing. The self-published version was so successful that John Wiley & Sons picked it up. It's sold more than 200,000 copies and is in 24 languages now, testimony to the way in which working visually is being received around the world. Patrick has gone on to created a consulting business called Business Models Inc. and is integrating The Grove's SV process and Graphic Guides with the canvas and is getting a huge response from clients.

BUSINESS MODEL GENERATION

This best seller by Alexander Osterwalder and a huge network of colleagues bases its approach on a graphic template called the Business Model Canvas (see next page for an example). The book advocates using visual facilitation as an integral part of the process of coming up with the models.

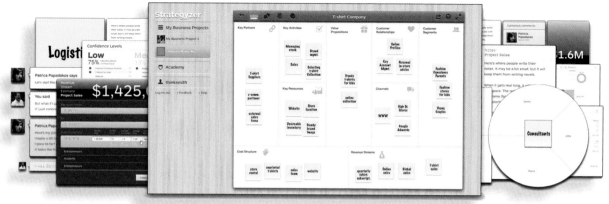

BUSINESS MODEL CANVAS

This image shows all the different screens linked to Strategizer.com's Web version of the Business Model Canvas, the graphic template at the heart of the best seller, *Business Model Generation*. It appeared initially as an iPad app, still available as the Business Model Toolbox. But the future, in creator Alexander Osterwalder's opinion, is Web applications in the cloud.

This assumption is born out by another new start-up, Mural.ly. It allows users to map out content on a large, virtual wall. You can collaborate real-time with others and then show off your ideas as a presentation. According to CEO and co-founder Mariano Suarez Battan, the startup's goal is to "become the GitHub of Visual Ideation." One of its initial examples was a Mural.ly implementation of the Business Model Canvas, but without the ability to run the numbers.

The success of the Business Model Canvas in helping organizations think through their business models is a leading indicator. Alexander insightfully understands that the visualization revolution is moving to the Web, and he has led his network to develop a Web application, Strategizer.com. By working out the functionality of sticky notes and linking them with software that does the math regarding size of markets, expected revenue, and the like, he and his team have created a tool that literally tells you whether you can make money. This can all be done on paper, of course, but the app facilitates the process. All of the category headings have drop-down instruction sets and predesigned menus to facilitate the process.

Moving to the Cloud

The next development for graphic templates will be tools such as these available through subscription services. Although all presentation software programs have many graphic templates you can choose to use, few if any of the traditional ones were designed to support interaction and group process. This is changing rapidly. The Business Model Canvas app supports collaboration. So does Prezi, the zooming presentation software designed in Hungary and growing at a million users a month. So does Mural.ly, a pinboard style mural-making platform competing with Prezi. All of these allow a user to e-mail others and invite them to join in the co-creation of a visual display of some sort. The new applications have large virtual displays, but access through screens still does not support group oriented panoramic thinking and doesn't yet have the impact that a room and paper templates can have. Perhaps we just have to wait for the walls to catch up.

10. Decision Rooms
Making Choices in a Big-Picture Context

So far we've been considering visual practices as graphic tools that work either in your imagination or on surfaces. But we humans live in spaces, and something magical happens when you begin to consider your entire meeting space as a visual environment. "Big-picture thinking" is a figure of speech drawn from the experience that people have of being able to imagine much more when the pictures are really big! Let's look at how you can get this effect to work for you as a leader in your organization.

Good Decisions Require Understanding the Larger Context

Much of leadership is focused on guiding people to do things that will produce superior results for the organization. This is a process of maintaining a big picture of the context and then making astute choices of what to do next. Many times these choices will be yours alone, depending on what kind of unit you are leading, but often in regard to very critical, organization-shaping choices, you will need to involve others and bring your team along. One of the truisms in planning is that you can make decisions quickly and spend time dealing with slow implementation or spend more time up front involving and aligning everyone so that you can implement more quickly. In addition to speeding up implementation, the quality of decisions tends to improve when you as a leader are open to listening to other opinions, even if you will ultimately make the final decision. Decision rooms help.

MANAGEMENT TEAM
DECISION ROOM

Most executive conference rooms are not optimized for visual display. A decision room is. Below is a model of one of The Grove's conference rooms, reconstructed in Second Life, a three-dimensional virtual environment that allows easy simulations. You can see the SV Model and four of the related Graphic Guides on the wall, supported by electronics that allow for remote participants to attend by Web conference. Graphic templates on the wall are mirrored in tabletop worksheets and online graphic templates.

VIRTUAL DECISION ROOMS

Two of the most common ways of working virtually are on a computer Web conference, either with or without telepresence, and using graphic tablets to do virtual visualization. All of the graphic templates and processes described so far work in these environments, with the limitation that they cannot be seen side by side at scale, and hence cannot encourage panoramic thinking.

In recent years many companies have begun supporting special environments that allow for rapid decision making. These usually have abundant space for visualization, excellent technical infrastructures, and facilitation staffs that are well versed in different kinds of innovation, planning, and problem-solving processes. If your organization has such an environment, this would be a good place to hold a special meeting as a way of finding out how the environment works.

Create a Memory Theater

Decisions rooms have a link to traditional theater. Prior to printed books, when information and knowledge was shared orally for the most part, theatrical presentation was a critical means for getting people to remember stories and cultural lessons. Churches used graphic imagery for this purpose as well. In plays, the Greeks and others would use various parts of the stage to represent different elements. An all-seeing narrator, for instance, might always occupy one part of the stage, with certain comedic elements happening in another. If you think about meetings you have attended in which people have been charting, have you ever noticed that people will gesture at a space where some chart was originally created, even though it has been moved? Humans remember large amounts of information by creating memory theaters in the brain. In fact, this technique is actually taught to persons who are training for memory competitions. A decision room is precisely this type of tool. It creates a shared memory theater and encourages people to look at things from multiple points of view.

On the next page is an early illustration of The Grove's Strategic Visioning Model, showing it placed in such a room. In this case the future orientation is on the right wall. The past is on the left, and the actions that need to be taken in the present are front and center. You need to imagine a U-shaped table arrangement facing the far wall.

Making Choices Is the Play

Choices are the focus of decision rooms. Decisions are the result of choosing one option over another. There are always implicit or explicit reasons or criteria. The essence of a visual decision room is creating ways to keep both the criteria and the options visible and be able to move the options around to determine priorities.

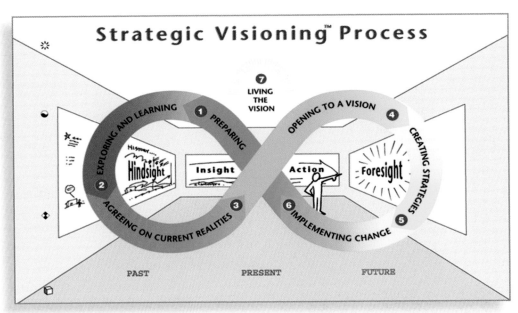

A good metaphor is the computer spreadsheet. Before it was invented, accountants and financial people had to manually calculate different scenarios. Changing factors meant redoing the entire display. With an electronic spreadsheet, an analyst can easily create different scenarios, engaging in "what-if" thinking, and see the impact of changes immediately. This type of exploration is what any designer does during the prototyping phase of design. Sticky notes combined with graphic templates and staged in a decision room environment create a huge spreadsheet capability for a whole group to participate in this kind of exploration during decision making.

A vice president (VP) of marketing in a large New York bank used this approach to cut $2 million in expenses from his budget. He didn't want to make the cuts unilaterally, so he had his entire team of direct reports—about 15 people—participate in a two-day meeting to figure this out. The centerpiece was a huge display that graphically displayed all the parts of the organization that required resources. It wasn't an organization chart exactly, but more a set of boxes arranged so that the units that worked together were near each other. Representatives of each unit

SV IN CONTEXT

An early version of the Strategic Visioning Model included an illustration of a decision room environment that used the walls to represent past (left), future (right), and present (middle). By using the walls consistently for different charts, leaders can create a "memory theater" that helps everyone link and remember the different elements of a planning and decision-making process.

AD HOC DECISION ROOM

This drawing illustrates a temporary decision room created in a hotel during the meeting of a tech firm determining where to allocate the next year's research budget. It focused on a graphic template called Sow-Grow-Harvest-Plow developed by Rob Eskridge, a consulting associate of The Grove. R&D leaders presented their suggestions on the template and then created a unified version for the entire R&D function. Adding a multiyear chart allowed the group to think in phases as well, and resolved some of the budget conflicts by allowing phased funding..

received an allotment of small sticky notes representing their budget and was asked to "spend" those dollars. This created a visual map of where people thought the resources should flow. Once the group interests were visualized, everyone could then move into a negotiation phase and argue for this or that approach, with the overall map as context. It was a very painful meeting, but the VP achieved his purpose and came out with an agreement that everyone understood and was willing to support. Without a decision room environment he would have had to dictate the cuts, or work them out with just a couple of his direct reports.

A Portfolio Decision Process

A common practice is to create a temporary decision room in a hotel. A high-tech firm supported an R&D portfolio planning process this way. (A portfolio is the name for a folder or folio, used as a metaphor for the sets of products and services an organization offers.) Determining what is in and out of a portfolio becomes an important job of leadership. In these deliberations decision rooms are essential. On this page is an illustration of an arrangement the leader of R&D for a large technology firm in the Portland area created to get his research and development leads to agree on budget for the following year. He was a very demanding boss and quite capable of deciding by himself, but he wanted everyone to go along and agree. So he, like the VP of marketing, decided to do this as a group. His process was the following:

1. **Defining Criteria for the Portfolio Categories:** The Sow-Grow-Harvest-Plow portfolio template becomes meaningful when everyone agrees on what the categories

mean. They should link to overall organization strategies. *Sow* meant "start something," but the group had to look to its larger organizational goals to know what things were important to start. The same went with *grow* and *harvest*. The *plow* category took discussion. In some cases it simply meant "stop this." In others, it meant redeploying or repurposing resources. All these criteria were defined in advance.

2. **Portfolio in Advance:** The leader asked each R&D manager to create a portfolio of current resource expense in his or her area before the meeting and come with a 4' by 4' version that could be shared.

3. **Presentations:** Each R&D manager presented his or her portfolio to the others, answered any questions of understanding, and posted the portfolio on the wall.

4. **Shared Portfolio:** Everyone them co-created an organizational portfolio that drew from all the individual ones.

This process was intended to take a full day. As it began, the R&D director and the graphic facilitator he'd involved realized they were going to have a problem agreeing on one portfolio for the following year. Can you imagine why?

Be Prepared to Improvise

Decision making isn't mechanical. It is a function of our understanding of timing as well as relationships to other factors. Projects often last more than several years, and in some cases, they cannot be evaluated in the first year because they haven't produced any results. As thoroughly as you may analyze and lay out all the information, it is people who have considered all the factors who decide. In the R&D case, a time-oriented way of thinking needed to be integrated with a prioritization-focused way of thinking that the portfolio template reinforces. The solution was creating another chart, on the spot, that showed several years with channels for each of the R&D units. When the group disagreed about the next year's investments, the leader could settle the issue by deciding how much of that item would get to start or stop based on the multiyear phasing.

THE PROBLEM OF AGREEING ON PLANNING LANGUAGE

Certain words having to do with planning have so many different definitions that people involved in organizational planning get confused. Here are some of the ones that need to be defined on graphic templates, and in general communications.

VISION: This generally means a picture of a preferred future. Sometimes the word aspiration is used instead of vision.

MISSION: Sometimes this means the underlying purpose of the organization that is unchanging, but sometimes it means the big goal. Military groups have specific missions, for instance.

OBJECTIVE: Sometimes this refers to the biggest, overall direction (as in the OGSM model), but other organizations use this word to mean the specific aspects of a goal.

GOALS: This word is sometimes the top-level word and sometimes is the detail supporting an objective.

DELIVERABLES: These are usually specific, tangible outcomes.

MEASURES: These are the objective means by which a group can see whether goals are met.

STRATEGIES: This word is used for the way in which an organization intends to meet its goals. But sometimes this word is used to indicate the big goal itself.

INITIATIVES: This means the specific projects supporting goals.

TOP MANAGEMENT
WANTS ALIGNMENT ON
KEY DECISIONS

At Otis in 2008, John Schiavo (standing) was CEO, Ahmade Hamade (left) was chief financial officer, and Jerry Reardon (right) was executive VP in charge of sales and marketing. They ran the company but wanted an alignment meeting to bring along all the functional leads.

Alignment Meetings

A great example of using a temporary decision room occurred at an alignment meeting that John Schiavo called in 2008 after all the Otis functional groups had completed their annual plans. He wanted to see everyone's priorities in one place and then determine the trade-offs. This was a departure from creating independent plans and having top management make the decisions.

To make the alignment meeting work, he asked all of the function managers to come with a big version of the OGSM chart illustrated on page 125 (some are visible in the photo to the left). These clearly showed the overall objectives of each function for the following years, as well as goals, strategies, and measures. They were staged on walls around a big conference room in a hotel near the company's headquarters. You may notice sticky notes on the maps in the photo. During each presentation, notes were created for two reasons. One, written in green, noted requests for help from other functional groups or the top management team. The other sticky notes, written in purple, indicated specific decisions that needed to be made to clear the way for action and implementation. It took most of the day to go through the dozen functional presentations. By the last hour there were dozens of specific decisions items identified. The last hour completely focused on making them.

1. Three "buckets" were created on a big chart in front of the group (see next page). They were Top Management, Functional Responsibility, and Strategy Teams.
2. Each decision sticky note was retrieved from the functional charts (after photos were taken), and the group was asked in which bucket each went. Did it need top management attention, functional attention, or a special team to decide?
3. In one hour all the decisions had been sorted, owners assigned, and teams formed. John orchestrated the dialogue. The top team would huddle now and then, and then share their decision. Functional owners stepped up. Everyone walked out agreeing on the full sweep of

FUNCTIONAL MANAGERS

Leads from all of the functions were in the Otis alignment meeting. Here are some shown sitting under the Otis Vision Map, a Storymap that included history, vision, and current overall strategy. It provided the big-picture context for the planning.

decisions. Being able to see everything at once made it possible—and efficient.

4. Following the meeting all charts were digitally copied and compiled in a book that looked just like the charts that everyone had seen during the meeting.

Leadership Is Required for Convergence

In both the R&D portfolio meeting and the Otis alignment meeting case, leadership played a critical role in getting the final decisions made. In both cases the active, engaged discussions and charting allowed the leadership to have a much clearer idea of the overall context, and as a result, more wholesale acceptance of the outcomes. This is why decision rooms are so helpful.

ALIGNMENT TEMPLATE

The chart below shows the simple structure used.

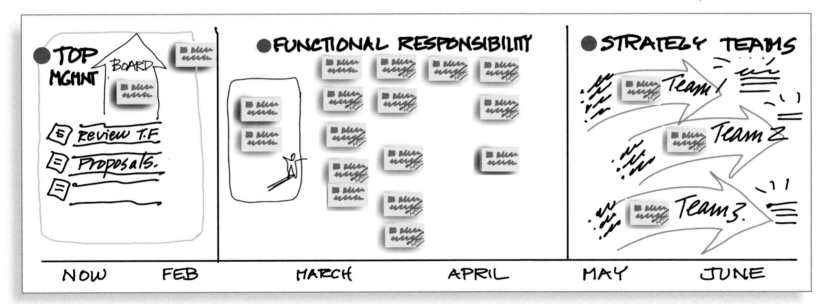

Project Rooms & Rapid Decision Support

A type of decision room is the project room that many design firms create for big projects. Ed Fredrichs, the former CEO of Gensler, says "We always had a project room. We need to see the entire project laid out visually." Moreover, he went on to say that, in some ways inspired by earlier work The Grove had done with the firm, they began to produce large graphic banners that summarized everything on the project. It would contain the following:

- Drivers
- Big ideas
- Goals and strategies
- Tactics
- Roadmaps

"It was basically a project room in our pocket," he said. "We would go over every aspect of it with our clients and design teams to make sure everyone was aligned on all the critical elements."

Another testimony to the effectiveness of these approaches is the fact that large consulting firms are marketing "rapid decision support" and "accelerated decision support" as a service. They have learned that visual meeting strategies are critical to full engagement and ownership of decisions.

Decision Rooms for Large Groups

When groups get larger than 50 to 60 people it helps to bring technology into play. CoVision is a leader in designing large, interactive meetings. It uses tablets and laptops—ideally one device per three participants. Its software platform is an easy to use, browser-based application, that allows meeting participants to respond to presenters, brainstorm, harvest small group work, sort

Decision making isn't mechanical. It is a function of our understanding of timing as well as relationships to other factors. Projects often last more than several years, and in some cases cannot be evaluated in the first year because they haven't produced any results. As thoroughly as you may analyze and lay out all the information, it is people who have to consider all the factors and decide.

and rank items, vote in polls, and record comments anytime during a meeting. Questions are introduced at different stages in the meeting, with simple response boxes available on the same input devices. All entries are then readable by everyone on the same devices, on large projection screens, or by a specially formed theme team, depending on the design of the meeting.

CoVision's approach supports the cycle of "describe and decide" that the R&D managers and Otis functional leaders experienced. The diagram on this page illustrates the process.

1. Information is presented and then a question posed.
2. Participants in their table groups discuss the question for 5 to 10 minutes and post replies. There are quickly hundreds of comments that everyone can read when they are finished.
3. A theme team of key managers reads the ideas as they come in and identifies and prepares themes that are shown to the whole group.
4. The presenter or panel responds to the themes and sometimes moves to a large-group dialogue about them. Comments made during this larger, town hall meeting are often visualized on large projection screens so that people can see that their input is being recorded.

This cycle of ideation and response can happen any number of times. Lenny Lind, founder of CoVision, says, "The devices are just enabling tools. The focus of everyone's energy is in the small group discussions. The software merely records the small groups' ideas so that they can be distilled and shared with the whole group."

Working with The Grove, CoVision combines large-scale visualization with the fast-feedback process by recording the themes discussion on large displays. The approach was used to involve 80 stakeholders in reviewing Nike's corporate responsibility plan. It was also used by the California Independent Systems Operators to involve more than 100 stakeholders in a

COUNCIL PROCESS SUPPORTS ACCELERATED FEEDBACK

CoVision is a leader in large interactive meeting design. This is a diagram it uses to illustrate the cycle of input and feedback that allows very large groups to integrate small-group and large-group dialogue and come to alignment. CoVision's software supports small table groups having dialogue around carefully designed questions, and then entering answers into portable computers or tablets. Once entered, all input can be viewed by everyone in the meeting, themes identified, and town hall meeting dialogue used to build understanding and alignment.

WORLD ECONOMIC FORUM RANKS PROBLEMS

In the open plenary of the 2005 World Economic Forum in Davos, Switzerland, 700 world leaders used CoVision's method, with America Speaks facilitating, to identify and rank the major problems facing the world at the time. The theme of the gathering was "Making Tough Choices." In less than three hours, everyone was engaged in meaningful deliberations and reached consensus of this list of problems:

1. Poverty
2. Equitable globalization
3. Climate change
4. Education
5. Middle East
6. Global governance

These priorities were then fed into the Forum topic tracks and reviewed at the end of the conference in a plenary session.

contentious review of plans for redesigning the energy grid in California. Both the structure of the grid systems and the plan to upgrade them were complex, with many elements. These two aspects were visualized in large murals that oriented meeting participants. CoVision was then used to solicit broad feedback to specific questions posed by the planning staff and to find agreement where possible.

Other Technologies for Polling

Decision support technology is a field unto itself with rapidly evolving choices. People are experimenting with using Twitter and its hashtag functions to allow participants in large meetings to respond to issues. Many companies offer polling tools that use special keypads or smartphones to allow even very large groups to vote quickly. Results are calculated immediately and formatted into nice graphs that illustrate the consensus (or not) in the room. These tools allow large groups to experience the same kind of rapid feedback that smaller groups get from using sticky dots and large displays. The primary limitation of all these tools is being confined to a small screen, where the current information disappears as soon as a new set is displayed. For complex decisions leaders often need to think about this fresh information for more than a few minutes.

Supporting Implementation

In general, decision room environments support your and your leadership's commitment to key decisions. Something to keep your eye on in regard to decision process is the growth of the "unconference" movement. It's driven by younger people who are used to free flowing, open space types of gatherings, where decisions emerge out of very dynamic, improvised interactions. These dynamic processes may well benefit even more from visual decision room staging to encourage consensus. Regardless of the decision process, the next step is aligning on how to implement it. That's where roadmaps and Storymaps come into play, as we'll see in the next two chapters.

11. Roadmaps & Visual Plans
Managing Milestones & Swim Lanes

Visualizing takes a turn when the focus is on implementation. Think about planning processes in which you have participated. In the beginning when all possible ideas are being discussed, the focus is broad and permissive. But put up a calendar when people have to start thinking about timing and what kinds of deadlines they will have to endure, and the energy definitely shifts.

Mapping Activity against Time

Roadmaps are the charts that map your plans against a timeline. The term is a metaphor, of course. Unless you are actually traveling somewhere, the "road" is some depiction of a series of activities over time. In most projects and programs, these flows of activity are visualized as channels or what some like to call "swim lanes"—another metaphor. It's one that arises due to the fact that project activities are always dynamic, like water, but within boundaries, like the lanes in a pool (or the banks of a river, as was suggested earlier in Chapter 5).

Project planning of this type can be very objective if you are building something physical. But if what you are implementing is an organizational change, a new marketing effort, or some innovative new program for talent development, then many elements are hard to describe precisely and, as a result, challenging to schedule. So how do you go about this?

The first thing to appreciate is that a certain amount of structure is your friend. Consider the Roadmap Graphic Guide on this page. It takes as a default that having three channels of activity, each with designated leaders, is a useful focus. It also assumes that there will be milestones or subgoals every so often. The process is a bit like planning a hike in the mountains. You plan specific rendezvous points and times but don't try to plan every detail in between.

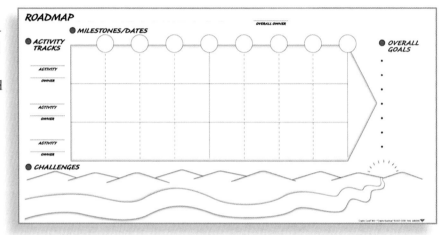

ROADMAP GRAPHIC GUIDE

Roadmaps are charts organized on a calendar with various channels of activity. The name itself is a metaphor, of course, but one that is so familiar that most people do not even think about it. Milestones historically were rocks that used to mark the miles; the term has also become widely used for the different objectives that you have on your way to your overall goals. This image is The Grove's Graphic Guide from its Strategic Visioning templates, available at www.grove.com.

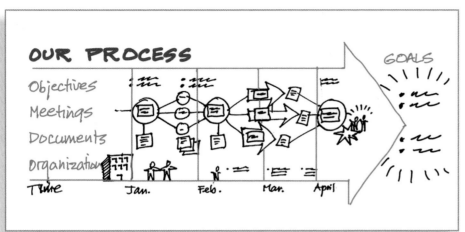

ACCORDION DESIGN

This style of mapping a planning process grew out of work of Interaction Associates (IA) in the late 1970s, when it was collaborating with The Grove on some large projects. It's now a standard design for process maps called the accordion model.

Planning processes invariably occur over a series of meetings. The first meeting will develop agreements that will change the second one, and so forth. A visual that helps depict this dynamic is what Michael Doyle at Interaction Associates named the accordion model(shown to the left). It illustrates the big meetings and smaller meetings, and can flex like an accordion in regard to time. This is the pattern reflected in the process map suggested in Chapter 6 as a personal exercise. Visualizing your roadmap not only helps you think through its details, even if timing changes, but also provides a useful way to communicate these changes by sending out new versions to everyone as shifts occur!

How Do You Co-Construct a Roadmap?

It may seem simpler at first to just tell people what to do on a large project. But with experience you will soon realize that keeping everyone aligned during a dynamic process is a real problem if people don't share the same big picture of what is important. Thus, it is well worth it to agree on phases and desired results in advance. Let's look at two ways to go about this, one that involves using the graphic itself as an excuse to get alignment and a second where specific meetings are held to co-construct a roadmap. Let's consider the first approach.

Converting an Army Base to a National Park

In 1988 the Presidio of San Francisco, the base of the United States' Sixth Army, was included on the base-closure list that passed Congress. A clause in the law that created the Golden Gate National Recreation Area (GGNRA), the large national park mentioned earlier in connection with the Headlands Center for the Arts, said that if the Presidio was ever decommissioned, it would become part of the GGNRA. Suddenly leadership at GGNRA was thrust into one of the biggest planning projects in its history. Because GGNRA had been a nontraditional form of an urban/wilderness park in the National Park System (NPS), the leadership it attracted was not from the mainstream mega-parks, but rather from some of the new experiments in urban parks. Brian O'Neill, the superintendent, came from the Heritage Conservation and Recreation Service. He had experience as an innovator and supported a partnership approach to development. He was also familiar with visual practice as a result of the Headlands Center for the Arts, which he actively supported. He recommended that Roger Brown, the NPS planner leading the transition planning team, use The Grove's visual approach.

The NPS has a very developed planning process, and getting citizen input is an essential first step. It was planning six large visioning meetings around the region as a kickoff in 1990. You need to appreciate that public meetings like this are tough in a community like San Francisco with very avid stakeholders. The Presidio was a case study. Its premier location at the northern tip of the city attracted dog walkers, wind surfers, bicyclers, Army historians, beach walkers, wealthy neighbors, the City of San Francisco, and the NPS itself, to name just a few. What would happen without the military police? Could NPS afford it (the budget would be three times that of Yellowstone National Park, the NPS's largest)? How could 250 historic buildings be rehabilitated?

To understand what was being asked of The Grove, we had to understand this project in the context of the total planning effort. They explained the process. It was aimed at updating the General Management Plan of GGNRA. "But what happens when a person comes to one of these meetings and wants answers about a specific building?" we asked. "That can't be answered until after the amendment is accepted," they said. To succeed with the input meeting, the NPS needed to explain the whole process, not just the planning part. Out of this insight grew the large roadmap illustrated on the next page.

PRESIDIO NATIONAL PARK

The Presidio vision workshops would be difficult in a community with very avid stakeholders. Its premier location at the northern tip of the city attracted the widest possible range of stakeholders, and many of them, like the city of San Francisco itself, had a great deal of influence. (This is a real roadmap, by the way).

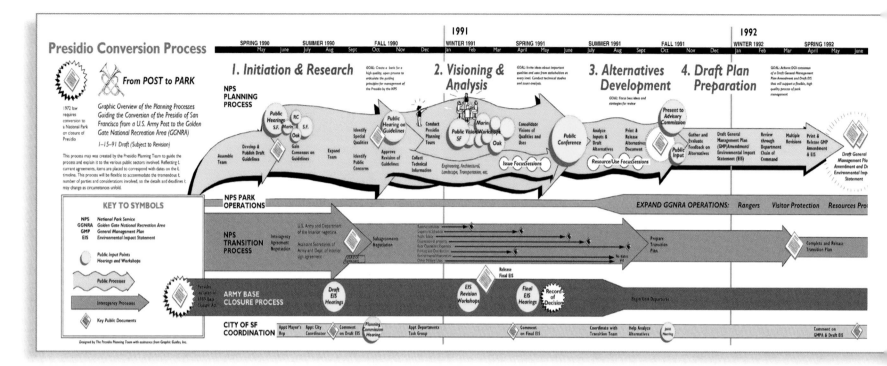

From POST to PARK

1972 law requires conversion to a National Park on closure of Presidio

Graphic Overview of the Planning Processes Guiding the Conversion of the Presidio of San Francisco from a U.S. Army Post to the Golden Gate National Recreation Area (GGNRA)

1–15–91 Draft (Subject to Revision)

This process map was created by the Presidio Planning Team to guide the process and explain it to the various public sectors involved. Reflecting the current agreements, items are placed to correspond with dates on the timeline. This process will be flexible to accommodate the tremendous number of parties and considerations involved, so the details and deadlines may change as circumstances unfold.

KEY TO SYMBOLS

NPS	National Park Service
GGNRA	Golden Gate National Recreation Area
GMP	General Management Plan
EIS	Environmental Impact Statement

Public Input Points
Hearings and Workshops

Public Processes

Interagency Processes

Key Public Documents

Designed by The Presidio Planning Team with assistance from Graphic Guides, Inc.

SPRING 1990 May June · **SUMMER 1990** July Aug Sept · **FALL 1990** Oct Nov Dec · **1991 WINTER 1991** Jan Feb Mar · **SPRING 1991** April May June · **SUMMER 1991** July Aug Sept · **FALL 1991** Oct Nov Dec · **1992 WINTER 1992** Jan Feb Mar · **SPRING 1992** April May June

1. Initiation & Research

2. Visioning & Analysis

3. Alternatives Development

4. Draft Plan Preparation

NPS PLANNING PROCESS

NPS PARK OPERATIONS — EXPAND GGNRA OPERATIONS: Rangers Visitor Protection Resources Pro...

NPS TRANSITION PROCESS

ARMY BASE CLOSURE PROCESS

CITY OF SF COORDINATION

THE PRESIDIO CONVERSION PROCESS MAP

This diagram illustrates five parallel planning processes related to the conversion of the Presidio Army Base into a national park. The yellow circles are all of the meetings in which public input was possible. Blue is the National Park Service (NPS) planning process. Green is the Presidio park operations process. Purple is combined NPS and Army. Brown is the Army base closure process. The bottom line is the City of San Francisco.

A Single Document Alignment Process

In addition to agreeing that the roadmap should conceptually illustrate the actual implementation, so that questions about building assignments could be answered, everyone felt it should also reflect the other four planning processes taking place at the same time! A draft of this roadmap was circulated to all five planning teams for confirmation. It was the first time any of them had seen the whole picture in one place. Eventually everyone agreed on the content, with particular emphasis on the public meetings, shown in yellow on the map.

This version of the roadmap was printed out on a 4-foot by 24-foot mural and presented at each of the public visioning workshops. An NPS leader was, in about 10 minutes, able to review the

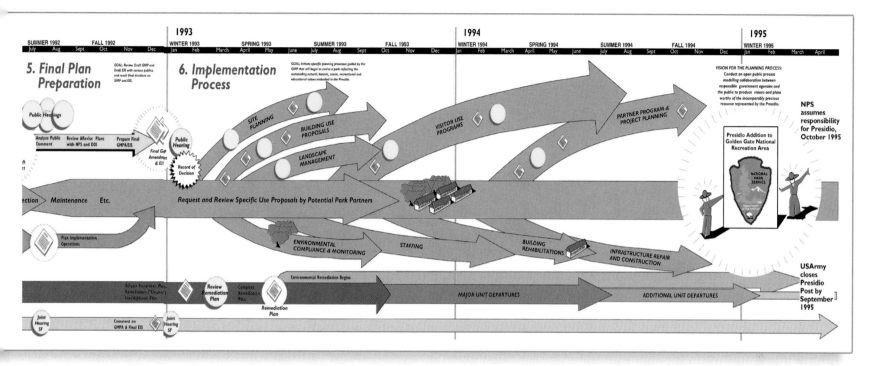

The timeline diagram contains the following labels and text:

SUMMER 1992 | FALL 1992 | **1993** WINTER 1993 | SPRING 1993 | SUMMER 1993 | FALL 1993 | **1994** WINTER 1994 | SPRING 1994 | SUMMER 1994 | FALL 1994 | **1995** WINTER 1995

July Aug Sept Oct Nov Dec | Jan Feb March April May June July Aug Sept Oct Nov Dec | Jan Feb March April May June July Aug Sept Oct Nov Dec | Jan Feb March April

5. Final Plan Preparation

GOAL: Review Draft GMP and Draft EIS with various publics, and reach final decisions on GMP and EIS.

6. Implementation Process

GOAL: Initiate specific planning processes guided by the GMP that will begin to evolve a park reflecting the outstanding natural, historic, scenic, recreational and educational values embodied in the Presidio.

VISION FOR THE PLANNING PROCESS: Conduct an open public process modelling collaboration between responsible government agencies and the public to produce visions and plans worthy of the incomparably precious resource represented by the Presidio.

Public Hearings

Analyze Public Comment | Review & Revise Plans with NPS and DOI | Prepare Final GMPA/EIS

Final GIP Amendment & EIS!

Public Hearing

Record of Decision

SITE PLANNING

BUILDING USE PROPOSALS

LANDSCAPE MANAGEMENT

VISITOR USE PROGRAMS

PARTNER PROGRAM & PROJECT PLANNING

Presidio Addition to Golden Gate National Recreation Area

NATIONAL PARK SERVICE

NPS assumes responsibility for Presidio, October 1995

...ection Maintenance Etc.

Request and Review Specific Use Proposals by Potential Park Partners

Plan Implementation Operations

ENVIRONMENTAL COMPLIANCE & MONITORING | STAFFING | BUILDING REHABILITATIONS | INFRASTRUCTURE REPAIR AND CONSTRUCTION

Release Hazardous Waste Remediation ("Cleanup") Investigation Plan | Review Remediation Plan | Complete Remediation Plan

Remediation Plan

Environmental Remediation Begins

MAJOR UNIT DEPARTURES | ADDITIONAL UNIT DEPARTURES

USArmy closes Presidio Post by September 1995

Joint Hearing SF | Comment on GMPA & Final EIS | Joint Hearing SF

---

entire process and field questions. It worked like a charm. Everyone saw that the process was organized, knew where the vision workshops fit, and were able to see where they could participate if their interests were further along in the process. It didn't matter that the outlying steps were conceptual.

You might note that the data here are presented in bands, or what some call swim lanes, which are designed to graphically reflect the nature of each process. NPS planning would be more open and flexible, hence the blue arrows are wavy. The implementation process, in green, would be diverse and branching and less detailed in the farther-out years. The Army base closure process was very regulated and formal and is illustrated that way, as is the base closure process. Each band was wider and narrower depending on the amount of effort required at each stage.

CODA

The Presidio was ultimately organized as a separate trust reporting directly to the Department of the Interior. In exchange for financial independence from the NPS budget process, Congress required it to be self-sufficient financially by 2013. This outcome underlines the fact that conceptual roadmaps, such as this one, largely are helpful for alignment at the beginning of projects, and necessarily need updating as things continue. The shift to the trust happened toward the end of this particular roadmap.

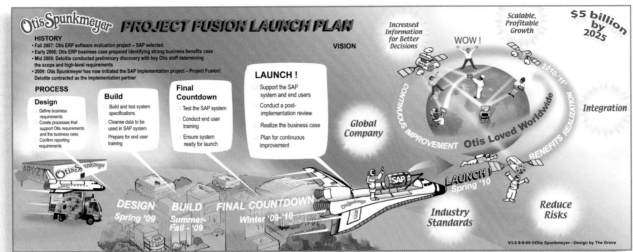

PROJECT FUSION LAUNCH PLAN

The project team at Otis Spunkmeyer responsible for a large technology implementation project needed to communicate benefits (illustrated on the right side of the graphic above) and the phases and key milestones for the project (in the talk balloons). The graphics are derived from an earlier illustration of the company vision (see photo on page 135), and shows the Otis cookie truck launching a spacecraft that will empower global communication. Linking metaphors and imagery across several large-scale visuals begins to create a visual language in the company that can be used very effectively by leaders to sustain attention on large projects.

Technical Roadmaps

Following its extensive use of visual methods during its big planning processes in 2006–2007, an Otis Spunkmeyer team in the information technology function that was leading a large enterprise data-system implementation decided to use a visual roadmap to help align the project team and communicate to all employees the process and expected benefits. The end result is shown above. The original content grew out of a one-day workshop with all of the subject matter experts and project team leads who had been working on the specifications for weeks. The roadmap design meeting allowed them all to lift their collective heads up from the detail and stand in the shoes of the large employee base that needed to know the big-picture story. The graphic invited the project team to craft the general story, with a clear focus on the benefits for everyone involved.

Once the content was developed, the process moved to creating and responding to versions that the project team was able to refine in many internal conversations and negotiations. Everyone realized that publishing this map would, in effect, commit everyone to that schedule. The leaders of the project were delighted to have this happen, as you might guess.

Using version numbers links this type of process metaphorically to the process of upgrading software. This experience is so widespread in business now that most people immediately understand and know that version 1.0 visualizations will improve with feedback.

Roadmap Murals Help Cascade Key Messages

Leaders at Sutter Health wanted to bring clarity and excitement to its transformational vision and strategies for implementing them. A Storymap process yielded this roadmap (see next chapter for more on Storymaps). Sutter Health is a 45,000-employee nonprofit organization. Cascading its message to this many people required something that would stand out from other communications. The image shown here provided that focus. Subelements were used to support strategy presentations at a big Destination 2012 management symposium when the map was introduced. The event organizers even constructed a large wooden "bridge to the future" as the entrance to the symposium, bringing this metaphor to life much like John Schiavo had at Otis with his plane flight (see Chapter 7).

Roadmaps Allow Feedback on Progress

On the last page of this chapter is a large image of the roadmap used to organize the annual strategy development processes for RE-AMP, a large consortium of nonprofits and foundations in the upper Midwest aimed at clearing up global warming pollutants in the energy industry. The implementation team for this project was featured in *Visual Teams* as an example of a high-performing team. It was also very savvy about the use of visualization to support alignment and communication. This roadmap was created in Adobe Illustrator and updated at the end of the year to reflect the actual work completed. Notice how circles are used for meetings, computers for Web conferences, and colored bands for the different working groups.

SUTTER HEALTH ROADMAP & VISION

This detailed roadmap was printed large and used as a key component in a 2,000-person management symposium called "Destination 2012." It figured in the CEO's opening presentation, as well as in strategy information booths. It combines a clear visionary element on the right with a roadmap and bridge metaphor on the left.

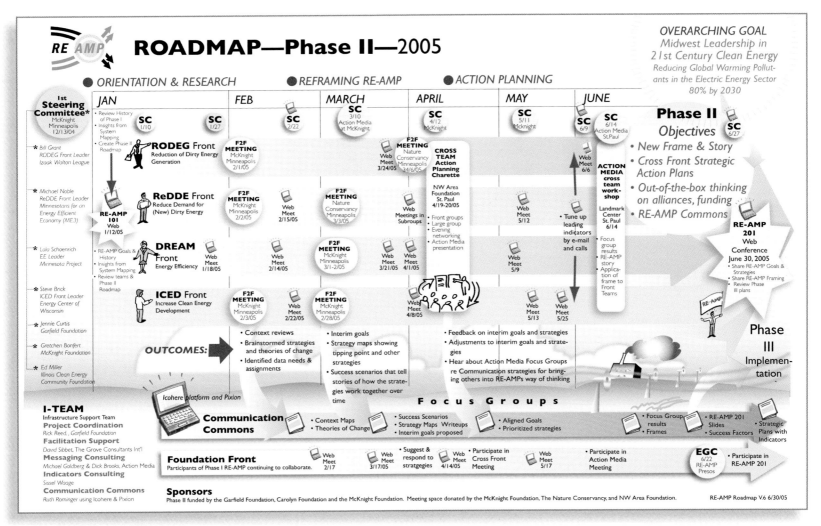

RE-AMP ROADMAP

This is the actual report of 2005 work accomplished.

Circles are meetings. Computers are Web conferences. Colored bands are work teams. Documents flow to the commons.

The two long, vertical bars in the middle are the two cross-group meetings used to integrate everyone's work.

12. Graphic Storymaps
Connecting Plans with Culture

Graphic Storymaps comprise the sixth essential tool set in this section on essential tools. Storymaps is a name The Grove Consultants International uses for large murals that are designed to support leaders telling critical stories about new directions. Storymaps use words and imagery to help everyone remember not only plans but also the culture and values that make their implementation meaningful. Chapter 1 relates a classic example by describing the Quality Journey of HealthEast. The previous chapter on roadmaps included more examples. This one explains how you can use this tool for your own leadership communications.

On this page is a Storymap created for a nonprofit called Save the Redwoods League, an organization credited with inspiring today's widespread parks systems. It was created as part of an in-depth alignment process between the board and advisory committees. The redwoods were, for this organization, not only an icon of what they were saving but a metaphor for how they would like the organization to operate. Mapping guiding principles and programs to this image made complete sense to the organization. It's a great example of using a powerful, valued metaphor.

Integrating Words & Graphics in Large Murals

The practice of using large, graphic murals to integrate great amounts of information has a long tradition, if you consider the hieroglyphics in Egyptian tombs or the stained glass windows in cathedrals as examples. But the contemporary, tight integration of words and graphics in large murals is a relatively recent development. They evolved from an approach used by a Swedish firm Celeme in the 1980s. In one case it worked with Volvo to create a poster of a new car that would help train salesmen. It illustrated the new car and all its parts in an explosion drawing, like the instructions in a model kit. Unlike model instructions, no parts were labeled on these maps. The labels were all around the edges! Teams of salespeople then worked to match the labels with the parts and thereby learn the new car! This process did not require trainers delivering informa-

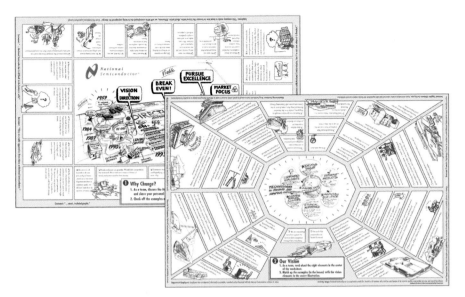

NATIONAL SEMICONDUCTOR LEARNING STORYMAPS

During National Semiconductor's turnaround in the early 1990s, thousands of people needed to understand the new vision and strategies depicted in a large Storymap mural (illustrated on page 160 at the end of this chapter). Segments of the vision were embedded in a second level of information that learning teams needed to associate with the central images. This discovery-learning approach is one of the ways large infographic murals are used.

tion but used facilitators who could work with large numbers at once. In educational circles this approach is called discovery-based learning. *Learning Maps* were popularized in the United States and the term registered by Root Learning in the 1990s. Root used the posters to teach companies about their customers, marketplace drivers, and most interestingly (and proprietarily) how the business made money. These business model maps were sometimes associated with decks of cards and other learning materials to create a real, discovery-based, team-learning environment. (The examples to the left were created for this purpose.)

The Grove realized early on that this same kind of visualization could support leadership-based storytelling following strategy formation processes. By using visual meetings methods to develop the imagery in a collaborative manner, the Storymap design process itself became a way to reach engagement, alignment, and commitment to the new ideas. Let's look at a couple of examples. Like graphic templates, these large visuals emphasize either spatial/structural relations between vision and plan elements, such as the maps on this page and the Yosemite vision on page 153, or they emphasize time, such as the Visa history on the following page. Let's begin to understand the Storymap tool by studying the Visa history.

New Employee Orientation at Visa

In the early 1980s Visa needed to share its unusual history with new employees. It had grown from a Diners Card amenity in the 1950s into a billion-dollar international company. No one had captured the history of its growth and success, except in profit charts and reams of financial reports that sat on several shelves in the headquarters' archives. There was a story to be told for those who had participated in Visa's creation, as well as for those who would share in its future.

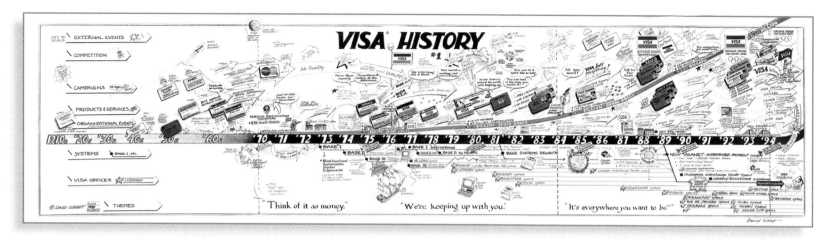

The Storymap process began with the company creating a list generated by top management of who in the corporation was familiar enough with the past to bring the group into the present. This group included recent retirees, top management, and some new executives. They gathered for an initial meeting to tell the story. A long roll of white paper across one entire wall in a conference room captured their storytelling. It included information about the growth of their computer infrastructure, international offices, products, marketing campaigns, competition and external events. Ranny Riley, a consultant associated with The Grove, interviewed additional senior managers who were unable to attend the initial meeting and briefed The Grove on what should be included. A first-draft graphic was created and circulated for critique and additions from the core group of leaders. A half-dozen versions later the image you see on this page emerged.

Visa printed the history as a 4-foot by 24-foot mural and used it as a backdrop for new employee orientation. Key leaders could come into those meetings with very little preparation and bring the very engaging and human stories to life. All the facts they needed were on the mural. Participants received smaller versions to help them remember the session. In addition, the initial map was framed and given as a holiday gift to all of Visa's key member banks and partners. The Visa storytelling sessions were so successful that Visa has updated this history two times since its initial creation. On the next page is the most recent version.

VISA HISTORY

Visa successfully competed with the big bank's MasterCard offering back in the 1970s through a network of smaller banks. Visa's founding leader, Dee Hock, organized the effort around some guiding principles that have allowed the organization to develop organically in what Hock now calls a chaordic pattern. In 1994 leaders created this chart to orient new employees, allowing anyone in Visa to tell this story. All of the main facts are on the chart, so the role of the leader was to bring it to life and convey the emotion and life of the organization. The mural organizes the information on eight tracks of activity, each of which has a distinctive graphic treatment. The evolution of the large transaction systems and overseas offices illustrated below the timeline supported the product development, shown as actual portraits of the cards. Organizational efforts are arrows. Marketing campaigns are in talk balloons. External factors show along the top.

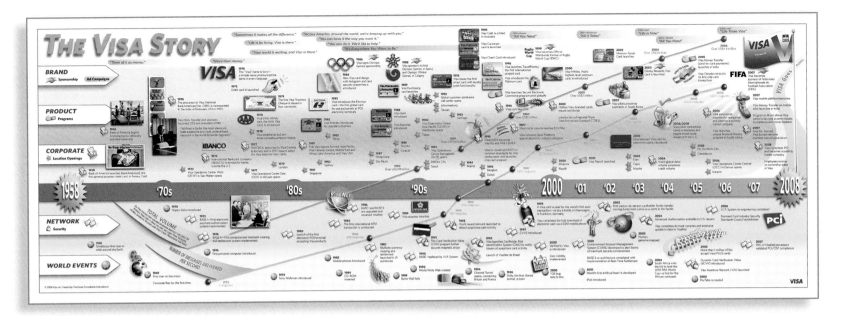

VISA HISTORY EXTENDED

In 2008 Visa decided to refresh its Storymap with this extended version. It was created in Adobe Illustrator and provides a nice comparison between the original handdrawn version on the previous page and the more formal image above. Printed out large and in smaller poster form, both graphics served the same purpose in a different style. In crafting these kinds of visuals, considering the overall look and feel is as important as aligning on the content and the messages. They need to resonate with the people using them.

Connecting with Culture Is Critical

Facts about an organization by themselves don't mean much to people. For instance, the content of the Save the Redwoods League and Visa examples shown here might not mean much to you if you have no relationship to or interest in these organizations. Facts take on life through the interpretations that people give them through storytelling. Leaders work with these stories, elevating the ones that serve current strategies and ignoring others.

If you had to script every leader who conveys an organizational story in a new employee meeting or a critical off-site or Web conference, you would need a very large staff to keep it all aligned. However, getting leadership to agree on the overarching story in a graphic form and then linking key symbols and icons from the culture creates a very flexible backdrop for storytelling that does keep everyone aligned. Over the years this approach has worked very successfully for a wide variety of organizations.

Envisioning Priorities at Yosemite National Park

Don Neubacher is a great example of a visual leader who understands the power of getting everyone enrolled in a story about priorities. He is the superintendent of Yosemite National Park, one of the jewels in the National Park System in the United States. He came there from Point Reyes National Seashore, and before that he was a planner at the Presidio. There he was exposed to visual practice working with Brian O'Neill.

Yosemite, like many of the grand national parks, is run by an organizational culture very influenced by the military, in that many of its rangers and employees have prior histories in the military. Hierarchy and discipline are valued. But Don is a younger, more collaborative leader. He wanted his branch chiefs to understand and agree on priorities, not just follow orders. To do this he needed a process that would engage them appropriately. He chose to generate a strategic vision Storymap.

It began with his direct reports, a group of about eight managers responsible for the major functions of the park. They met for two days to look at the history of Yosemite, its current environment and pressing issues, and potential visions for the park. The park has, as do all national parks, a master plan and guiding mission. This really wasn't up for debate. The immediate issue was determining priorities for the next five years in a time of shrinking resources and increasing public demand on the system. Yosemite is reaching 4 million visitors a year at this point, and the park, as big as it is, it is reaching its carrying capacity.

YOSEMITE LEADERSHIP

Don Neubacher, superintendent of Yosemite National Park, gathered his leadership in a two-day workshop to co-create a vision and determine priorities for the next five years at the park. They were aligned on the overall mission and their long-term, general management plan, but nearer-term priorities posed a challenge. Demand for park access was increasing and resources were shrinking. Because the way forward was not obvious, Don needed every bit of organizational intelligence focused on identifying and aligning on priorities. Here the leadership team is exploring potential graphic metaphors for organizing a large vision Storymap they intended to use to engage the branch chiefs in subsequent meetings (see the map on page 156).

DON ORIENTS BRANCH CHIEFS

Don Neubacher engaged three dozen of his branch chiefs in critiquing and making suggestions to the Yosemite vision and five-year plan. You can see it in this picture. Don is orienting everyone to the special meeting focused on the vision and preparing the branch chiefs to help with more detailed action planning. The map was covered with sticky notes by the end of the meeting and went through six versions in the process of getting everyone aligned.

Getting All Yosemite Leadership Involved & Aligned

Two subsequent meetings with branch chiefs and then with all managers evolved the vision shown on the following page. Both the words and the images were the source of much debate and discussion. Each of the functional areas wanted critical icons that would serve as talking points. The image itself is not a photograph, but a composite showing the various ecosystems within the park, with a homage to the valley floor, which is the park's iconic signature. As an example of the scrutiny that went into the map, the chiefs wanted to make sure that the Grizzly Giant sequoia tree on the right side of the vision was as tall as the tower granite face of El Capitan on the left, balancing their interest in the "charismatic granite," as they called it, and the mega fauna represented by the giant sequoias. They also made sure that a person was showed doing a controlled burn, another innovation by the park.

Action Planning & Visual Plans

To anchor this big picture in specific objectives, the functional leaders all signed up to develop explicit action plans for each of the emphasis areas. They followed a report template that the leaders co-developed. Led by the internal communications director, Tom Medema, the park subsequently created a printed and digital visual plan with many additional images and photos. The quality of this effort attracted considerable attention within the park service and helped continue Yosemite National Park's thought leadership in their field.

The entire journey took about six months and is still alive. Members of the leadership team have moved on to other parks. New faces have joined. The stories are being told and retold. But now the park has a map that combines values, issues, visions, and immediate priorities. It literally illustrates how it supports its park-specific mission: The Stewardship of Yosemite Inspires the World.

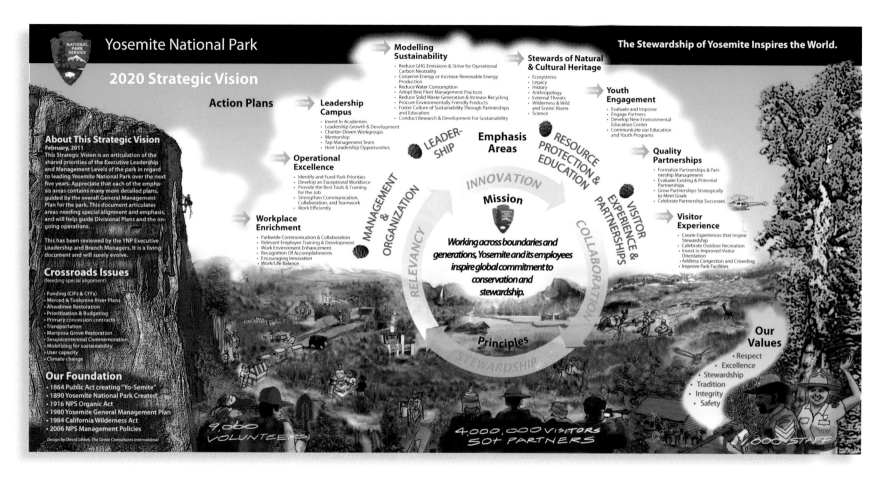

Yosemite National Park

2020 Strategic Vision

The Stewardship of Yosemite Inspires the World.

Action Plans

Modelling Sustainability
- Reduce GHG Emissions & Strive for Operational Carbon Neutrality
- Conserve Energy or Increase Renewable Energy Production
- Reduce Water Consumption
- Adopt Best Fleet Management Practices
- Reduce Solid Waste Generation & Increase Recycling
- Procure Environmentally Friendly Products
- Foster Culture of Sustainability Through Partnerships and Education
- Conduct Research & Development For Sustainability

Stewards of Natural & Cultural Heritage
- Ecosystems
- Legacy
- History
- Anthropology
- External Threats
- Wilderness & Wild and Scenic Rivers
- Science

Youth Engagement
- Evaluate and Improve
- Engage Partners
- Develop New Environmental Education Center
- Communicate our Education and Youth Programs

Leadership Campus
- Invest In Academies
- Leadership Growth & Development
- Charter-Driven Workgroups
- Mentorship
- Tap Management Team
- Host Leadership Opportunities

Quality Partnerships
- Formalize Partnerships & Partnership Management
- Evaluate Existing & Potential Partnerships
- Grow Partnerships Strategically to Meet Goals
- Celebrate Partnership Successes

Operational Excellence
- Identify and Fund Park Priorities
- Develop an Exceptional Workforce
- Provide the Best Tools & Training for the Job
- Strengthen Communication, Collaboration, and Teamwork
- Work Efficiently

Visitor Experience
- Create Experiences that Inspire Stewardship
- Celebrate Outdoor Recreation
- Invest in Improved Visitor Orientation
- Address Congestion and Crowding
- Improve Park Facilities

Workplace Enrichment
- Parkwide Communication & Collaboration
- Relevant Employee Training & Development
- Work Environment Enhancement
- Recognition Of Accomplishments
- Encouraging Innovation
- Work/Life Balance

About This Strategic Vision
February, 2011
This Strategic Vision is an articulation of the shared priorities of the Executive Leadership and Management Levels of the park in regard to leading Yosemite National Park over the next five years. Appreciate that each of the emphasis areas contains many more detailed plans, guided by the overall General Management Plan for the park. This document articulates areas needing special alignment and emphasis, and will help guide Divisional Plans and the ongoing operations.

This has been reviewed by the YNP Executive Leadership and Branch Managers. It is a living document and will surely evolve.

Crossroads Issues
(Needing special alignment)
- Funding (CIFs & CFFs)
- Merced & Tuolumne River Plans
- Ahwahnee Restoration
- Prioritization & Budgeting
- Primary concession contracts
- Transportation
- Mariposa Grove Restoration
- Sesquicentennial Commemoration
- Mobilizing for sustainability
- User capacity
- Climate change

Our Foundation
- 1864 Public Act creating "Yo-Semite"
- 1890 Yosemite National Park Created
- 1916 NPS Organic Act
- 1980 Yosemite General Management Plan
- 1984 California Wilderness Act
- 2006 NPS Management Policies

Design by David Sibbet, The Grove Consultants International

LEADERSHIP

Emphasis Areas

RESOURCE PROTECTION & EDUCATION

INNOVATION

Mission

MANAGEMENT & ORGANIZATION

RELEVANCY

Working across boundaries and generations, Yosemite and its employees inspire global commitment to conservation and stewardship.

COLLABORATION

VISITOR EXPERIENCE & PARTNERSHIPS

Principles

STEWARDSHIP

Our Values
- Respect
- Excellence
- Stewardship
- Tradition
- Integrity
- Safety

9,000 VOLUNTEERS

4,000,000 VISITORS 50+ PARTNERS

1,000 STAFF

The success of this process resulted in similar techniques being used for two big river planning efforts in the park for the Tuolumne and the Merced rivers. Citizen involvement is critical for these projects, so recording in the public meetings serves as a visual demonstration that the park personnel are listening. The various alternatives are then shared and critiqued visually as well. For natural resource planning, visual-meeting methods are tried-and-true tools.

YOSEMITE VISION

This is the final version, as approved by three dozen branch managers and leadership at Yosemite National Park and featured in a colorful internal plan that included all the emphasis area action plans.

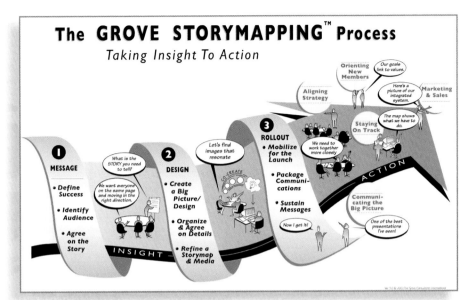

STORYMAPPING PROCESS MAP

This is a Storymap used to illustrate The Grove Storymapping Process. The blue arrow represents ongoing work in an organization. The spiral is the process of creating a Storymap graphic. It begins with message development, then design, and finally support of a rollout communication process. The benefits are listed on the far right. The substages are shown as bullet points in the spiral. The talk balloons show what people along the way might be saying.

Implementing a Storymap Process

If you are interested in having your organization use Storymap methods, here is how you would go about it:

1. **Message Development:** This is where you and your leadership team determine what it is that you need to communicate. You would, during this process, identify who your audience is and who you would want to involve in the co-creation process. Your leadership team or a selected group would then be involved in developing and agreeing on the overall story. It may be that you have completed a planning process and have a new vision and strategy to communicate. You might want to communicate about your history, customer interests, marketplace, or your business model, apart from a special planning process.

2. **Conceptual and Final Designs:** Once the message is clear, then finding the right graphic metaphor and overall design is the next step. This is a wonderful place to involve key stakeholders. Playing with the graphic imagery invites everyone to start thinking about the organization as a whole system and the characteristics in the culture that leadership would like to support. This is what HealthEast did in its Quality Journey Process (pages 21 to 23) and Yosemite National Park in its strategic vision map development (page 151 to 153).

This step usually requires involving information designers who know how to work in a collaborative way. They work with an internal design team that reviews different examples and decides how best to represent the organization. At National Semiconductor, the metaphor of *Star Trek* rang true and was understood by its employees (see page 156). At Save the Redwoods League it was a redwood grove. HealthEast chose a soulful image of a nurse. Designers will generally provide you with some conceptual sketches and work with your design team to find the right overall look and feel. You would also decide whether you want

The three graphics shown here are versions of an illustration of a Storymap from a public policy center in a major corporation. The challenge was showing the flows of information.

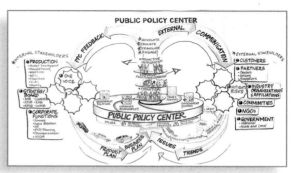

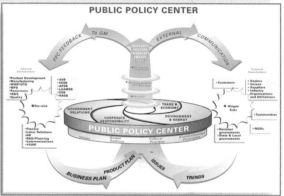

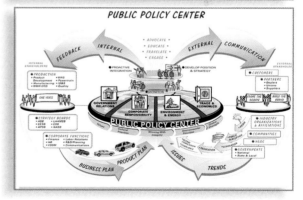

it polished and computer generated or drawn by hand. (The latter invites more interaction when you review things. The former may have more authority.)

After the concept is approved, a detailed workup of all the content is included in a first version of the map. Now the process proceeds, shaped by how important it is to involve other people. If alignment is a real concern, more reviews are better. In general, once the design, or what is sometimes called the architecture, is complete, then making changes in the details, or the interior decorating part, can easily go through many rounds. The more people who have a hand in this, the more ownership will be experienced.

When the content and design stabilize, a final version is created.

3. **Rollout Process:** Graphic murals are often used in explicit communication campaigns, sometimes called rollouts. These might be processes in which your leadership teams review the map with their units and solicit feedback about what is compelling and what could be improved. It may be that the rollout is at a large annual gathering and reinforces a vision and strategy presentation. The variations are numerous. Usually associated communications go along with the map itself. It's common for organizations to create a book that explains the map in more detail, pulling examples from the map as illustrations. Key leaders make videos explaining the story. It's also common to have the image appear online, linking to additional information. These links can be embedded right in the image to allow information to pop up when a cursor rolls over it.

Sustaining communication of this nature is important. If you treat these maps as a type of organizational thinking software, then version 1.0 is like version 1.0 software for computers. It can improve. If you republish the mural the following year as version 2.0, reflecting changes and inputs from the larger organization, you can begin to support what amounts to an organization-wide interactive dialogue on vision, direction, and values. It's a slow and deep process rather than fast and flickering, and it can have a lot of impact.

The following page illustrates a set of National Semiconductor (NSC) vision maps. These went through a series of revisions over four years when Gil Amelio was chief executive officer. The

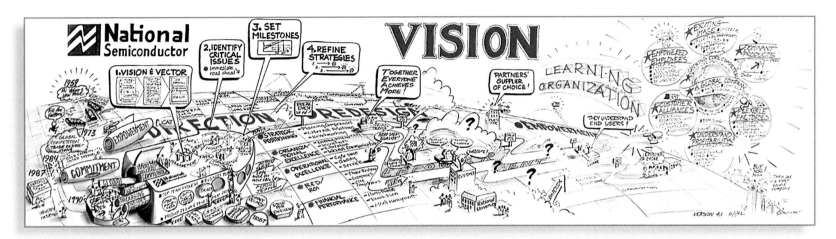

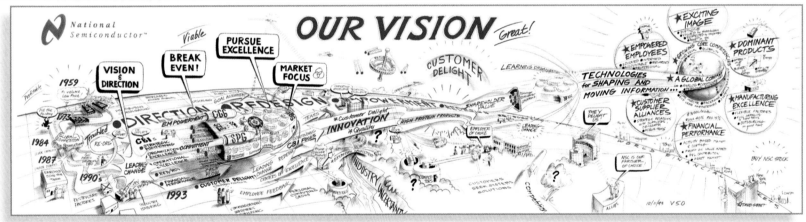

VISION OF NSC

Gil Amelio and the change team at National Semiconductor used large Storymaps to drive a turnaround in the early 1990s. Annual versions illustrated progress in the process as well as worldwide input from Leading Change workshops.

vision had a 95 percent recognition rate worldwide, as assessed in employee surveys at the time. The change team at NSC included a creative internal communications leader, Mark Levin, who linked magazine articles, videos, and case studies to these graphics. A half-dozen other members of the change team learned to work visually leading many strategic visioning sessions internally. They subsequently went on to support many other high-tech companies with visual practice.

13. Video & Virtual Visuals
Mobile Video, Tablets, Animation, & Panoramic Display

A seventh set of power tools for visual leaders is the array of media now available for online communication and education, featuring rich multimedia and animation. Historically these have been beyond the reach of most managers, and expensive! But that is not the case now. As you'll see through another set of real-life stories, the visual revolution is exploding in this area. This chapter should help you at the big-picture level begin to understand your choices. We'll start with video, then look at virtual visuals in online meetings, animated whiteboard videos, and the prospects of panoramic display in virtual settings. The following section in this book will be devoted to how you as a leader can actually apply these tools well and guide your organization in making the right choices. Let's look at what the media can accomplish first.

TEDx VIDEO EXPLOSION

The popular TED conferences (for Technology, Entertainment, & Design) now license their approach to regional TEDx conferences. Check this map of all the events in just one month worldwide!

Video for Education & Messaging

Short, affordable videos are transforming education and messaging as inexpensive, highly sophisticated tools become generally available. How they can be used in organizational settings is being foreshadowed by the TEDx phenomenon. If you don't know about it, look closely at the graphic on the smartphone on this page. The dots represent TEDx events in *one month* worldwide. The TEDx model is expanding so rapidly it suggests that regular use of video for leadership communications is just around the corner.

TED began in 1984 as a one-off event organized by information designer Saul Wurman for his friends, a pretty special list of people in technology, entertainment, and design. It caught on and became the go-to, edgy conference for these communities. Saul charged a lot, and everyone received a lot. A format of 18-minute talks developed, and 50 people a year were invited to blanket whatever theme was chosen that year. TED became so popular that it overflowed its location in Monterey, Califor-

TEDx SANTA CRUZ

This is the theme image from the September 2012 TEDx Santa Cruz. It explored the concept of "openness" in technology, communications, knowledge, and organizations. The self-organizing nature of the Web has become an organizing metaphor and point of belief for many people who feel that if systems were free to self-regulate they would flourish. There are, of course, many counterarguments, since nature itself is shown to move on after disasters and not necessarily regenerate or return to homeostasis.

nia, and began to organize smaller gatherings linked by satellite. Because of the quality of both participants and presenters the event kept growing. In 2001, Chris Anderson, publisher of *Business 2.0*, bought TED through his nonprofit foundation and took it to a whole new level. TED adopted the motto Ideas Worth Spreading and made videos of all of its talks available free online. In addition, in 2009, it began to license the idea to regional organizations that were willing to adopt the format. They are called TEDx conferences, and are required to create and post videos of all talks that are given.

Video Is Now Affordable & Supporting Interactive Engagement

David Warren, a retired professor of visual communications in Santa Cruz, discovered the TEDx format and found "the most exciting work I have ever done" taking on the lead role in organizing TEDx Santa Cruz. It offered its first event in 2011, and to David's surprise, completely sold out the 300-seat auditorium at Cabrillo College. The next year saw an increase to over 350 attendees in a bigger space.

David says it cost them about $8,000 at the time to provide professional video for the event—a requirement to be TEDx. They invited 25 presenters. If you divide the video costs, this runs to $320 a video! Part of what has fueled the explosion of TEDx organizations is the offer of free streaming online by Livestream for all TEDx conferences. TED has also supported the effort with well-presented manuals that show organizers how to launch an event. David says that there are four in his core group and another 10 in an extended group who spend the year organizing the event, and some 50 volunteers help run it. Although it may seem that video is a relatively passive entertainment medium, this network of engagement around the TEDx events and TED itself is creating a new type of community of sharing and concern. It makes the medium interactive, with videos themselves perpetrating online, allowing for continued response and comment.

Visualization Is a Big Feature at TED

In 2008 Autodesk supported TED with a demonstration of a huge touch screen setup in partnership with Perceptive Pixel, the organization that makes the large touch screens on television used to show voter data and other interactive mapping graphics. All 50 presentations at the central TED event were recorded on Wacom tablets (see below), with about 16 drawings apiece for each presenter during the three days of the conference. This was a bit of a stunt, but it provided a very good look at how everyone was communicating. Listening to all the presentations so intently revealed a range of visualization practices on the part of presenters.

1. Simple Slide Images: The predominant format was very clean, simple slide presentations that supported rich storytelling (For guidance on how to do this, look at Nancy Duarte's book *slide:ology*. It's state-of-the-art. Her firm creates presentations for Apple.)

2. Demo Videos: When presenters wanted to show an experiment or prove that a phenomenon works, video was the choice. In many presentations you therefore had videos embedded in videos.

BIG VIZ AT TED

In 2008 Autodesk, Perceptive Pixel, and The Grove teamed up to record all the TED presentations in the Big Viz demonstration booth. We used Sketch-Book Pro, the Autodesk sketching software, and a big touch screen wall programmed just for the event by Perceptive Pixel. Drawings, when saved, would attach to one of the predrawn presenter portraits (see bottom of picture above). A tap on them would show all of the associated graphics (see small drawings in the lower left). Tapping on one magnified theme (main screen), where they could be moved, sorted, grouped, rotated, and resized. Such walls will become available in organizational settings in the next 10 years much like video conference rooms are now for larger organizations. To see a video of this event, check out www.grove.com/site/ir_vid.html (The Grove's video library).

YOUTUBE

YouTube, the free video posting service on the Web, is another leading indicator of the video revolution. Google reported in mid-2012 that one hour of video was being uploaded to YouTube **every second!** That upload rate—equivalent to 60 hours of video per minute—represents an astonishing tenfold increase from its 2007 rate. This amounts to 86,400 hours of video a day! If you search for graphic recording or graphic facilitation, you can see the flood of samples that are now posted. For instance, this image is from a World Café meeting in Bilbao, Spain, and explains how graphic recording supports a World Café. The Grove inspired this practice when Tomi Nagai-Rothe recorded one of the first Cafés at founder Juanita Brown's home.

3. **Flipchart Talks:** A number of presenters would use two or three simple drawings on a flip chart (clearly, black-pen people). These were often little mental models of some sort.

4. **Computer Simulations:** A widely viewed example is Hans Rosling's famous data visualization presentation relating countries and standards of living over time. He illustrated them as expanding and moving circles on a huge x and y axis which he stood behind.

5. **Pure Storytelling:** Some presenters used no visuals at all, other than the ones they conjured through very adept storytelling. Humans still find stories very compelling.

6. **Maps and Charts:** Many presenters would use the many formats depicted in the Group Graphics Keyboard to present data and help the audience see patterns.

Notably missing was large-scale, panoramic visualization of the sort described in this book. Although TED is a breakthrough phenomenon, it is still working in the broadcast modality, and not truly co-creative in its use of visuals during the conference itself.

Video Is Fast Becoming a Key Instructional Medium

Salman Khan is another visual leader who is fostering a transformation in online education with inexpensive videos made from screen capturing his drawings. Salman is a former hedge fund manager who set out to tutor his young cousin in math with a homemade video he posted online. From this grew the Khan Academy, and more than 3,400 videos as of the writing of this book, all of which he posts free online. They offer instruction on everything from algebra to computer science to art history. According to a *Time* magazine online article, running the nonprofit academy is now Khan's full-time job, and he plans to expand the enterprise further, adding more subject

areas, more faculty members (until now, all the videos have been narrated by Khan himself) and translating the tutorials into the world's most widely used languages.

Annie Paul writes in *Time* in November 2012:

> The real revolution represented by Khan Academy ... has gone mostly unremarked upon. The new availability of sophisticated knowledge, produced by a trusted source and presented in an accessible fashion, promises to usher in a new golden age of the autodidact: the self-taught man or woman. Not just the Khan Academy, but also the nation's top colleges and universities are giving away learning online. Khan's alma mater, MIT, has made more than 2,000 of its courses available gratis on the Internet. Harvard, Yale, University of California at Berkeley, Johns Hopkins and Carnegie Mellon are among the other elite institutions offering such free education. When Stanford announced last August that it would be opening to the online public a course on artificial intelligence, more than 70,000 people signed up within a matter of days. The course's two professors say they were inspired to disseminate their lessons by the example of Salman Khan. Khan Academy's own videos now go well beyond basic algebra to teach college-level calculus, biology and chemistry.

The Khan Academy's work is an example of what is inspiring David Warren and Santa Cruz TEDx Open program. It's empowered by the Internet, of course, but it is safe to say that without visualization and video, this would not be happening. How soon will all this be standard in organizations? Judging from the booths at a recent ASTD conference in Denver, business education is moving steadily in this direction as well. Already on YouTube it's possible to search for how-to videos on almost anything you can look at directly. It's now possible to have this same support at work. Many human resource development professionals are encouraging their leaders to begin using this medium. It is interesting that Salman used everyday technology to set his example. The picture on this page uses a pencil and lined paper to demonstrate. Shot with digital video and uploaded to YouTube, very little is standing in the way of this kind of sharing.

THE KHAN ACADEMY

The Khan Academy has 3,400 lessons posted free online, like this one where Salman Khan is demonstrating how to draw a binary tree. He has four degrees from the Massachusetts Institute of Technology (MIT) and Harvard. He got a perfect score on the math portion of his SAT. Several years ago he quit his hedge fund job and began creating online math and science programs in a back room, using his computer, drawing tablets, and videos of him drawing on paper, as in this example. Through his Khan Academy, he has taught more than 85 million lessons to students all over the world and has triggered a widespread re-thinking of online education.

TABLET INNOVATIONS

Rachel Smith creates affordable graphic recording animations using the ability of a Brushes iPad app to capture the sequence of a drawing in a file that she can export to a video editing program. The picture above shows her sketching a panel for one of her movies. This approach circumvents the expensive post-production work needed to create traditional videos.

Rachel is also an accomplished virtual visualizer on Web conferences, using a Wacom tablet, as shown in the photo to the right, of her creating an agenda at a Visual Meetings workshop

Animated Graphic Recording Movies

Ever since RSA Animate in Great Britain began animating graphic recording on whiteboards as a visual way to amplify a talk, the method has caught on and many communicators are now using this medium. It's been used in some popular commercial advertising but is now spreading out to become a new tool for regular leadership communications. It's a branch on the traditional animation tree, but affordable enough that you might consider this approach if you want to have special presentations stand out from more traditional video. Graphic recording or whiteboard movies as some call them, show illustrators working on paper or a whiteboard, and then speed up the drawing and add special effects in post-production on the computer.

Rachel Smith at The Grove has developed a way to use the painting application Brushes for doing the animation (see example to the left). Brushes captures and replays line-by-line versions of drawings. Movies done this way don't show a hand drawing the images but have the little pictographs and illustrated text emerging as the narrative line proceeds.

Graphic recording movies are still used in a noninteractive, broadcast mode, but they are using the power of visualization to get across ideas that benefit from understanding how parts interconnect dynamically. The simple graphic images allow for a story-book feeling, sparking the imagination of the listeners and creating a very different energy and level of attention than traditional slide presentations, which do not usually have animation.

Graphics Augment Telepresence Meetings

Telepresence is another growing use of interactive video. This term refers to a technology that combines two or three screens to simulate people sitting across the table from one another at a meeting. Virtual visualization is an emerging complement as teams find that focusing on the work itself rather than the video images is helpful, especially for teams that know each other.

Telepresence rooms are fairly expensive and have clearly been designed with a slide presentation modality in mind. A common visual use of telepresence is to edit slides as a group, with one person entering comments and ideas in the notes section of the slide software and sometimes actually changing the slide itself if it isn't too difficult. This activity works well if the purpose of the meeting is to fine-tune a presentation and align on the message. It doesn't really work well in the beginning stages of ideation. That is where active visualization on graphic tablets is more helpful. Since graphics are on the same channel as presentations, you have to choose one or the other. Some organizations are pairing telepresence setups with SMART boards to get a full video-graphic capability, but those are still not common.

Contrasting with higher-end telepresence rooms, most Web conference services can now handle video fairly well. Skype allows screen sharing and if you have a tablet connected, it can show active drawing. It isn't interactive, but it is visual. However, active recording on a tablet doesn't work

BASIC TELEPRESENCE ROOM

Telepresence involves using higher end video to link one or more sites, with images of participants shown lifesize across the table on screens. The graphics are handled on monitors as shown here. Also illustrated is an example of using graphic recording interactively in such a conference.

HAKUHODO VOICE VISION TEAM

The Hakuhodo Voice Vision team meets online to discuss how they could use visuals to report results from customer focus groups back to clients in Tokyo. This image shows everyone linked by video in GoToMeeting, a Web conferencing service. The pictures along the top were plenty big enough to provide everyone with real-time feedback during the communications, as well as look at the shared whiteboard, where notes were being created graphically with Autodesk's SketchBook Pro software.

Kayo Ootaka, leader of the team, participated in some Strategic Visioning workshops in the early 2000s and became convinced that working with visualization in social media would open up some new possibilities.

well if you also turn on the video. The same is true of other lower-end platforms. Adobe Connect, however, has designed its Web conference service to handle more robust video and it works well with graphics and video both connected.

As with any emerging technology, if you are persistent about learning its quirks, you can accomplish a lot. A team called Voice Vision from Hakuhodo, the second biggest advertising company in Japan, held a Web conference with me on GoTo-Meeting, a popular Web conference service. We could see members of the team on the video cam images across the top of their screens (see opposite page). The images were low resolution, but we could easily see our gestures and the expressions on each person's face. I was in San Francisco and they were in Tokyo. We worked with a translator, but the Japanese team members knew enough English to understand a lot of what was said. We all could discern a lot just from watching each other's gestures and expressions. In some ways it was easier to see faces than it would in a meeting where some are off to the side rather than in the direct line of sight.

Can Other Essential Tools Work Online?

The preceding chapters include many examples from face-to-face meetings. Without question, the level of engagement and quality of big-picture thinking is superior if you can get people together in person. But most teams have remote members now, and many organization encourage virtual work. Fortunately, there are many ways to get good visual value from working online.

7. **Metaphors with Meaning:** Well-designed videos and animated talks can bring to life a central vision, strategic plan, or change process and become a point of attention. As with print posters, their ability to attract attention depends on differentiation from other communications. A big mural works when it is new and fresh. An animated graphic recording movie has the same impact. An evolving edge for this kind of work is to use online forums

to invite contributions of what kinds of media, metaphors, and messages work. This is what the Voice Vision team is doing with its work at Hakuhodo (see prior page).

8. **Visual Meetings:** Online visual meetings can be quite effective if visualization is central to the work, as in a process design meeting. Having everyone's ideas graphically illustrated during creative sessions provides interesting feedback. But straight graphic recording of text while people talk may not be very interesting to media-savvy Gen Yers. Vivian Wright, a visual leader at Hewlett-Packard (HP), says that "online meetings need to be like radio—continuously changing and inviting contribution." She likes to use the whiteboard and text-entry features to have the participants provide content on simple graphic templates (like the ones shown in the sidebar), around which she then invites dialogue. In a leader role you might need to engage someone else to handle this part of the Web meeting if you aren't familiar with the technology. It takes some preparation to orchestrate an interactive Web conference. Online visual meetings are most likely to be useful in meetings focused on designing something or in critical decision-making meetings that need alignment.

9. **Graphic Templates:** Simple graphic templates work very well in virtual meetings online. Timelines, four-box grids, maps, and rating scales are easy to create in real time. If you are the leader and want to have your team experience you listening to their suggestions, these tools will help. You can also use graphic templates by sending them out in advance and assigning individuals or subgroups to fill them out. Your online meeting can then revolve around each person sharing his or her ideas and then creating a composite view.

10. **Decision Rooms:** Creating a real decision wall virtually is still hard to do. What you can do in Web conferences is use polling and voting to provide immediate feedback. If you orchestrate the meeting so that information is clearly numbered and options are understood, then rating and ranking activities can provide the same kind of feedback that you would get from dot voting on sticky notes in a face-to-face meeting. If three-dimensional environments improve, it will be possible to stage decision rooms that have some of the same impact as a real-life conference room.

Most Web conference software will allow participants to type in bits of content on whiteboards. You can then create a simple graphic template and have everyone sort the information using their cursors.

MAPS

FOUR-BOX GRID

RATING SCALE

TIMELINE

When everyone can contribute and stay engaged instead of multitasking, everyone focuses and gets more out of the exchange.

Follow this process:

1. Explain to everyone the purpose and goals of the session.

2. Invite contribution using whatever tools your Web conference software provides.

3. Draw a simple graphic template.

4. Have everyone post and sort information and discuss what it means.

ONLINE ROADMAPS

The chart above reflects the notes taken during a Web conference with the Otis Spunkmeyer human resources team as it reviewed its 2010 roadmap. The source document was a slide created with The Grove's Roadmap Digital Graphic Guide. It was brought into SketchBook Pro and the comments were noted on the screen using a Wacom tablet as the meeting progressed. Robyn Meltzer, the team leader, went on to solicit ideas for the following year. The meeting took a total of 1.5 hours.

11. Roadmaps: Progress meetings are often held in teleconferences and online. Although most of these probably default to using a list or a spreadsheet to indicate tasks and action items, it is possible to work with graphic roadmaps effectively. *Visual Teams* describes Robyn Meltzer's use of the roadmap with her human resources team at Otis Spunkmeyer (page 153). The team was spread all over the country. She would call a Web meeting and review the prior year's roadmap, with a graphic facilitator checking off items as they were discussed (see illustration shown on the computer here). She would actively ask questions and provide feedback to everyone. The group would brainstorm items that needed to go in the next year's plan. After the conference, she and a subteam would draft a roadmap for the following year, and hold a second Web conference to allow everyone a chance to respond, upgrade with new ideas, and commit to the plan.

12. Graphic Storymaps: Increasingly, organizations are using graphic murals aimed at supporting leaders sharing visions and directions of the company, and allowing employees to self-orient to company plans and goals. Rich graphics such as these can be designed with rollovers that pop up a second layer of information on screens. If you wish to create a Storymap for your plans, investigate whether your information technology people understand how to create an interactive version online. It's technically quite possible, but as with anything technical, the people involved have to know how to do it.

Online work is very helpful during the many dialogues and discussions required to agree on the content of a Storymap. Having online review sessions with recorded inputs allows a much larger network of people to feel ownership of the final result. Co-designing with tablet-style computers is coming, so bear that in mind as you are planning murals.

7. Video & Virtual Visuals: That is what this chapter is about. Imagine working on four interconnected SMART Boards like the picture on page 168 illustrates, with supple access to video, interactive visualization, working drawings, and all the information available to your organization. This is the dream that the technology companies are moving toward, and that you as a leader should be ready for.

Virtual Leadership Development

Vivian Wright is another visual leader who has taken video and online visualization seriously. She was a talented young manager in Hewlett-Packard's (HP) formatter factory in Boise in the 1980s when she attended a Group Graphics workshop and became a skilled practitioner. She moved to the San Francisco Bay area and continued as an internal manager using many creative methods to get her colleagues to collaborate and align on plans. With HP's emphasis on virtual work, she became an accomplished leader of online meetings and workshops. Her current role as business learning partner in HP's global finance organization has led to innovations that are forerunners of what will become a regular way of working.

Several years ago she teamed up with a video-based leadership development firm to bring coaching to the Web. The results have been extraordinary, she reports. The participants get to work actively with online coaches, conduct role-plays, receive feedback, have breakout discussions, and receive playbacks and transcripts (since many members speak English as a second language).

"You have to let go of some tried-and-true in-room things when you go virtual," Vivian reports. "You have to have high engagement on the other side when people are watching or they will multitask and do their e-mail. They have to be co-creators of the content. You make *them* the focus, not yourself as performer." She gave an example of how one of the modules works. Actors create a video of a disgruntled high performer. Participants watch a short video and are then invited to role-play. Volunteers come on camera, with a live video feed from their video cams. Right next to them on the screen the actor appears and in a live dialogue interacts with the person around the issue. "It is enormously engaging," Vivian reports.

THREE-DIMENSIONAL INTERFACES

The image below is of HP Finance's Career Visions Portal, created for the finance function by a firm specializing in three-dimensional interfaces for conference events. These kinds of digital spaces, evolutions of early platforms like Second Life, will eventually be accessible on tablets and open up another level of visual subtlety to virtual communications. Many are assuming that business education materials will be converted to e-book and other digital formats in the near future if not already. These kinds of environments will assuredly integrate video, forums, search, graphic recording movies, and many other media channels.

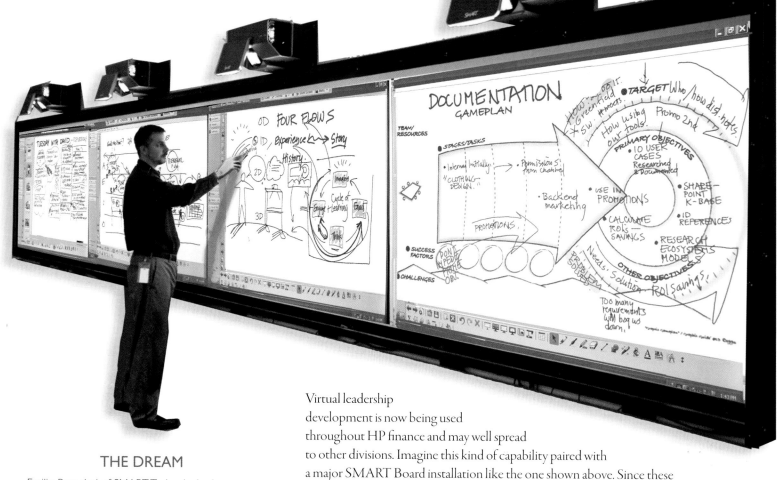

THE DREAM

Emilio Bernabei of SMART Technologies in Calgary, Canada, demonstrates how images can be shown side by side on a long panorama wall composed of four SMART Boards. This is the closest yet to a system that has all the advantages of a computer and the big-picture capacity of walls.

Virtual leadership development is now being used throughout HP finance and may well spread to other divisions. Imagine this kind of capability paired with a major SMART Board installation like the one shown above. Since these interactive whiteboards reflect whatever is on your computer, it could just as easily be a coaching session that uses large-scale graphics.

The next section is about what you as a leader can do to both take advantage of current realities in visualization and prepare for the future ones. The choices are really amazingly broad, as you will see from the graphic overview of new media included in the next chapter.

Part Four:
Managing the New Media

WHAT'S LEADERSHIP
IN AN "ANY TIME,
ANY PLACE" WORLD?

ARIGATO
GOZAIMASU!

Part Four:
Managing the New Media

14: Technology & Visualization How do you make choices about what media to use for your communications? Which will support visual work? What are the critical requirements that when met, will clear the way for your people to work more visually? This chapter will provide some principles and practices for meeting these challenges. It suggests that in your role as a leader you can support your organization by being able to focus, work in a collaborative way, and get results by reducing the fragmentation and chaos that distracts energy and attention from the work you need to accomplish.

15: Virtual Leadership This chapter focuses on you as a leader and how to make the best use of all the choices now available for virtual communications. As a leader you need to be able to communicate clearly in the midst of all the changes. You also need to stay oriented yourself, keep people's attention on the right things, make sure that your critical messages are getting through and that everyone feels engaged and committed. It's tough in a distributed environment, but there are some emerging best practices.

14. Technology & Visualization
Enabling the Right Tools

This section began with images of a portable computer, tablet, and smartphone. We are all being directly affected by these new technologies, or what some call the new media. This chapter shares principles and practices that have emerged from immersion in this new world and from being surrounded by the high-tech culture of Silicon Valley. It's important to be knowledgeable but not hypnotized. Those of us who aren't digital natives still have some perspective on what is gained and lost. Let's start with a visual flyby of all of the media choices and how they tend to bias in regard to supporting or not supporting visualization. This overview is not at the level of specific software, but a little higher, looking at the available media and platforms for visual communication. In the following chapter we'll explore some ideas about how you can begin to use these tools to provide effective leadership in an increasingly networked and virtual world.

Small and Fast versus Large and Slow

Many of the tools suggested so far as essential for visual leadership encourage you and your teams to work bigger and slower—at least in the "making sense" stages of things. Leaders familiar with visual facilitation know that visual meeting methods bring more engagement and deeper understanding and result in more aligned and capable teams when it comes to implementation.

But big and slow is not the world of new media. It seems as if the trend is to get smaller and faster. Frame cuts in contemporary ads, like the ones shown on television at big sporting events, explode with visual effects. Many seem designed with fast-forward television recorders in mind. The images become a flicker in the mind. Because our brains are focused heavily on pattern identification, changes in imagery, sound, and point of view keep us attracted. But the price of fast-paced imagery and constantly changing content is shallow engagement in anything new. Ad graphics play to what we already know, care about, and are biased to think is attractive. A website that coaches advertising people on how to keep

LET'S JUST TWEET
WHY FIGHT IT?

THIS IS TOO
SMALL FOR
OUR VISION

WE COULD NOT GET
THE TAGLINE IN!

FOUR FLOWS & MEDIA

Media is the name for the means by which people communicate to large numbers of other people. As you think about using different types, bear these four-flows questions in mind.

❏ **Attention**: Is my communication capturing and holding attention?

❏ **Energy:** Is my communication compelling at the feeling level; can people trust the "vibe"? Does it excite and inspire? Is it interactive?

❏ **Information:** Is my media helping or hindering presentation of content? Does it need scale and size? Does it need zooms and drill-downs? Should it reflect movement?

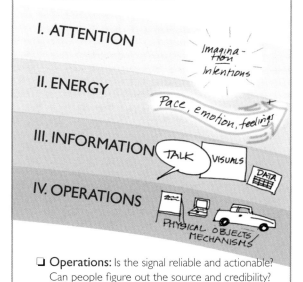

❏ **Operations:** Is the signal reliable and actionable? Can people figure out the source and credibility? Is it current?

the attention of an audience specifically cautioned against including anything that might be controversial. So how do you handle this? Just going with what is trendy won't necessarily get you where you need to go as an organizational leader.

Let's Imagine the Choices

The next six pages provide a visual overview of media in common use in organizations in the early twenty-first century. The spreads list pros and cons from the perspective of how they support visual leadership. Some are purely channels or what some would call platforms. That word is used to refer to an environment that supports many kinds of content. A Web conference service or telephony service is such a platform. So is YouTube, Twitter, and a website.

Other types of media are specific visualization tools that can be used on multiple platforms. (It's not only the technology that is confusing.) Presentation software is an example, as would be video itself, graphic recording, and templates. All of these are also considered media. The new media would be those supported by digital technologies. All require some understanding on your part if you are to provide leadership regarding which will best serve your organization..

How Does It Feel to Face All These Media and Know They Are Evolving?

You will probably have a very visceral feeling scanning the next six pages. They are purposely laid out in a scannable fashion so that you can experience the full sweep of what organizations are facing. Many of these choices are emerging not as a result of organizations thoughtfully choosing this or that medium, but because technology companies are busy enrolling everyone they can in new products, often through retail channels. There are now regular upwellings of new media into organizations. Not only that, but each of the types of media is evolving within its own technology and user base.

What Media Do You Use?

Which of these media types do you understand enough to use regularly? Which would serve your leadership goals? Read the descriptions and check the ones that seem relevant.

1. Think about your experiences with each of these media. Which are you comfortable enough with that you can use them competently? Rate yourself on the scale 0 to 10, with 10 being "completely comfortable."

2. Think about what you need to communicate to the larger organization. Rank the media as to how relevant they are to what you need to accomplish.

3. Now think about your own organization. Where do you have staff that are competent in each of the types?

4. Think about the need to differentiate from other communications in order to attract and hold attention. Which media would serve you best in that regard?

	1. PHONE & TELECONFERENCE	2. E-MAIL & LISTSERVS	3. TEXTING	4. VIDEO CONFERENCES

	Includes desk phones and mobile phones	Includes e-mails with attachments	Includes smartphones and computer texting	Includes multiple video images simulating real life
	Pros + Ubiquitous + Quick + Intimate + Call in from anywhere	**Pros** + Understood + Quick and global + Archivable + Can attach visuals	**Pros** + Very quick + Gen Y platform + Readable in meetings + Can attach photos	**Pros** + Feel real + Some whiteboard capability + Recordable
	Cons – No direct visual support – Requires hard copies in advance for visuals – Varying fidelity	**Cons** – Overused – Frequently ignored – Impersonal – Must open visuals	**Cons** – Not easily archived – Limited space – Mostly nonvisual	**Cons** – Expensive – Require advance setup – Limited visualizing tools
YOUR INTENTION	Quick team meetings, negotiations, broadcast	Communicate generally to your team	Quick checks	Save travel money
YOUR EXPERIENCE	1-2-3-4-5-6-7-8-9-10	1-2-3-4-5-6-7-8-9-10	1-2-3-4-5-6-7-8-9-10	1-2-3-4-5-6-7-8-9-10
YOUR PREFERENCE	RANK 1-24	RANK 1-24	RANK 1-24	RANK 1-24

OTHER INTERACTIVE MEDIA

TYPE OF MEDIA	5. VISUAL MEETINGS	6. WEB CONFERENCES	7. INTERACTIVE WHITEBOARDS	8. WEB FORUMS	9. ONLINE TEAM ROOMS
VISUAL ICON					
DESCRIPTION	Face to face and online graphic facilitation	Includes free and fee-based platforms	Includes large and small collaboration solutions	Refers to online sites for posting and comments	Includes both internal and service provider sites
PROS	Pros + Imagery inspires + People feel heard + Support big-picture thinking + Group validated record	Pros + Allow slides, chat, white-board, polling + Fairly well understood + Recordable	Pros + Multiple inputs + Recordable + Digital-ink overlays + Can create panorama with linked displays	Pros + Participate at will + Archivable + Can attach images	Pros + All info in one place + Archiving reports + Multimedia capability + Supported by IT in larger organizations
CONS	Cons – Need paper or tablets – Require understanding of basic visual formats	Cons – Require computer – Drawing is basic – Tech support needed	Cons – Learning curve – User skill required – Limited graphic tools	Cons – Visual functions limited – Slow paced – Require encouragement	Cons – Requires buy-in – Not real time – Small screen for visuals
YOUR INTENTION	Engage and really think through a situation	Save travel money; review plans, methods	Co-design, work on versions of images	Gather opinions	Coordinate and syn-chronize projects
YOUR EXPERIENCE	1-2-3-4-5-6-7-8-9-10	1-2-3-4-5-6-7-8-9-10	1-2-3-4-5-6-7-8-9-10	1-2-3-4-5-6-7-8-9-10	1-2-3-4-5-6-7-8-9-10
YOUR PREFERENCE	RANK 1-24	RANK 1-24	RANK 1-24	RANK 1-24	RANK 1-24

VISUAL MEDIA WITH LONGER PRODUCTION PROCESSES

TYPE OF MEDIA	10. SLIDES	11. MURALS & STORYMAPS	12. VIDEO & MOVIES	13. PLANS & REPORTS	14. WHITEBOARD ANIMATION
VISUAL ICON					
DESCRIPTION	Includes all presentation software and hard copies	Includes large-scale graphic charts and murals	Indicates informal and formal productions	Refers to noninteractive printed or PDF reports	Also called graphic recording animation: speeded-up drawings
PROS	Pros + Available everywhere + Support individuals doing active visualizing + Convenient templates + Produce hard copy	Pros + Engaging/memorable + Big-picture capability + Stand out + Support alignment in the creation process	Pros + Cameras easy to get + Capture motion + Record emotion + Highly visual	Pros + Tangible and durable + Handle color and visuals + Archivable + Convenient to read	Pros + Captures attention + Combines verbal/visual + Triggers imagination + Shows connections
CONS	Cons – Overused – Not interactive – Small screen format	Cons – Take time to create – Don't fit small screens	Cons – Not interactive – Visuals disappear – Technical to produce	Cons – Take time to produce – Not interactive – Heavy to carry	Cons – Challenging to produce – Not interactive – Images don't persist
YOUR INTENTION	Organize your thinking quickly	Support leadership storytelling	Convey passion and commitment	Commemorate important information	Attract attention/encourage visual thinking
YOUR EXPERIENCE	1-2-3-4-5-6-7-8-9-10	1-2-3-4-5-6-7-8-9-10	1-2-3-4-5-6-7-8-9-10	1-2-3-4-5-6-7-8-9-10	1-2-3-4-5-6-7-8-9-10
YOUR PREFERENCE	RANK 1-24	RANK 1-24	RANK 1-24	RANK 1-24	RANK 1-24

SOCIAL MEDIA

TYPE OF MEDIA	15. ORGANIZATION BLOGS	16. CHAT NETWORKS	17. FRIEND NETWORKS	18. INTRANET SOCIAL MEDIA	19. VIDEO/PHOTO SHARING
VISUAL ICON					
DESCRIPTION	Indicates blogs on your organization's website	Includes Twitter and other chat services	Refers to Facebook and dozens of similar sites	Internal social networking systems	Includes dozens of sites optimized for visuals
PROS	Pros + Easy to update + Can include visuals + Allow linking to other information	Pros + Quick + Mobile and global + Can link to sites + Allows hashtags	Pros + Popular + Can include photos and links + Connect to other networks	Pros + Private + Supports spontaneous organization + Searchable	Pros + Established + Highly visual + Supports video + Searchable + Link to other sites
CONS	Cons – Limited interaction – Small screen graphics – Requires tech support	Cons – Limited entries – Only link to pics – Hard to reference	Cons – Very public – Not focused – Hard to control data	Cons – Hard to focus – Expensive to create – Requires tech support	Cons – Images are public – Massive # of choices – Not really interactive
YOUR INTENTION	Communicate personally with many people	Point people to other sites; support meetings	Reach unlikely contacts	Encourage informal but private networking	Share videos and visuals globally
YOUR EXPERIENCE	1-2-3-4-5-6-7-8-9-10	1-2-3-4-5-6-7-8-9-10	1-2-3-4-5-6-7-8-9-10	1-2-3-4-5-6-7-8-9-10	1-2-3-4-5-6-7-8-9-10
YOUR PREFERENCE	RANK 1-24	RANK 1-24	RANK 1-24	RANK 1-24	RANK 1-24

OTHER AVAILABLE MEDIA

TYPE OF MEDIA	20. E-LEARNING	21. E-BOOKS	22. MOBILE APPLICATIONS	23. GAMES & SIMULATIONS	24. VIRTUAL REALITY
VISUAL ICON					
DESCRIPTION	Refers to self-paced learning on any device	Includes electronic books and interactive iBooks	Includes smartphones and tablet computers	Includes games, data viz, and demonstrations	Three-dimensional (3D), interactive environments
PROS	Pros + Convenient + Go at own pace + Can include video and other multimedia + Supports learning	Pros + Links and layers + Interactive visuals + Portable + Low-cost reproduction	Pros + Portability + Interactivity + Game-like designs + Links to other sites	Pros + Portray sophisticated visual dynamics + Interactive + Immersive	Pros + Immersively visual + 3-D and animated + Portable + Easily updatable + Links to other media
CONS	Cons − Expensive to create − Tied to computer − Requires tech support	Cons − Standards aren't set − Designing interactivity is expensive	Cons − Difficult to create − Expensive − Crossplatform conflicts	Cons − Expensive and technical − Computer-based − Less human interaction	Cons − Nonintuitive interfaces − Requires special software − Can be impersonal
YOUR INTENTION	Think about structure? Think about hierarchy?	Provide portable support for learning	Engage younger employees	Access experiences that are hard to obtain	Invite nontraditional communications
YOUR EXPERIENCE	1-2-3-4-5-6-7-8-9-10	1-2-3-4-5-6-7-8-9-10	1-2-3-4-5-6-7-8-9-10	1-2-3-4-5-6-7-8-9-10	1-2-3-4-5-6-7-8-9-10
YOUR PREFERENCE	RANK 1-24	RANK 1-24	RANK 1-24	RANK 1-24	RANK 1-24

Each type of media just described is also changing within itself. Consider these few examples:

- E-mail became popular in the early 1990s. Now this functionality is embedded in every social network site and is migrating to the cloud. Some say that e-mail is already passe with the younger generation, which prefers to text and tweet. As texting spreads, chat formats are evolving. Some new apps explicitly focus on using pictures, and some allow digital-ink annotations. Each change requires behavioral adjustment.

- Travel restrictions after the 9/11 attack on the United States, accelerated by the 2008 global financial crisis, encouraged large organizations to work virtually. This accelerated the development cycle of Web conference media. Skype made free Web conferences widespread on the low end. Fee-based offerings provide ever more sophisticated services on the high end.

- Remember when graphical user interfaces (GUIs) replaced the old C-prompt, text-oriented Internet? Now ZUIs, or zoomable-user interfaces are evolving rapidly, driven by touch-screen technology and early leaders like Prezi. It's a presentation program from Europe that allows zooming into tiny details in a graphic, either with preset paths or manual navigation. ChronoZoom is a program that allows zooming on timelines. Mural.ly provides pinboard capability and collaborative presentation design with zoomable features.

If you feel overwhelmed, so are your people. This is why leadership in this area is required.

Treat Media as a Portfolio Problem

Organizations that take on too many products and services have what in strategy work is called a portfolio problem. Letting things run wild with media will surely leave you in this kind of predicament. What you need to do is determine priorities. But this is more complex than mandating a single platform. You need to be very careful when picking the tools that you expect everyone to use. Each, to be effective, requires skill building and behavior change—probably the hardest part of making good use of emerging technology. Picking a platform is like pouring the foundation to a building. If the capabilities are too limited, you can create substantial roadblocks to ever being very visual. If they are too complicated, people might not take the time to learn.

The Challenge of Large-Scale Infrastructure Decisions

Some types of infrastructure are what are enterprise-wide. As a young leader you will probably not have influence on these, but you might be part of a task group looking to upgrade. Increasingly, these environments do allow for websites, video, archiving, forums, and most of the forms of digital media described here. Most are still not as developed as they could be for handling zooming and large-scale graphics, but that is evolving. The dimensions described on the portfolio template shown here generally shape the big choices. Do you pick programs that are standard for everyone or allow units to pick their own? Do you adopt open-source software or customize your own? What do you allow inside and outside the firewalls that are increasingly needed to protect data? A key question to ask, in addition to those listed at the beginning of this chapter, is "Where will stability be our friend?"

Standardization Can Empower Application Flexibility

In the late 1990s the information technology (IT) function at Hewlett-Packard (HP) gathered its leaders to take a historic, three-decade look at its accomplishments. What the group appreciated, looking backward, was the importance of discriminating between infrastructure and application-level leadership. (Infrastructure in this case meant the platforms that were common to everyone. Applications were the programs that worked on them.) In the mid-1970s, mainframe computing was giving way to mini-computers and HP was active in the market. There were, of course, many varieties, but the HP 3000 was one of the leaders. The company decided to standardize internally on that platform.

MEDIA PORTFOLIO EXERCISE

A great way to involve your team in aligning on appropriate visual communications is to have it collaborate with you in determining a media portfolio. Follow this process.

1. Review the strategies and goals for your unit and where you need to communicate and collaborate.

2. Determine some dimensions to your portfolio (some are suggested in the graphic below).

3. Identify candidate media types you want to use on sticky notes (perhaps using the new media overview in this book).

4. Sort them on the portfolio graphic shown below.

5. Decide on which you want to standardize and which can be optional for different teams.

6. Identify the pros and cons of each choice.

7. Prioritize your choices on a timeline.

This concentrated the available IT energy on the application layer, and soon HP was one of the first companies to have truly global e-mail. Many other innovations flourished. This level of focus came unraveled in the late 1990s with the introduction of nine enterprise resource management projects in different divisions that were installing the popular SAP database management platform. Unfortunately, leadership did not insist on standardization. Engineers focused their creativity at the infrastructure level and most of the projects did not deliver on the promise of integrated data management.

Infrastructure-Like Decisions You Can Control

The principle of settling infrastructure and platform issues in order to have creativity flow to the application programs and work itself applies to your picks of how to support visualization.

❏ Settle on common calendaring so that less energy is spent setting up meetings?

❏ Choose a robust Web conference platform that allows for both video and interactive drawing so energy isn't tied up in technical work-arounds on Web conferences?

❏ Create common plan reporting templates so creativity goes into cross-comparing plans and thinking of the larger organization rather than competing on look and feel?

❏ Create standard tagging and version numbering conventions on graphics to streamline time-wasting archiving and retrieval activity?

❏ Agree on the pacing and frequency of key update communications in regard to change processes so that no energy is spent wondering who does what, when, and where?

There are, of course, many other opportunities for having standardization support flexibility. How you determine what will work for you depends on assessing where you are wasting time that is a result of not having a standard in place. This, of course, all flows from knowing your goals.

15. Virtual Leadership
Communicating with Intention & Impact

Is there such a thing as virtual leadership? Let's see what's possible when you take charge of new media tools rather than have them take charge of you.

Leaders as Buoys & Beacons

By definition you and your leadership team are expected to provide direction for overall work efforts. Even in self-managed environments, leadership is supporting the values and conditions that make this possible. This means that regardless of your aims, you need to know how to focus organizational attention, and this means understanding how to work through whatever media you choose to provide reliable connection with your people.

If you have ever heard foghorns on a foggy bay, then you know that in soupy, dynamic conditions on the ocean, ships need buoys and beacons to navigate. The same is true of employees in an organization. The details of actually moving your ship is handled by your crew, but as a captain or navigator, you need to know your bearings. Do you know how to create a reliable signal in the fog of information that serves to orient everyone to the right path forward?

Win Trust Through Positioning

Warren Bennis has been one of the lead authors on leadership since the 1980s. Prior to publication of *Leaders: Strategies for Taking Charge* in 1985, he described his research of 90 well-known leaders to the Commonwealth Club in San Francisco. His insights apply to the new media. According to Warren, all of these leaders shared four characteristics (you might notice they map to the Four Flows):

1. **Vision:** They inspired with a compelling story of possibilities. (This underlines the importance of intention and a personal sense of purpose.)

2. **Personal Trust:** They have positive self-regard and positive regard for others. All were

---

HOW TO BE A BUOY IN A FOGGY SEA OF POSSIBILITIES

1. **Rise above the noise:** Foghorns get attention no matter what else is going on. Key communications need to stand out.

2. **Use consistent & rhythmic signals:** Buoys and beacons repeat their signals on a set rhythm that everyone can count on.

3. **Use clear and simple messages:** Buoys and beacons are not complicated.

4. **Be redundant; use multiple sources:** In the bay, it is a system of foghorns with different signals that orients the ships and provides some level of certainty about where they are.

THAT'S WHERE THE ROCKS ARE!

"people champions" who never talked down about the people on which they counted. (Visual listening helps embody this principle.)

3. **Communicating Meaning:** The leaders Warren studied focused on interpreting what events meant and not on just communicating information. (This is the importance of understanding other people's experiences with metaphor and models you use.)

4. **Trusted Positioning:** People want to know in what direction you are going, and when you change position, they want to be forewarned and guided through the change. People get nervous with brilliant people who are wrong 30 percent of the time. (This underlines the importance of making clear, consistent infrastructure choices, for instance.)

In his talk, Warren called the last characteristic consistency. By the time *Leaders* was published, he changed it to *positioning*. The word *consistency* suggests he was agreeing with the buoy principle. If people are going to trust you and your leadership team, then they need to be able to orient consistently to what you are asking of them. This requires eliminating the "noise" and chatter of too much media. The word *positioning* is a better name. It indicates that some flexibility is needed. But when changes are made, they need to be announced in advance, then again near the change, then at the turn, then after the turn, to underline the new position. All this argues for being quite intentional about your use of media.

How Intention Shapes Your Use of New Media

Cutting through the clutter requires focusing on something other than technology—most important, what you are actually up to as a leader. In fact, it may require a radical rethinking of what it means to lead. In the past, when information and knowledge were less accessible, a big part of leadership was guiding people in how to do their work. Managers hired employees, helped develop them, set goals, demanded performance, and meted out rewards and punishment. There

Cutting through the clutter requires focusing on something other than technology—most importantly what you are "up to" as a leader. In fact it may require a radical rethinking of what it means to lead.

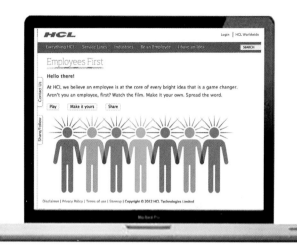

was a time when managers believed their organizations could work like well-oiled machines: just apply scientific management and match the right people to the right jobs and thrive.

Those days are long gone. With monsoon levels of information available and market circumstances so dynamic that people at the home office may be the last to know what is happening, many organizations are finding that the leadership role is turning upside down.

Total Transparency at HCL Technologies

Vineet Nayar was one of the "management mavericks" at Gary Hamel's Inventing the Future of Management conference in 2008 in Half Moon Bay, California. Some three dozen thought leaders in the field gathered to explore how management could be as innovative as technology. (The last chapter of *Visual Teams* tells this story if you want more detail.)

Vineet is relevant as an example of just how different management might be with the new media. He has advocated a culture of total transparency at HCL and a philosophy of "Employees First." HCL is one of the fastest growing digital information technology (IT) service provider companies in India. In 2008 it received the Hewett Best Employers award for best employer in Asia. All 55,000 employees post their 360-degree feedback of each other online for all to see. Individual comments aren't recorded, but the overall evaluations are. In addition, Vineet described a system of job requests, or tickets, made online to other teams and people from which a unit needs help. All responses are also posted so that everyone can see just how quickly different units respond to each other. Among other innovations, he instituted a blog in which any employee can post a question. All of the answers are required to include names. He reported 3,500 posts at that point. He also reported that HCL was growing at 40 percent a year. "Transparency creates trust," he said. "Employees are the most precious resource, and you win their trust with transparency."

HCL TECHNOLOGIES

The fastest growing IT service provider in India has an employees-first policy and radical transparency for key interactions. Vineet Nayar, the chief executive officer, may be a model of what virtual leadership will look like in a more networked future.

Managers Support the Front Line at Nordstrom

Empowering employees doesn't necessarily involve digital technology. How you interact as a leader with your people is ultimately what matters most. At Nordstrom, Betsy Sanders was a young vice president and general manager who saw the upside-down triangle that the company used to orient new employees and believed it. It had the customers on the top and the managers supporting the frontline workers, who were encouraged to do whatever it took to create great results. Against all odds she took on the Los Angeles region for Nordstrom and, in a now legendary turnaround, applied the upside-down principle and ignited a firestorm of inspired employee contribution and customer loyalty. Her book, *Fabled Service: Ordinary Acts, Extraordinary Outcomes*, details how making customers feel like gold is good business.

A reigning assumption is that new media will help in the process of aligning and inspiring employees. You need to appreciate that media itself doesn't make the difference. Your intention does, when aligned with visible behavior. "Most managers don't see their roles as upside down," Vivian Wright relates. "If they did, then they would act like consultants and treat their employees like volunteers. Moving to increase the power of the institution and one's own role takes the aliveness out of situations. Working to increase the power in your team brings it back in."

Leading Interactively with Consultative Opportunities

The fact that the environment posed by new media is confusing opens a very big door of opportunity if you choose to step into it with a collaborative, consultative orientation. If your intent is to support communications with an appropriate-tools environment, think of involving your people in this choice as an opportunity to develop their capacity to think, make decisions, and solve problems themselves. Get your direct reports and other stakeholders involved in helping you figure out the right platforms for your work. Following are some ways you can do this.

A reigning assumption is that new media will help in the process of aligning and inspiring employees. You need to appreciate that media themselves don't make the difference. Your intention does, when aligned with visible behavior.

❏ **Collaborate on website design:** You know that having an organizational website, and perhaps a blog or forum capability, might be desirable. Instead of hiring an outside firm to design it for you and deliver something beautiful, insist that the design process involve you and your people in a round of design sessions. If your designers don't work that way, then find some who do. If people help create the site and its interfaces, then they will use them.

❏ **Co-create Storymaps and visual plans:** The story about HealthEast demonstrates how those leaders expertly used people's interest in agreeing on what to put on the Quality Journey Map as a means of engaging the whole organization. All of the revision loops provided chances for important internal conversations. Don't default to just getting out an end product.

❏ **Choose a team-room platform:** There are many choices for having a central information and project management resource for your teams. Rather than picking one and mandating it, invite a task group to take on the challenge of involving people and recommending something. Your leadership would be to make sure that any givens and constraints are communicated. It may be important to integrate with other parts of the organization, and you need to insist on that as design criteria. But constraints are friends of innovation. If people actually have some say, then they will rise to the occasion.

❏ **Co-design a decision room:** Rather than mandating a work environment for critical meetings, either virtual or face to face, pull in some of your up-and-coming people to help think this through with you. If they are allowed to have input, what do you think it will be like the first time they use the environment?

❏ **Empower regular use of video:** Get your more media-savvy workers to start making videos to communicate important ideas and learning. Get them to interview customers and

DESIGN THINKING

Designers often work in teams, by creating prototypes and concepts together. The Grove's Graphic Guides support this type of thinking in planning sessions. Why not treat your media development as a "design thinking" challenge and really get people to buy in to what you create together?

bring back video reports. Interview partners. Create your own internal YouTube of "how-to" help. Probably all it will take is making sure people can get video equipment without much trouble, and maybe getting some training in post production software. It's incredibly accessible now. You don't have to know how to do this to get it started, but you would have to champion the approach if it's not your organization's normal way of working. You might have to spend a little money up front on equipment and organizing a secure, online location for archiving.

Is Collaboration Necessary?

Tools all have biases in that they are designed to serve purposes. But tools can be put to many uses designers never anticipated. Visualization of the sort described in this book is intended to support collaboration and understanding, spreading the story of what you want to achieve and how you want to work so widely that everyone can figure out how his or her job can aid in the larger effort. Living systems embed the DNA in all of the cells, not just some.

But the very same tools can be used to create a focused, driven environment that is not very collaborative. It's possible for high-growth organizations, and even some specialized and institutionalized organizations, operating in a machine-like way, to yield results. If you are the boss and have the power, you can certainly use media as your alignment tool without a lot of collaboration. People do want to keep their jobs and will do what they are told if being fired is the alternative.

However, regeneration, co-creation, and transformation are not possible without widespread engagement of your people and general understanding of process, cultural values, and the other critical elements of organization life. Even though overly directive approaches to leadership can succeed, in response employees become skilled at keeping back a portion of their commitment energy, refusing to invest 100 percent. Acknowledgment, involvement, and respect for your people is the path to full commitment, according to most who write about leadership.

Regeneration, co-creation, and transformation are not possible without widespread engagement of your people and general understanding of process, cultural values, and the other critical elements of organization life.

SMART BOARDS

With SMART's Bridgit software you can link up to 64 boards, tablets, and computers.

Making Intelligent First Moves as a Visual Leader

Let's assume that you are interested in tapping the collective wisdom of your people and want to lead in a more consultative, learning-leader sort of way. How can you get started? Following are some scenarios. These may be the focus of a collaborative design meeting to set specifications.

❏ **Support a video-friendly Web conference service:** Adobe Connect is an example of a Web conference service designed to support heavy video use. This means you can have people on their webcams and at the same time do some collaborative drawing and visualizing without slowing things down. While Skyping is relatively free, it doesn't support doing both at once. If it is easy for your group to have robust, visual Web conferences, then they will begin to do that.

❏ **Train a cadre of graphic facilitators in your organization:** Every organization has its black-pen people (see page xiii) who love to draw and record. If you invest in training several internal people, then you can begin having visual meetings on those occasions in which you would really benefit from being visual—such as in annual planning or a special problem-solving workshop. You would want to make sure they have access to large paper, markers, and digital cameras for recording and sharing their work.

❏ **Invest in an interactive whiteboard network:** SMART Technologies has developed Bridgit software that will allow you to link a SMART Board with a PC, Mac, or tablet and have all the different nodes able to interact and draw. The investment is in the $10,000 to $15,000 range. If your organization needs to engage in collaborative design, it is a great way to go. As a leader you would need to take some initiative to install this capability.

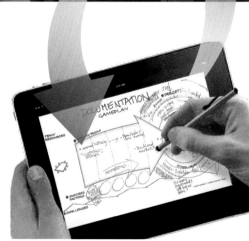

❏ **Create a Storymap of your vision and strategy:** Break away from slides and create a large, graphic mural of your next vision and strategic plan, if you have one. This would involve working with an internal or external information designer for the mural itself and working with your facilitators for the message development. You will be surprised at how engaged people become in helping shape and edit these graphics (see Chapter 12).

WORKING WITH A GRAPHIC FACILITATOR

Professional graphic facilitators are people who regularly lead and record meetings and help design visually oriented group processes. Following are the steps you would go through to work with these resources:

1. Have your staff identify two to three possibilities and ask for samples of the facilitator's work.

2. Have a telephone interview to assess level of experience, approach to consulting, and the role you would like the facilitator to play. Is he or she a good listener, or worked in your industry?

3. Have an initial design meeting in which you clarify the desired outcomes, agenda, roles, and rules.

4. Ask graphic facilitators how they would handle specific issues you know are likely to arise, and specify the degree of involvement you would like them to have in clarifying things.

5. Be sure you are the "voice of the outcomes" in the design sessions and the meeting.

6. Have the facilitator be the "voice of the agenda" in managing the timing. He or she should be like a chauffeur taking you, the rider, to the airport.

7. Make sure you are clear about the documentation you would like after the meeting. Are simple digital photos enough? Do you need to have the information typed up? Do you want to involve other staff in helping the facilitator?

❏ **Pilot using online team rooms:** Pick a team that needs to work at a distance and that would benefit from having a single place to put critical documents, calendars, timelines, and exchanges regarding a project. If you invest in a little training, then you can create an example that could replicate well in other parts of your organization. Get the team involved in helping research the options. (*Visual Teams* has a great deal of information about these types of tools.)

❏ **Organize a visual summit:** Every so often it is important to get a larger group together to align on new plans, bring new employees into the culture, and strengthen the personal relationships among everyone. Organize a summit in which you create a visual history, involve everyone in small breakouts looking at current issues and driving forces of change, do some visioning, and establish priorities. The HealthEast Quality Journey Mapping Meeting is that kind of event. These settings allow you to create a real theater of ideas.

❏ **Encourage video case studies:** Purchase video cameras and encourage teams that are doing things others should know about to make informal videos featuring interviews, explanations, and key models and frameworks used for their work. Arrange with your IT people to have a place where these can be stored and streamed or contract with an outside vendor who can do this for you. You should also find a firm that can do the video editing inexpensively or train someone internally who is interested in this. That will probably require some equipment expense. Video editing requires large hard drives and a fairly big computer capability. Laptops can handle this if they have enough memory and use portable hard discs.

❏ **Begin using OARRs charts in regular meetings:** Get in the habit of making sure your outcomes, agenda, roles, and rules are recorded visibly and that you take being clear about these seriously, not just a pro forma drill you race through.

❏ **Use graphic templates in your planning meetings:** Use graphic templates to visualize the different steps in a planning process. Create a summary mural of priorities and have it available for posting online or physically in work spaces. Then build your next planning cycle by reviewing the graphic work from the last one (see Chapter 9).

The Challenge of Social Networks

Leaders are busy. Most don't have much time to spend on social networks. But there are ways to using them effectively as a leader. The sidebar on this page lists guidelines if you are new to social media or you are finding that your current use of it isn't very effective. At The Grove we know that our clients and associates are interested in developments in the field of visualization, especially anything connected with strategic facilitation, working with groups, and supporting collaboration. Focusing on these themes, we regularly post on Twitter, Facebook, and LinkedIn (the more professionally oriented social network), pointing out online resources, magazine articles, books, and graphic examples that are relevant. We do this about two to four a week, rather regularly. It doesn't take long if you use applications that will put one post on several networks at the same time. If colleagues refer a special article or website, we can send a link message out to our network. It takes less than a minute to do. It's having a focus and knowing what people will find valuable that makes the difference.

If you are a leader who likes to use video, you can use your social networks to point people to the key videos you want to make sure they see. If you like using big murals to communicate your vision, you can have these as PDFs and send them as attachments in e-mails. If you like to blog, you can use the social network to link to the blog you wrote. It may be that your gift is knowing a lot of others who are experts and who have the ability to pick the ideas that matter the most. This may be the focus of your network activity.

In *The Tipping Point: How Little Things Can Make a Big Difference*, Malcolm Gladwell describes connectors, mavens, and salespeople as three types of leaders who make a difference in getting new ideas going. When situations are dynamic, it often takes only a little push as the right time to get things to "go viral" (notice the cellular mental model).

GUIDELINES FOR SOCIAL NETWORKING

Social networks are busy and diverse, even ones that are internal to your organization. To get a buoy effect and have people pay attention, follow these principles:

1. **Focus:** Determine a very clear focus for your posts—i.e. company plans, progress, acknowledgments.

2. **Frequency:** Determine a regular frequency so that people can understand how to tune in. Will you post daily, weekly, or monthly? The constancy may be more important than the volume.

3. **Brevity:** Keep your posting to the point. If you are using Twitter, then you must be brief. Forums and blogs aren't so constrained.

4. **Links:** One of the great values of social networking platforms is being able to link, or point at, other sources of information. If you use your role as leader to create posts that function as little beacons pointing at relevant documents, then you can help everyone stay oriented to what is important.

5. **Relevance:** Keep your posts helpful and relevant to the work people are doing. As the leader, your behavior is amplified. Make sure you are amplifying what you want to see more of.

6. **Acknowledgment:** Social networks are a mini-spotlight that you can shine on things that are working. Positive reinforcement creates change.

- **Connectors** are people with large numbers of people they know.

- **Mavens** know the most about a given subject and are relied on for thought leadership.

- **Salespeople** are persuaders who have the ability to bring others along and love to translate ideas.

You may be any one of these types of leaders. What helps is to link with your complements, and together, create attention around ideas that matter. If you are a salesperson type, you might want to send things to connectors to amplify. If you are a maven, you might want to recruit salespeople to help. The basic principle is to establish an identity online that others can trust.

Knowledge in the Network

Fans of new media believe that we are entering a time when collective sense-making is possible through increasing linkages and networks. There is little question that factual information is at everyone's fingertips, literally if you have a smartphone that can connect to the Internet. But is this knowledge—the kind that knows how to use information—the kind that gets results? And how much of it is helping us understand systems and interconnections of things, using our visualization capabilities? Speed and brevity in communications doesn't support deep understanding of organization the way co-creating visuals does.

In the last chapters of this book we will turn back to the very human challenge of leading change. If you talk to people experienced in implementation of new technology of any sort, they will admit that changing behaviors, norms, and attitudes is *much* harder than changing the technology. Let's look at this problem closely, and see how visual leaders would handle it.

Fans of new media believe that we are entering a time when collective sense-making is possible through increasing linkages and networks. There is little question that factual knowledge is at everyone's fingertips, literally if you have a smartphone that can connect to the Internet. But is this knowledge—the kind that knows how to use information—the kind that gets results?

Part Five:
Leading Organization Change

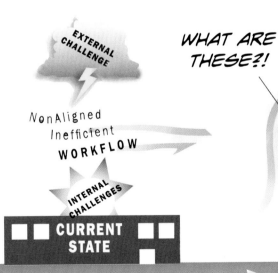

EXTERNAL CHALLENGE

NonAligned Inefficient **WORKFLOW**

INTERNAL CHALLENGES

CURRENT STATE

WHAT ARE THESE?!

I THINK THEY ARE COMPONENTS OF A CHANGE PROCESS.

FUTURE STATE

Part Five:
Leading Organization Change

16: Anticipating the Need to Change Change and transformation, by definition, take you into territory in which your organization will be having new priorities, require new behavior, and be implementing new processes. It's confusing for all if there are no guides to how this will happen. This chapter explains a useful framework for anticipating the stages of change by using a Storymapping approach.

17: The Chrysalis Effect Because organizations are full of human beings who have awareness, feelings, a wide diversity of skills, and real constraints in terms of how much change they can handle and how fast it can happen, we'll end this book looking at the heart of visual leadership—how you create the conditions of trust that allow your organization to transform. Borrowing from the analogy with the caterpillar becoming a butterfly, we'll look squarely at how visual leadership can help enormously with this challenge. We'll also look at what you as a leader can do to make sure your people are having fun and seeing results as you help them develop their visual IQ and capabilities.

16. Anticipating the Need to Change
Putting Visual Tools to Work

So far we've looked at many tools and methods for raising your and your organization's visual IQ. These tools and practices come alive when they are integrated over time in a specific planning or problem solving process. They are most important when your organization needs to change. This chapter is a chance to see how the tools and methods described in this book come into play in your own real-life situation. Let's look at how this can happen if you are involved with, or decide to enter into, large-scale organization change.

In the following pages is a graphic framework that steps through at a general level the types of stages a change process goes through, and the types of activities and tools that generally come into play. This is a general map, of course, and is illustrated as a Storymap with accompanying descriptions. But in this case, your organization is the territory. To make these ideas come alive you should actually put the tools shared in this book into practice and literally create your own map, using this framework as a starting point. It's as simple as getting several sheets of paper and marking off a set of columns representing the different stages. As you read through the descriptions, translate the general points and tips into your specifics. You can do this either in regard to a past change process, or about one you want to imagine in the future. In either case, what you include and omit will flow from the specifics of your own circumstances, your goals for change, and what kind of resources you have to work with.

Visualizing Predictable Patterns in Change

The transformation framework is a result of needing a map like this to provide a reference point in large consulting projects. It reflects an evolving model of how things work that integrates a number of assumptions. In use, it's an illustrated checklist. Back in Chapter 5 we looked at a higher level version of a similar kind of map, the Sustainable Organizations Model (SO Model). Its intent is to think about choices for organizational form. The transformation model zooms in on the specifics of how you would implement one of those changes. You would take on such a process when you begin to feel that your current organization has lost its vitality and effectiveness or needs to be more efficient.

GREINER CURVE

It is widely accepted that stages of growth in an organization are a series of evolutionary developments interrupted by revolutionary periods of change. Larry Greiner popularized this idea in the 1970s with this graphic. The SO Model (Chapter 5) echoes this underlying pattern.

Keep this oscillating pattern in mind, for it will also echo in the more specific transformation process you might be leading. Think of the organization transformation model as a zoom in on one of the revolutionary times. The same pattern will apply. Expect jumps and then integrating times, more jumps, and more integration. Your specific journey will, of course, be unique. These kinds of conceptual models can guide your attention but shouldn't keep you from seeing the unique patterns in your specific situation.

Putting Insights into Practice

Many different drivers can trigger your need to change your organization. Which of these might apply to you?

❏ Are you a startup that needs to focus on a lead product or service and generate some real cash flow or flow of new supporters?

❏ Are you happy being a high-growth organization but need to have a different service or product be the lead?

❏ Are you a specialized organization but the mix and performance aren't quite right?

❏ Are you leading an institution that is simply needing to trim down and get more efficient?

❏ Are you a very process-oriented organization that is a bit stuck in its own procedures and needs to become more innovative and co-creative, perhaps allying with other organizations?

❏ Do you simply have to get better at doing what you know you need to do and increase levels of motivation and skill development?

❏ Or is the crisis and challenge you face in your own leadership? Maybe you need to figure out how to be more of an enabling manager rather than doing everything yourself?

In any of these cases, mapping out how you might go about the change is a way of beginning it. As we step through a complete change process, and how the different tools and methods of visual leadership apply at each stage, pay attention to what resonates. Bear in mind that there are also nonvisual aspects that are very important, like providing time for people to let go of old ideas, providing times for deep dialogue, and listening that isn't conceptual or explicit. The graphics illustrate each stage and provide a list of the generic features that usually attend these stages. The text will review the tools that will help. The colored rainbow running through the graphic suggests the ongoing flow of work that needs to continue during any change process. This graphic depiction is purposefully dynamic to reflect the riverlike, fluid nature of organizational change.

1. Visualizing the Call for Change

Whatever type of crisis you may be in, the drivers will be some combination of internal and external challenges. Visualizing these is the first step in understanding what is required. Following are some of the things you can do at this stage:

❑ **Change process orientation:** Share the SO Model or Greiner framework with your team and share what might be involved if you want to begin working on change.

❑ **Issues scans & interviews:** List the internal and external challenges that are leading you to think about change. Interview customers, other companies, or internal people to develop a sense of what is happening in the larger environment. Look at your employee surveys. Pick out a graphic template and ask staff to report back in a manner that allows you to visually compare and contrast the data in a decision meeting.

❑ **Facilitated scoping sessions:** Involve some others in mapping out what you think change might involve after you've created your first draft. How much investment do you need in aligning leadership and stakeholders? How much work do you need to wake up your employees to what you are seeing? A visual scoping session will bring all of these issues to the fore, and simultaneously begin galvanizing your change team (Step 2).

❑ **Graphic history mapping:** Take a longer view of your organization's history and the roots of change. Create something like the Visa maps for your own organization and engage people in a dialogue about core values, past times of change, and best practices. In any of these sessions your overarching goals are to make the need to change very visible and to create as much consensus as possible.

Call for Change

• Voices for change step forward.

• Some awaken to needs.

• Outmoded thinking is challenged by circumstances.

• A few articulate a desired future state.

EXTERNAL CHALLENGES

Nonaligned Inefficient WORKFLOW

INTERNAL CHALLENGES

■■ CURRENT ■■
STATE

• Change Process Orientations
• Issue Scans and Interviews
• Facilitated Scoping Sessions
• Graphic History Mapping

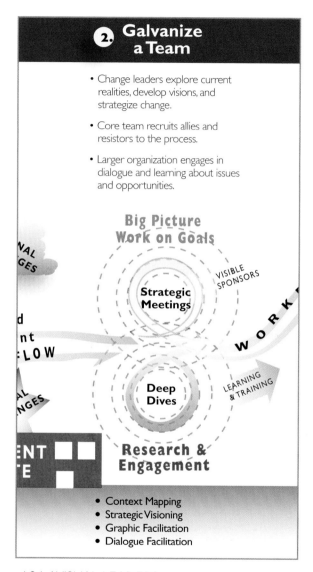

2. Galvanize a Team

- Change leaders explore current realities, develop visions, and strategize change.

- Core team recruits allies and resistors to the process.

- Larger organization engages in dialogue and learning about issues and opportunities.

Big Picture Work on Goals

VISIBLE SPONSORS

Strategic Meetings

WORK

Deep Dives

LEARNING & TRAINING

Research & Engagement

- Context Mapping
- Strategic Visioning
- Graphic Facilitation
- Dialogue Facilitation

2. Galvanize a Team

If you are certain you need a concerted transformation effort, then you need to have a team of aligned leaders to help you. Visible leadership is essential to overcoming resistance. The graphic suggests doing some things at the big-picture level through strategic meetings and scoping sessions and simultaneously doing deeper dives into the organization to build momentum at lower levels. In addition to all the individual enrollment needed, here are some tools you might use:

❏ **Context mapping:** Revisit the issues identified and draw out the drivers of change. Map them on a large chart showing the interrelationships. This can combine internal and external factors (see template on page 122).

❏ **Strategic visioning:** Explicitly take your leadership team through a Strategic Visioning process, with review of history, context, SPOT analysis, visioning, potential bold steps, and gameplans. Viewing the big picture from multiple perspectives is critical at this stage.

❏ **Graphic facilitation:** Use visual meeting methods to document discussions and input. In change processes, people need to be heard and respected for their concerns. Listening to people furthers the chances they will listen to you.

❏ **Dialogue facilitation:** You will want to make sure that your efforts at this point allow people a chance to connect on the feeling and personal relationship level. Your graphic sessions should always support real dialogue. In change new ideas emerge from listening.

How long this stage takes and how many meetings and individual conversations are needed can vary widely. Organization cultures that are very collegial many need a great many cycles at both the top levels and organization-wide. More hierarchical cultures might concentrate more energy at the leadership level, making sure a core group is aligned and committed to all the work that change requires.

3. Test Vision & Know-How

The core work of your organization needs to proceed during change, but you also need to test and strengthen whatever visions and initiatives come out of your strategy meetings. Quick wins are helpful to build momentum. You and other key leaders need to visibly support change, and you need to build the internal capabilities of staff groups and other resources. Following are some explicit things you can do:

❑ **Leadership coaching:** It's very helpful to have other leaders and yourself practice telling the story of Why Change? and What's Our Vision? People also want to know that there is a framework for the change. Many organizations will develop a storymap of the change process at this point and have leaders practice explaining it.

❑ **Facilitation & team training:** With the number of meetings and Web conferences a big change requires, training an internal team of facilitators who understand visual meeting practices and have a grounded understanding of team dynamics is usually critical. In larger organizations, executives will often empower a change team to lead the process. If this group uses visual methods, then they can learn by doing.

❑ **Experiential training:** To the extent that you can, initiate projects that give people actual experience with new behaviors and attitudes that will help accelerate the change. At Nike, a large change in the global procurement organization is supported by teams that are testing the new processes and sharing their learning with other teams. At the Headlands Center for the Arts, tangible enactments were essential to get funding.

❑ **Action-learning design:** If you and your managers are clear about the things that require special task forces and teams, then challenge your younger leaders to take them on as a form of action learning. Having these teams use visual tools to plan, and then report back graphically, will help you share their learning.

3. Test Vision & Know-How

- Initiative teams take on the most pressing issues.
- Leaders call for learning.
- Organization acquires needed people and skills.
- Vision and goals drive planning for new norms, organizational designs, and systems.

VISIBLE SPONSORS · WORKFLOW · QUICK WIN · QUICK WIN · LEARNING & TRAINING

- Leadership Coaching
- Facilitation & Team Training
- Experiential Training
- Action-Learning Design

4. **Commit Real Resources**

- Leadership takes stands on people, culture, and designs.
- Managers agree on and communicate new priorities.

Make Decisions

SUPPORT MORE WINS

Leadership Meetings

W

Change Teams

CHANGE INITIATIVE

Organize Initiatives

- Change teams are empowered and resourced to act.

- Decision Support
- Change Team Facilitation
- Initiative Action Planning
- Cascade Design

4. Commit Real Resources

There comes a time when you and your organization needs to make a complete turn into the change and go beyond simple pilots and stretch projects. This is the inflection point that Process Theory and the SO Model graphically depict. Again this needs to happen at both a top-leadership level and throughout the organization, usually through some well-orchestrated, visual processes. This is how John Schiavo cleared for takeoff—in a real plane.

❏ **Decision support:** It's at this point that staging a real decision room makes sense. Bring decision tools into the process that allow rating and ranking. The scale of commitment you make may be technological, and hiring a big consulting firm is the step that commits your organization. It might be a decision to invest in a new line of products or enter a new market. It might be a decision to redo your business model. Whatever level of decision you make, you can count on some people feeling like they have much at stake. You'll need to keep reinforcing the reasons you are changing and the benefits.

❏ **Change team facilitation:** Specifically organizing and tasking change teams that work across the organization is a common strategy at this stage. In large technology installations, a project team of experts will help characterize the processes needed, but special teams need to train others, prepare for change, and focus on other special tasks that surround the big decision.

❏ **Initiative action planning:** Graphic templates are a terrific way to get your initiative teams clear and aligned and to stay in touch with them through visual reporting.

❏ **Cascade design:** One type of action is to have managers explicitly socialize a new vision and strategy and solicit feedback from the organization. This may have been done on a smaller scale before. California AAA's Storymaps allowed it to go out to all its call centers and brief everyone on the process.

5. Amplify & Align

One of the most effective ways to provide momentum for change is to amplify and support anything that is moving in the right direction. This is what Tom Mehlone was doing at North American Tool & Die with his refrigerator awards. It's what your internal communication people can do by featuring initiative teams that are getting results. Just as important, you and your leadership team need to show up aligned in action. The most common reason for change projects failing is nonaligned leadership support. It doesn't take much to empower inertia rather than change. It is very easy to unintentionally send out double messages if you aren't aligned. One powerful manager who doesn't comply can compromise an entire culture change process.

❑ **Storymap murals:** These are very effective at helping align leadership and others during the process of their creation and then again during critical conversations (Chapter 12 explains this approach).

❑ **Change roadmaps:** These kinds of graphics are invaluable for providing a sense of order in the midst of whatever turbulence arises as the change takes hold (see Chapter 11).

❑ **Process mapping:** Most organizational change involves changing how things are done over time. Using special teams to graphically characterize, analyze, and improve specific processes commonly happens at this point.

❑ **Process redesign:** Whatever process you lay out at the beginning of a change will begin to evolve based on real-life events. If you and your management team begin iterating your strategy charts, visions, and process maps, people will see that you are guiding and responding in an organized way. Doing this also provides a way for you to support keeping leadership in a learning mode to balance out the very tempting practice of becoming more directive as challenges arise. The more you can get the DNA of the change story into all parts of the organization, the more innovation and improvisation you will see.

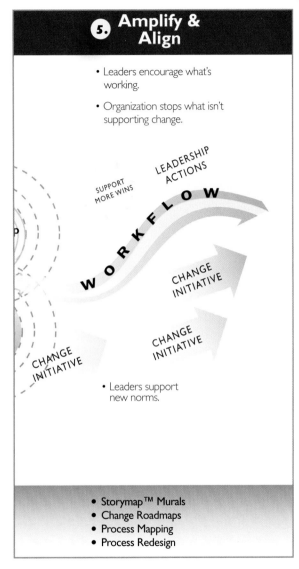

5. Amplify & Align

- Leaders encourage what's working.
- Organization stops what isn't supporting change.

SUPPORT MORE WINS

LEADERSHIP ACTIONS

WORKFLOW

CHANGE INITIATIVE

CHANGE INITIATIVE

CHANGE INITIATIVE

- Leaders support new norms.

- Storymap™ Murals
- Change Roadmaps
- Process Mapping
- Process Redesign

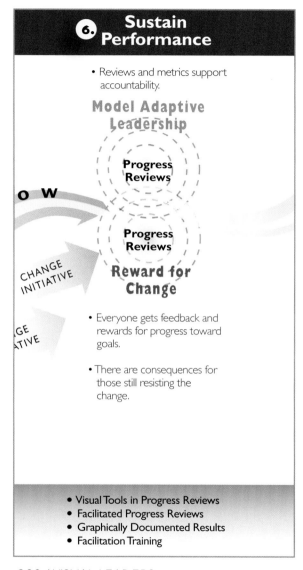

6. Sustain Performance

• Reviews and metrics support accountability.

Model Adaptive Leadership

Progress Reviews

o w

Progress Reviews

CHANGE INITIATIVE

Reward for Change

• Everyone gets feedback and rewards for progress toward goals.

• There are consequences for those still resisting the change.

• Visual Tools in Progress Reviews
• Facilitated Progress Reviews
• Graphically Documented Results
• Facilitation Training

6. Sustain Performance

Once a change begins to "lock in," then you as a leader should move to support and acknowledge it. The point of change is to have a new set of behaviors and orientations become accepted organization-wide. Holding progress reviews at all levels and keeping organizational attention on the right factors is the role of leaders. By this time people should be able to see tangible, visible results of all the work they've put in. Following is how you can support at this stage.

❏ **Use visual tools for progress reviews:** Provide platforms for virtual exchange that allow good visual exchange and encourage the design of templates for project tracking that help you and others see how things are going.

❏ **Facilitate progress reviews:** Provide facilitators who can support special reviews with visual meeting strategies so that critical teams feel supported and essential processes stay on track. Teams that are heading out into new territory won't get everything right. An environment that encourages experimentation and innovation will also support making mistakes. Managers who are under pressure for results need the balancing support of facilitators who are focused on good, effective group process.

❏ **Document results:** Providing regular feedback on progress to the entire organization, investors, and supporters is invaluable. Post regular video communications, enroll internal-communications people to provide a steady drumbeat of results information, and make strategic updates to key Storymaps.

❏ **Use facilitative leadership training:** When an organization turns the corner and is fully in the momentum of change, the role of leadership also shifts to a much more supportive role. If you've worked hard to create an adaptive organizational environment, where responding to change becomes a competency, you will need to go beyond just providing visual tools and make sure your leaders are trained and supported.

7. Create a New Culture

If Charles O'Reilly is correct that culture trumps strategy, having your change become the new culture is a desirable end state. This means that everyday expectations support behaving in a way that supports new ways of working. The lessons from the change process now need to be integrated into ongoing training and development programs, talent management practices, and the way you and other leaders show up for both regular and special meetings. Here are examples.

❏ **Facilitated learning sessions:** During the three years it took to spin off Agilent Technologies from Hewlett-Packard, the information technology (IT) department of Agilent cloned every single business system. It was the biggest process of this type ever attempted. To acknowledge this effort, Agilent created a huge storymap of the process and involved all of the people who made it possible. These types of facilitated learning sessions can double as acknowledgments and celebrations.

❏ **Celebration events:** Staging very special events that dramatize change means a great deal to the people involved. This can work even in smaller changes. Milliken Carpet is famous for organizing sharing rallies that honor teams and people who have contributed to change. Leadership's central involvement has made these rallies feel like the Oscars for the people involved. These are especially important in organizations that provide lots of services and products to a wide range of people, such as Nordstrom, where the attitude of employees is a key differentiator.

❏ **Learning systems development:** Reflecting your new culture in the training and development your organization does ensures that it becomes part of the makeup of all new and emerging employees, as well as the people who were directly involved in the change.

❏ **Case study development:** Graphic histories provide an interesting way to reflect on a long process and harvest learning. These can support videos, storybooks, and other media that bring forward the practices and tools from the change just completed.

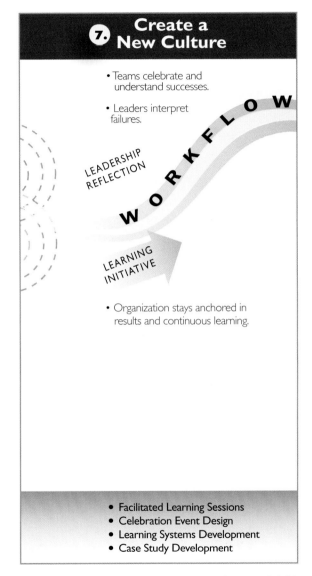

7. Create a New Culture

- Teams celebrate and understand successes.
- Leaders interpret failures.

LEADERSHIP REFLECTION

WORKFLOW

LEARNING INITIATIVE

- Organization stays anchored in results and continuous learning.

- Facilitated Learning Sessions
- Celebration Event Design
- Learning Systems Development
- Case Study Development

THE GROVE ORGANIZATION TRANSFORMATION MODEL

Commanding the High Ground of Interpretation

On this page is the entire process in one graphic. At this point you should appreciate that these types of visual frameworks for thinking about change are to the real work what pianos are to music. The keyboard is arranged logically, based on real harmonics and finger sizes. But music endlessly varies. Stages may repeat. Some may be extended. Others may be compressed. There are discordant parts and harmonies. If you worked through your own change map you'll appreciate these visual models as being a type of mental instrument, and will learn to trust what you see through them and not be too obsessed with trying to have your circumstances fit *into* them. Your people will experience this map/territory dichotomy when you create a mural about your vision and change process. The real world won't flow exactly that way. That is why you need to know how to explain and talk about relationships between thinking and acting.

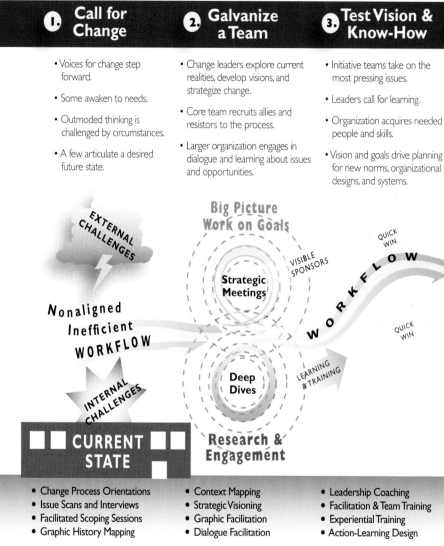

1. Call for Change
- Voices for change step forward.
- Some awaken to needs.
- Outmoded thinking is challenged by circumstances.
- A few articulate a desired future state.

2. Galvanize a Team
- Change leaders explore current realities, develop visions, and strategize change.
- Core team recruits allies and resistors to the process.
- Larger organization engages in dialogue and learning about issues and opportunities.

3. Test Vision & Know-How
- Initiative teams take on the most pressing issues.
- Leaders call for learning.
- Organization acquires needed people and skills.
- Vision and goals drive planning for new norms, organizational designs, and systems.

4. Commit Real Resources
- Leadership takes stands on people culture, and designs.
- Managers agree on and communicate new priorities.

EXTERNAL CHALLENGES

Big Picture Work on Goals

Make Decisions

Nonaligned Inefficient WORKFLOW

Strategic Meetings

VISIBLE SPONSORS

QUICK WIN

WORKFLOW

Leadership Meetings

INTERNAL CHALLENGES

Deep Dives

LEARNING & TRAINING

QUICK WIN

Change Teams

CURRENT STATE

Research & Engagement

Organize Initiatives
- Change teams are empowered and resourced to act.

- Change Process Orientations
- Issue Scans and Interviews
- Facilitated Scoping Sessions
- Graphic History Mapping

- Context Mapping
- Strategic Visioning
- Graphic Facilitation
- Dialogue Facilitation

- Leadership Coaching
- Facilitation & Team Training
- Experiential Training
- Action-Learning Design

- Decision Support
- Change Team Facilitation
- Initiative Action Planning
- Cascade Design

5. Amplify & Align

- Leaders encourage what's working.
- Organization stops what isn't supporting change.

LEADERSHIP ACTIONS

SUPPORT MORE WINS

WORKFLOW

CHANGE INITIATIVE

CHANGE INITIATIVE

CHANGE INITIATIVE

- Leaders support new norms.

6. Sustain Performance

- Reviews and metrics support accountability.

Model Adaptive Leadership

Progress Reviews

Progress Reviews

Reward for Change

- Everyone gets feedback and rewards for progress toward goals.
- There are consequences for those still resisting the change.

7. Create a New Culture

- Teams celebrate and understand successes.
- Leaders interpret failures.

LEADERSHIP REFLECTION

WORKFLOW

LEARNING INITIATIVE

- Organization stays anchored in results and continuous learning.

FUTURE STATE

OVERARCHING GOAL

Compelling Vision of a Future State That Inspires & Motivates

---

THE GROVE ORGANIZATION TRANSFORMATION MODEL

Here is the combined model for change. It evolved out of the experience of 35 years of consulting at The Grove Consultants International and the insights of Peter Gaarn, a senior organization consultant deeply involved in change processes at Hewlett-Packard during the 1990s and 2000s. It is also informed by Arthur M. Young's Theory of Process and cross-calibrated with John P. Kotter's well-known change model. It is visualized with the stages of the familiar "S" curve in the background, because it is such a widespread backdrop for thinking about organizations. The graphics aim is to illustrate the way in which work must continue in and around change and the importance of working both at the top level and deep into the organization (the figure-eight images illustrate this). Like all abstractions, a real-life change process will reflect many variations, but these seven stages are ones that will inevitably be addressed at some point. The ways you as a visual leader can support your own change process are summarized along the bottom. To get the most value out of this kind of framework, take the time to map out an experience you are familiar with, using these stages as a guide to your reflections.

- Storymap™ Murals
- Change Roadmaps
- Process Mapping
- Process Redesign

- Visual Tools in Progress Reviews
- Facilitated Progress Reviews
- Graphically Documented Results
- Facilitation Training

- Facilitated Learning Sessions
- Celebration Event Design
- Learning Systems Development
- Case Study Development

SATURN TRANSFORMATION

In 1988 General Motors opened the first new car manufacturing plant built in the United States in several decades and needed to orient its 3,000 new workers to the history and vision of Saturn. The storymap shown here was sponsored by John Weigand, the senior organization consultant working with Skip LeFauve, the president of Saturn. John knew that getting leadership to agree on this history would engage it in an alignment conversation about the future. Three iterations and some very dramatic internal meetings accomplished just that. The blue ribbons represent the management history, yellow is labor, red is engineering, orange is marketing, and green represents finance. The ups and downs in the ribbons and roads represent periods of confidence and crisis, behind each of which is a story. The mural was so effective that three years later, Saturn commissioned an extension of this history.

Real Life Is Very Dynamic

Here at the end of a chapter focusing on general concepts and tools (hopefully anchored in the specific realities of your situation) is a picture of another organization's actual change. The early history of General Motors' Saturn organization illustrated on this page is a graphic reminder that the real-life transformation of organizations is dynamic and complex. This map was generated from a meeting of 20 of the founders of Saturn and vetted by internal attorneys, as well as meetings with top management and labor. Internal organizational consultant John Weigand used this mural intentionally to engage top management and labor leadership in the conversations it needed to have about the purpose and vision of Saturn at the point they opened a new plant in Spring Hill, Tennessee.

Saturn's evolution was a series of crises and improvisations, illustrated by the bunching up and smoothing out of the ribbons in the graphic. This up-and-down pattern reflects the arc of process the way a real musical composition will reflect the scales and abstract harmonic structures of a musical keyboard. Saturn had a remarkably successful stretch as a new kind of manufacturing culture, and was then reabsorbed into General Motors. It reflects the fact that if there is any truism about change, it is that everything will.

17. The Chrysalis Effect
Creating the Conditions for Transformation

A theme throughout this book has been the value of thinking about your organization as a whole system while you are working on the parts. Visualization, especially large-scale visualization and appropriate mental models, are central to experiencing this value in action. If you and your direct reports are the only people who can do this, then you are by default going to have to rely on command-and-control and top-down leadership. If you can bring your whole organization to a new level of visual literacy, then your chances of spreading key organization knowledge generally, like the DNA in living systems, is greatly improved. Is this possible?

What Difference Did Mapping Make at HealthEast?

Craig Svendsen is a medical doctor who was given the role of chief medical quality officer in 2005 at the beginning of HealthEast's Quality Journey process (see Chapter 1). He participated in the entire process and continues as its leader. So did its visual leadership make a difference? "Yes," he says. "In many ways."

1. **Bringing people together:** "It got everyone in one room as a contributor, collaborator, and organizational memory to understand our heritage, see where we currently are, and agree on where we wanted to go. It created a venue for discussion. This was incredibly valuable," he said.

2. **Common language:** "It created in one picture frame our past, present, and where we were headed. We could talk about the 'river of challenges,' what grounded us on the grassy part, and what on the road needed to move or change."

3. **Trigger for left-brain thinkers:** "A lot of medical people are very analytic and number-oriented. The graphic images triggered useful memories and metaphors, the way the smell of lilacs does."

TYING IT ALL TOGETHER

The Quality Journey Map at HealthEast allows Craig Svendsen, chief medical quality officer, to tell the story as one integrated vision. HealthEast's knot logo blends with the Quality Journey Vision's four strategies, and an image of the "spirit of nursing," standing on evidence-based medicine, reaching out the arms of caring and service, and measuring themselves again six quality measures in the big "Q," literally tied the story together. "We met our 2010 goal!" Craig says. (See Chapter 1 for how it got created.)

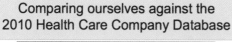
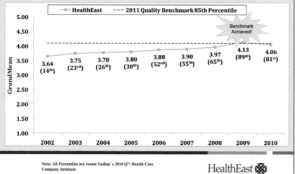
4. **Efficiency & flexibility in communications:** "The one picture allowed me to
    explain in five minutes or an hour to whatever audience that was appropriate for them."
5. **Video backdrop:** "We created a video of me giving the Quality Journey talk that was on
    our Infonet for all to view and comment upon."

As quality officer at HealthEast, Craig leads a virtual quality institute, composed of leaders who
have responsibility for quality. After the Mapping Meeting, they were able to know confidently
that leadership was aligned on four strategies. Before that meeting, when leadership set the 2010
quality goal, both he and Pam reported that they had a great deal of trouble deciding on how
they would measure progress. After the Mapping Meeting, they were clear. They needed to measure patient experience, employee experience, clinical performance, and operational efficiency—
the four main strategies on the vision. They got the results (see sidebar).

"We are currently looking at our next five years with a new CEO," Craig said in the fall of 2012,
"and we are using Pam's charts! We've engaged in a similar conversation about how we can put
our strategy into a graphic form. Because of the Quality Journey process, there is much more
willingness, and even eagerness, to do this one as effectively."

Craig describes himself as being "very left brain" as a doctor. He was surprised at his own response
to the graphics. "I found I could be very analytical with them," he said. "I wonder if strong left-
brainers are better at learning right-brain ways of thinking than the other way around?" There isn't
research on this, but Craig is reflecting the fact that visuals span a full spectrum of uses, from very
analytic to very impressionistic.

HealthEast Becomes a Visual Planning Culture

As the lead strategist at HealthEast, Pam Hull didn't stop being visual with the conclusion of
the Quality Journey process. She and her colleagues, Betsy Stites and Susan Nelson, became

proficient graphic facilitators and expert users of visual planning templates. They went further and licensed The Grove Graphic Guides for full organizational access on their Infonet. Not only has Pam become an adept visualizer (even though by her own admission her drawings are pretty basic), the whole organization is working this way in their planning. Here is what she reports:

- ❏ **Visual meetings:** "I don't go into any meeting with a flat agenda," Pam says.

- ❏ **Storymapping:** Bethesda Hospital conducted its own Quality Banner, using the Quality Journey Map as a template, and grounded out all the ideas in the specifics of their hospital.

- ❏ **Graphic templates:** Graphic templates are accessible to all on the Infonet and used in planning. "We use all of them," Pam says, "but find things like the SPOT (template) very powerful. It's almost diagnostic."

- ❏ **Video:** Not only did Craig put his Quality Map talk on the Infonet, but Kathryn Correia, HealthEast's new CEO, makes a regular video every two weeks that is posted for comment. "She will even get up at the flip chart and do drawings," Pam says.

- ❏ **Process maps:** HealthEast's Business Process Improvement Team uses the graphic templates, along with the Leader's Guides that accompany them. They use the Mandala and others for articulating future states and LEAN analysis.

- ❏ **Patient experience sessions:** "We get patients to create Lego-block arrangements of their experiences, and then we translate these into stories of patient experience," Pam says.

- ❏ **Visual IQ:** Craig and Pam both report real transformations in their thinking. Both spoke of their and others' experiences in boosting their analytic capability. The graphics invite focus and clarity. They also support seeing connections.

PAM HULL—A SUCCESSFUL VISUAL LEADER

"When I started this journey, I was a bullet point and sub–bullet point person, sending out 20-page strategy documents for review and comment," Pam Hull reports. "I'd get logical responses. Now they call me the 'circle lady'! I can't do anything without graphics."

Here's what she gained:

- ❏ **Involvement:** "We got 7,000 people coalescing around our vision and goals," she said.

- ❏ **Strategic articulation:** Caused her to think more clearly and succinctly.

- ❏ **Meaning:** People share what's in their heart, as well as their head, as they react to the graphics.

- ❏ **Memorability:** People point at the pictures in meetings and know what they are talking about.

Following are some of the best practices that you can take away from the HealthEast experience and implement in your own organization.

❏ **Galvanize for change:** Use visual meeting practices to bring together a critical mass of leadership around the need to change and a vision of what might be achieved.

❏ **Create a roadmap for change:** Just having a vision and values isn't enough. Specific milestones and initiatives need to be set and visually articulated so that they can be communicated efficiently and referred to frequently.

❏ **Focus on early wins:** Get specific groups to do their own visual processes and get results. HealthEast did the Bethesda Quality Banner and Business Process Improvement.

❏ **Ensure leadership commitment:** Make sure your top leaders are visible supporters of whatever processes and new tools you are using if they are different from standard practice.

❏ **Visibly measure & communicate progress:** Determine indicators of success and then communicate progress visually.

❏ **Provide visual tools:** Make templates and guides easily accessible to internal planners.

❏ **Use interactive media:** HealthEast's Infonet is a key part of their communication system. They allow comments in video sharing and comments on visual planning documents.

PREPARING A VISUAL PLAN

Pam Hull works visually as a regular practice now, supported by templates and her own willingness to just jump in and draw.

According to both Pam and Craig, one of the reasons why visual leadership was able to gain traction at HealthEast was the full support of leadership. Pam reports that people need to see it done, experience the results, *and* see that people in authority approve of the new way of working. In HealthEast's case, the fact that both Pam and Craig were visible—along with the CEOs of Bethesda, the acute care hospitals, the chief medical officer, and the CEO himself (and now herself)—gave everyone the confidence to jump in.

Let's look more generally at this issue of creating an effective framework and support for transformation.

The Chrysalis Metaphor

Within the community of people who think and write about transformational change, the metaphor of the butterfly has been instructive as an image of how organizations can achieve transformational change. As you must surely know, butterflies begin as caterpillars—very different creatures from the butterflies they eventually become, although their bodies have some similarity. The means by which this transformation occurs is a stage in which the caterpillar spins a pupae that hardens into a chrysalis, a picture of which is shown here. According to biologists, the cells of the caterpillar become loosened up and enter a state that is formless and soupy. In this state there are cells called imaginal cells. Some biological orientation allows these imaginal cells to find each other, link up, and eventually use the old caterpillar cells as nourishment.

The inference from this analogy is that there is a role for a trusted, firm structure that can hold cells together during the soupy stage. It is only within the reliable structure of the pupae that this can happen. In a change process, this pupae is the plan and the clarity of the "holding structure" that will guide the organization during the change. In organizational change the chrysalis is an image of possibility in everyone's imagination. Of course, there are changes to physical systems, personnel, and all kinds of other things, but the biggest force for change is everyone's orientation to and acceptance of plans and shared willingness to explore something new.

After setting its 2010 quality goal, the leadership at HealthEast thought it could go about things in an incremental way, improving this and that quality process. But the organization didn't really begin to change seriously until the Quality Journey Team planned the big Mapping Meeting. It was this process that provided the chrysalis for change, with Betsy, Pam, Craig, Susan, and others reinforcing its boundaries with clarity and persistence. During the dialogue and storytelling, people who could imagine the change began identifying each other and reaching out and connecting. Much of this happened during the informal parts of the process—the meals, the small groups, and the table sessions.

If you look closely at very successful large-group facilitation methods, then you'll see they all seek to create a safe environment for change. Some call this a container. Some might use the actual

IMAGINAL CELLS

The metaphor of the cellular transformation of a butterfly is supported by scientific studies of the role of imaginal cells in the process. Wikipedia reports:

> Imaginal cells or imaginal discs are one of the parts of a holometabolous insect larva that will become a portion of the outside of the adult insect during the pupal transformation. Contained within the body of the larva, there are pairs of discs that will form, for instance, the wings or legs or antennae or other structures in the adult. The role of the imaginal disc in insect development was first elucidated by Jan Swammerdam.

> During the pupal stage, many larval structures are broken down, and adult structures, including the discs, undergo rapid development. Each disc everts and elongates, with the central portion of the disc becoming the distal part of whichever appendage, wing, leg, antenna, and so on, it is forming. During the larval stage, the cells in the growing disc appear undifferentiated, but their developmental fate in the adult is already determined.

It is fascinating that scientists chose this name. How the cells find each other and link up to create the forms may have something to do with image. One of Arthur Young's students, Frank Barr, a medical doctor, found that glial cells on the membrane may serve a mapping function, communicating information from the outside world.

WHAT HOLDS THE CHANGE YOU ARE SEEKING TO MAKE?

In between the two processes of the caterpillar making a larva and the butterfly hatching is the soupy, hidden, messy stage when the imaginal cells need to find each other. What structures and processes provide this security for your change processes?

metaphor of a chrysalis. It's the idea of how the change process will work manifested a diagram or visual representing the stages and steps. Without these visual supports, it's hard to imagine what will happen. People tighten up and hold on, waiting for bosses and others to point the way. With shared understanding everyone can begin creating the new organization in a dynamic way.

The Power of Principles and Simple Rules

A September issue of the *Harvard Business Review* (HBR) had a number of articles on strategy and how it actually can be done more simply than many organizations practice it. Authors Donald Sull and Kathleen Eisenhardt in their article, "Simple Rules for a Complex World," distinguish between plans that are drawing on understood capabilities and working in markets that are pretty stable and plans that will inherently require flexibility and improvisation. In these second types of situations, simple rules may be much more effective as a strategy than an elaborate plan.

In some respects, the lesson from HealthEast and other storymap projects is that visual meeting processes can very effectively help organizations come to some understanding about what those rules need to be. In the HealthEast case, the Quality Journey Map specified very specific behaviors that should attend each strategic band. At National Semiconductor, the Analog Division decided to do the same thing and had one of the most successful processes. When Dee Hock formed Visa, he did it by getting all the small member banks to agree to a set of simple rules.

As you reflect on the full spectrum of mental models with which you can think about your organization (pages 58 and 59), this pattern of flexibility and choice being empowered by constraint in the right places shows up in all of them in some way or another. This interdependence of freedom and constraint is affirmed by people who work at modelling complex behavior. In 1986 Craig Reynolds wrote a software program to simulate the flight of birds on a computer. He called it Boids, and it became iconic for people who were excited about the way patterns of order can emerge from complex, dynamic systems. Imagine trying to program a computer to anticipate all the possible flight patterns of birds and have it be anything like a real flock of birds in flight. The challenge is not dissimilar to that of getting thousands of people in a large organization to all "flock" to a similar market or product and service orientation. But Craig didn't try to program all the little Boids. Instead he created a generic flapping bird icon and three simple rules that became the structure of constancy that empowered flexibility (see sidebar).

A key understanding emerging from studies of how living systems operate (meaning cells, plants, animals, and human systems) is that order can emerge from the overall dynamics without having to have central instructions. It's also clear that this needs some amount of structure. In the Boids case, it is simple rules. In the HBR strategy example, it's rules drawn from thorough immersion in markets, customers, and employee needs. In the HealthEast case, the agreed-upon graphic in the Quality Journey Map provided just enough guidance to "hold" the many individually inspired initiatives that followed.

If you come to any kind of understanding reading this book, appreciate how useful it is to, on the one hand, provide simple structures for people to work within, and on the other, invite engagement, interaction, and contribution as you move forward. When it comes to people thinking about organization and imagining change, images and frameworks that are visual can be explored and played with the way designers play with different concepts. When it comes to enacting these ideas, visuals become visible actions. People respond to other people, and the norms and examples of leadership are a powerful guide. Being a visual leader in this regard moves well beyond the wall, the tablets, and the computers. You and your fellow leaders are the buoys and beacons that point out direction and highlight what is "right" to focus on. In times as dynamic and uncertain as ours are now, your willingness to show up as a learning leader—someone who can listen as well as direct, who can explore and question as well as declare—is at a premium.

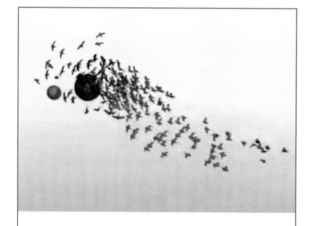

SIMPLE RULES CAN SIMULATE REAL LIFE

Craig Reynolds's famous Boids software program is a successful simulation in the field of "artificial life." It runs on three rules.

1. **Separation:** Steer to avoid crowding local flockmates. In other words "leave a little space."

2. **Alignment:** Steer toward the average heading of local flockmates. "Match speeds."

3. **Cohesion:** Steer to move toward the average position (center of mass) of local flockmates. "Head toward the center of the flock."

You can see this simulation on YouTube at www.youtube.com/watch?v=GUkjC-69vaw or just search for "Boids."

Visual tools provide the important complement to our fundamental storytelling nature and our ability to count, measure, and estimate with numbers and machines. It's visualizing that can provide us a sense of the whole, while still honoring and even celebrating the details out of which the whole arises.

More than one person has wondered why there is an empty, glowing sun on the cover of this book. Shouldn't it be filled with something? It should, but that is hopefully your imagination and aspirations. Each generation shapes its own sense of what is possible and needed and then works together to bring about yet another transformation. May these tools help you do just that with yours!

Part Six:
Links, Books, & Other Resources

Part Six:
Links, Books, & Other Resources

18: Websites & Bibliography This chapter provides you links to websites that are relevant content and to the authors who lie behind the ideas in this book. Each are annotated to give you a sense of which might be useful.

Appendix This short inclusion provides background on Arthur M. Young's Theory of Process and where the reader can find more information about his ideas.

Index Provides page references for key names, tools, and concepts.

18. Websites & Bibliography

Links

The literature on leadership is extensive. In thinking about visual leadership, you, the reader, should have access to some of the standards in the field. Following are also some key links to websites that will provide access to tools and take you deeper into some of the ideas in this book about systems thinking, visualization, and organizational transformation.

❏ **The Grove Consultants International:** The Grove is a full-service organization development and publishing firm in the Presidio of San Francisco. It has been offering tools for visual meetings since 1977, when it was formed. It offers an extensive line of Graphic Guides templates, Leader's Guides, and books for personal visioning, facilitation, team performance, and visual planning for anyone needing effective group processes based on visualization. The Grove regularly sponsors training in the Principles of Graphic Facilitation, Strategic Visioning, and Team Performance. It also carries all the supplies for visual meetings .
(www.grove.com; Facebook—The Grove Consultants International; Twitter—TheGroveConsult)

❏ **Arthur M. Young/Theory of Process:** This link is to a comprehensive website about the work of inventor and cosmologist Arthur M. Young, whose books on the Theory of Process and the nature of thinking have been seminal in the work of The Grove.
(www.arthuryoung.com)

❏ **Business Model Generation:** Alexander Osterwalder and a large network of collaborators are taking graphic templates to the Web. Their best seller *Business Model Generation* shows you how to combine visual meeting methods with business model analysis.
(www.businessmodelgeneration.com/)

❏ **Center for Creative Leadership:** Founded by academics, the Center has grown to offer one of the best selection of tools, assessments, and other leadership services.
(www.ccl.org/leadership/index.aspx)

COMPLEMENTARY MAPS FROM *VISUAL LEADERS*

If you would like to obtain free PDF posters of the Sustainable Organizations Model, Boulding's Seven Frameworks for Thinking, or the Organizational Transformation Model included in this book, visit www.grove.com/site/visual_leaders.html.

You can also find a wide range of tools for visual practitioners in The Grove Store.

❏ **Center for Graphic Facilitation:** Peter and Diane Durand have become a nexus of information about the revolution in visual practice. They are busy training and networking together a new generation of what they call rock star scribes. (http://graphicfacilitation.blogs.com/)

❏ **Cognitive Edge:** For those of you interested in the cutting edge of cognitive science, David Snowdon's network will get you to some of the best thinking in the field. It is focused on assisting organizations with truly complex problems and opportunities. (www.cognitive-edge.com)

❏ **Coro Centers for Public Affairs:** Coro was the seedbed for Group Graphics. Founded in 1948, it is one of the pioneers of experience-based education for leadership with centers in seven cities. Coro trains high school through professional leaders. (www.coro.org)

❏ **CoVision:** Pioneers in electronic decision support, CoVision provides web-based Council software for events like the Clinton Global Initiative, America Speaks community dialogues, and many organizational summits and planning events. Tools allow electronic brainstorming, sorting, grouping, ranking, and comments. (www.covision.com)

❏ **DavidSibbet.com:** This is my regular blog, where you will find posts about visualization, organizational development, cognition, technology, personal development, and information design. (www.davidsibbet.com; Twitter—DavidSibbet)

❏ **Digital Roam, Inc.:** Dan Roam's *Back of the Napkin, Solving Problems & Selling Ideas with Pictures* brought simple visualization to business. He's a prolific agent of visual thinking. (www.danroam.com/)

❏ **Duarte:** Nancy Duarte and her large design team are some of the most innovative presentation and communications people in the business. *slide:ology* is a state-of-the-art book on how to make presentation work for you if you are using slides.
 (www.duarte.com/)

❏ **Future Factor:** The publishing wing of Strandgaard & Co., The Grove partners in Denmark and Scandinavia, offers graphic templates, visual meeting materials, and links to Team Performance materials for Scandinavia.
 (www.futurefactor.dk/en/)

❏ **Heartland Circle: The Convening Company:** The Thought Leaders Circles growing in Minnesota and California are transforming approaches to tapping group intelligence.
 (http://heartlandcircle.com/welcome.htm)

❏ **Idea Connect:** Former partners with The Grove have branched out with their own suite of Grove-inspired tools to support learning about customers.
 (http://store.beideaconnect.com/)

❏ **Ideo:** This design company has been a leader in articulating what is meant by "design thinking." Their innovative processes are excellent examples of visual leadership.
 (www.ideo.com/)

❏ **Innovation Games:** Luke Hohmann is a pioneer in using gamification for planning and organizational communications. The Grove's Cover Story Vision is a game on his site.
 (http://innovationgames.com/)

❏ **Institute for the Future:** IFTF is an independent nonprofit research group working with organizations of all kinds to make more informed decisions about the future.
 (www.iftf.org)

❑ **Interaction Associates:** Interaction Associates wrote the book on group process, facilitation, and building collaborative cultures. Their courses are first rate. (www.interactionassociates.com)

❑ **International Forum of Visual Practitioners:** In 1995 a small group of graphic recorders held a conference to share ideas and support each other. This organization has grown and is now a worldwide network of graphic recorders, facilitators, and designers interested in supporting visual meetings. Their website is full of examples. (www.ifvp.org)

❑ **Khan Academy:** A leader in online learning and open source education, the Academy has more than 3,300 lessons on everything from science and math to history. (www.khanacademy.org/)

❑ **The Leadership Challenge:** Jim Kouzes and Barry Posner have created best-selling books, assessments, and leadership apps around their research. *The Leadership Challenge* is in its fifth edition and one of the best selling leadership books. (www.leadershipchallenge.com/home.aspx)

❑ **Neuland:** The Grove partnered with Neuland to take The Grove templates to the German market. They are makers of all kinds of meetings and equipment, including large portable walls directly inspired by visual practitioners. (www.neuland.biz)

❑ **Organization Development Network:** This network has roots in living systems theory. In the 1990s many schools began offering degrees in organizational development, and they continue to network through this association. (www.odnetwork.org)

❏ **Pegasus Communications:** The Pegasus conferences attract leaders, managers, and consultants interested in applied system thinking. Their site also has a large inventory of resources available to members.
(www.pegasuscom.com/)

❏ **Society for Organizational Learning:** SoL was formed in April 1997 to continue the work of MIT's Center for Organizational Learning (1991–1997). Peter Senge, author of *The Fifth Discipline: The Art and Practice of the Learning Organization,* says visioning, mental models, and systems thinking are three of the five.
(www.solonline.org)

❏ **TED:** This network explores the intersections of technology, entertainment, and design. Its motto is "Ideas Worth Spreading." It's one of the best examples of integrating face-to-face conferences, video, and online media for communication.
(www.ted.com)

❏ **Timeless Earth Wisdom:** Firehawk Hulen and Pele Rouge are dedicated to bringing forward Earth wisdom to our times. Firehawk is a gifted videographer and a wonderful example of the engaging power of imagery.
(www.timelessearthwisdom.com/)

❏ **Tony Buzan:** Inventor of Mind Mapping, Buzan is a prolific author and speaker who has done as much as anyone to popularize applications of visual thinking outside design.
(www.thinkbuzan.com/uk)

Bibliography

Axelrod, Robert M. *The Evolution of Cooperation*. New York: Basic Books, 1984. Print. A seminal work that changed the way experts view cooperation, based on analysis of the famous Prisoner's Dilemma game.

Bachelard, Gaston. *The Poetics of Space*. Boston: Beacon Press, 1994. One of this famous French philosopher's most popular books, originally written in 1958.

Bennis, Warren G. *Organizing Genius: The Secrets of Creative Collaboration*. Reading, MA: Addison-Wesley, 1997. Despite the myth of heroic leadership, the authors explore breakthroughs accomplished by group effort.

_____ and Burt Nanus. *Leaders: The Strategies for Taking Charge*. New York: Harper & Row, 1985. This is a report on the shared characteristics of 90 acknowledged leaders. It's still a classic.

Bois, Sam. *The Art of Awareness*. 3rd ed. Dubuque, IA: Wm. C. Brown Company, 1978. One of the best textbooks I know of on epistemology and general semantics—thinking about thinking.

Boulding, Kenneth. *The Image: Knowledge in Life & Society*. Minneapolis: University of Minnesota, 1956. This seminal work shaped my perceptions about mental models and their importance.

Bunker, Barbara, and Billie Alban. *The Handbook of Large Group Methods: Creating Systemic Change in Organizations and Communities*. San Francisco: Jossey-Bass, 2006. Founders of the field pull together the dominant practices.

Daniels, William. *Group Power I: A Manager's Guide to Using Task-Force Meetings*. Hoboken, New Jersey: John Wiley & Sons, Revised edition 1986. As practical and useful a guide as you will find for managing special meetings.

_____, *Group Power II: A Managers Guide to Conducting Regular Meetings*. Pfeiffer, 1990. This book includes practical advice on managing all the meetings by which you regulate your organization.

Gladwell, Malcolm. *The Tipping Point: How Little Things Can Make a Big Difference*. New York: Little, Brown and Company, 2000. Gladwell defines three types of information leaders and how they work together to influence change.

Hagel, John, John Seely Brown, and Lang Davison. *The Power of Pull: How Small Moves, Smartly Made, Can Set Big Things in Motion*. New York: Basic Books, 2010. The authors make a solid, well-researched case for how people use connections, knowledge, and resources to solve problems.

Horn, Robert. *Visual Language: Global Communication for the 21st Century*. Bainbridge Island, WA, 1998. This is a comprehensive history of the emergence and applications of text/graphic and visual language.

Jaworski, Joseph. *Synchronicity: The Inner Path of Leadership*. This is one of the better books looking at leadership from a holistic perspective.

Johansen, Robert, David Sibbet, Suyzyn Benson, Alexia Martin, Robert Mittman, and Paul Saffo. *Leading Business Teams: How Teams Can use Technology and Group Process Tools to Enhance Performance*. Reading, MA: Addison-Wesley Series on OD, 1991. This first-year report of IFTF/Grove's Groupware Users Project is still very relevant.

Kahane, Adam. *Power and Love: A Theory and Practice of Social Change*. San Francisco: Berrett-Koehler, 2010. Following *Solving Tough Problems*, Kahane digs in on the need to deal with power as well as trust and cooperation.

Kleiner, Art. *The Age of Heretics: A History of the Radical Thinkers Who Reinvented Corporate Management*. 2nd ed. San Francisco: Jossey-Bass, 2008. Kleiner's freewheeling portraits focus on corporate mavericks of the 1950s to 1970s.

Kouzes, James M., and Barry Z. Posner. *The Leadership Challenge*. 3rd ed. San Francisco: Jossey-Bass, 2002. The book's basic premise is that there are identifiable, critical skills that anyone can learn to become an effective leader.

Kotter, John P. *Leading Change*. Boston: John P. Kotter, 1996. Kotter classic is widely followed as a guide to thinking about leading change and was helpful in creating the Organizational Transformation Model.

_____, and Holger Rathgeber. *Our Iceberg Is Melting: Changing and Succeeding under Any Conditions*. New York: St. Martin's Press, 2005. This is a terrific example of using an extended metaphor to explain Kotter's change process.

Lakoff, George, and Mark Johnson. *Philosophy in the Flesh: The Embodied Mind and Its Challenge to Western Thought*. New York: Basic Books, 1999.

_____, and Mark Johnson. *Metaphors We Live By: A Leadership Fable*. Chicago: University of Chicago, 2003. A republishing of his classic 1980 work on metaphors with a new afterword.

_____. *Women, Fire, and Dangerous Things: What Categories Reveal about the Mind*. Chicago: The University of Chicago Press, 1987. This is an elaboration of his "experientialist" approach to thinking about cognition.

Mindell, Arnie. *Working on Yourself Alone: Inner Dreambody Work*. Portland, OR: Lao Tse Press, 2002. Combines perspectives from Jungian and Tibetan traditions to suggest ways of doing inner work by yourself.

Morgan, Gareth. *Images of Organization*. London: Sage Publications 2006. Describes how you can lead organization change by using metaphoric analysis systematically, i.e. organization as machine, as organism, as prison, or as brain.

Pascale, Richard. *Managing on the Edge: How the Smartest Companies Use Conflict to Stay Ahead*. New York: Touchstone, 1991. An insightful build on the McKinsey Seven "S" model showing how organizations sustain creative tension in approaches to strategy, structure, systems, staff, style, skills, and superordinate goals.

Sanders, Betsy. *Fabled Service: Ordinary Acts, Extraordinary Outcomes*. San Francisco: Jossey-Bass, 1997. This book details how Nordstrom created legendary customer service.

Schein, Edgar. *Organizational Culture and Leadership*. 4th ed. San Francisco: Jossey-Bass, 2010. Schein is one of the foremost thought leaders in organizational development and culture change.

Senge, Peter M. *The Fifth Discipline: The Art and Practice of the Learning Organization*. New York: Doubleday/Currency, 1990. Presciently identified and described the learning organization early and introduces systems thinking.

Sibbet, David. *Visual Meetings: How Graphics, Sticky Notes & Idea Mapping Can Transform Group Productivity*. Hoboken, New Jersey: John Wiley & Sons, 2010. This best seller provides a foundation of understanding for many of the visualization strategies described in *Visual Teams*.

_____. *Visual Teams: Graphic Tools for Commitment, Innovation, & High Performance*. Hoboken, New Jersey: John Wiley & Sons, 2011. Unpacks the Drexler/Sibbet Team Performance Model and shows how team leaders can use visual meeting methods through the whole arc of their work.

_____, and Ed Claassen. *Team Leader Guide: Strategies and Practices for Achieving High Performance*. San Francisco: Grove Consultants International, 2003. Comprehensive guide for first-line managers, covering leadership strategies, Drexler/Sibbet Team Performance Model, 80 best practices linked to the model, and 12 strategies that show how collections of best practices can lead to high performance.

Tushman, Michael L., and Charles A. O'Reilly III. *Winning through Innovation: A Practical Guide to Leading Organizational Change and Renewal*. Boston: Harvard Business School Press, 1997. This introduces the organizational alignment model.

_____, and Charles A. O'Reilly III. *Ambidextrous Organization: Resolving the Innovator's Dilemma*. Boston: Harvard Business School Press, 2009.

Young, Arthur M. *Reflexive Universe*. San Francisco: Delacourt Press, 1976. Anodos Foundation, 1999 Revised Edition. This is Young's seminal work on evolutionary process and how nature reflects universal principles. It deeply informs the Sustainable Organization Model.

Appendix

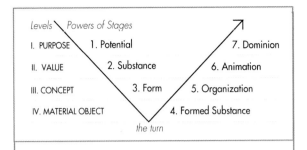

Levels | Powers of Stages

I. PURPOSE — 1. Potential — 7. Dominion
II. VALUE — 2. Substance — 6. Animation
III. CONCEPT — 3. Form — 5. Organization
IV. MATERIAL OBJECT — 4. Formed Substance

the turn

Arthur M. Young and the Theory of Process

Arthur M. Young received a degree in mathematics from Princeton in 1927 and studied relativity and quantum mechanics with Oswald Veblen. Young set out in the early 1930s to develop a unified theory of how universal systems relate to one another, caught up in the general efforts of the early twentieth century to describe a unified field theory integrating the major findings of science. In the process he spent a good number of years in the 1930s and 1940s grounding his thinking in the practical process of inventing and developing the world's first commercially licensed helicopter, the Bell 47.

He emerged from his work with Bell and parallel research believing that the unity of things cannot be found by examining forms and structures and deterministic rules, but by appreciating the nature of process—the actions of the photon and fundamental particles upon which all else is based. He came to see that all process in the universe is playing out a creative tension between freedom and constraint, between the potential of the photons of light and the constraints of cause and effect at the molecular level. When matter finds the combinatory rules at the molecular level, it can then turn back toward freedom through the evolved structures of plants, animals, and humans. This cycle is represented three-dimensionally by the torus and two-dimensionally in the arc of process.

The Theory of Process presents an integrated set of tools for understanding the evolution of life and consciousness in many fields of study. Students have applied the theory effectively in everything from the healing arts to international relations. Young evolved his theory of process by working deductively from basic principles and testing his ideas against both scientific fact and accepted theories over a period of 30 years. He was able to show that the process of nature is more fundamental than the structures it forms. He identified seven distinct phases of process that express themselves throughout seven kingdoms in nature.

In practice, Young's ideas are clear and sensible, once you appreciate how to bring the role of purpose back into the scientific method. The fourfold aspects of nature and the seven-stage arc pattern, key elements in the theory, turn up not only in mathematics, quantum physics, chemistry, and biology but also in philosophy and religion. Because Young chose to express his philosophical ideas using geometry (as well as engineering formulas and validation from philosophy and mythology), his work provides a basis for thinking visually about organizations, in this book's case, the evolutionary pattern that underlies the choices for sustainability. See www.arthuryoung.com for links to further resources or obtain a canonical poster and summary of the theory at http://store.grove.com/product_details.html?productid=1.

PRINCIPLES IN THE ARC OF PROCESS

- The universe is a process put in motion by purpose.

- The development of process occurs in stages, seven in all.

- Each stage develops a new power, retaining powers learned from prior stages.

- Powers evolve sequentially—in the natural world as kingdoms and substages.

- Early stages take on constraints until the "turn"; later stages regain freedom.

- Levels of constraint are the same on both sides of the arc.

- Stages of process alternate between innovation and recapitulation.

THE TORUS PATTERN

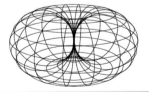

Index

DAVID SIBBET is president and founder of The Grove Consultants International, a firm leading strategy, visioning, creativity, future-forces, leadership development, and large-scale system change processes worldwide since 1977. He is author of the best-selling *Visual Meetings: How Graphics, Sticky Notes & Idea Mapping Can Transform Group Productivity* and *Visual Teams: Graphic Tools for Commitment, Innovation & High Performance.*

He was involved with the growth of Apple Computer in the 1980s, facilitated the change-management team at National Semiconductor during its turnaround in 1990, and worked at HP and then Agilent Technologies for many years, leading strategic-visioning sessions for groups and divisions, helping develop leadership programs, and designing Grove Storymaps for special kickoffs and change projects. He is currently doing extensive strategy and change work with Nike, Inc. He and The Grove facilitated the community-visioning processes and planning fairs connected with the conversion of the Presidio in San Francisco to a national park. As a founding director of Headlands Center for the Arts and tenant in the Thoreau Center for Sustainability, he has long experience as a park partner.

In addition to corporate and government work, David has sustained a diverse involvement with foundations, nonprofits, schools, and professional associations. Over the years David has helped design and lead many board/staff retreats, strategy sessions, and cross-organizational projects working on social change.

David is author and designer of many of The Grove's integrated process consulting tools and guides, including The Grove's Visual Planning Systems, the Drexler/Sibbet/Forrester Team Performance System, the Sibbet/LeSaget Sustainable Organizations Model, The Grove's Strategic Visioning Process and the related graphic templates, and The Grove's Facilitation Series. In 2007 the Organizational Development Network awarded David and The Grove its Membership Award for creative contributions to the field of OD.

David holds a master's degree in journalism from Northwestern University and a BA in English from Occidental College. He was awarded a Coro Fellowship in Public Affairs in 1965 to study metropolitan public affairs in Los Angeles. For eight years in the 1970s he was executive director and director of training for the Coro Center for Civic Leadership, designing experience-based education programs for young leaders. He began his own organizational consulting firm in 1977. David is a longtime affiliate with the Institute for the Future in Menlo Park, a member of the Global Business Network in San Francisco, a longtime member of both the Organizational Development Network and the International Forum of Visual Practitioners, and a member of Heartland Circle's Thought Leader Network. He is currently chairman of the board of Coro. David lives in San Francisco with his poet/teacher spouse. For additional information, explore www.grove. com and www.davidsibbet.com.